Nazneen Khan-Østrem was born in Nairobi and is a Kenyan Asian. She is a staff columnist for the Norwegian broadsheet *Aftenposten*. Raised in the UK and Norway, she has also worked as a television presenter for the Norwegian Broadcasting Corporation – NRK, enjoyed being a music journalist for *Aftenposten*, and as a commissioning editor for the publisher *Aschehoug* for several years. Nazneen graduated from the London School of Economics with an MSc in International Relations in 2000 and started working as an assistant professor in Journalism at Oslo Metropolitan University. Her first book, *My Holy War*, about Islam and identity, was published in 2005; and in 2007 she was selected for the Edward R. Murrow Exchange Program in Journalism by the US State Department. She has also contributed to the anthology *Not Quite Right For Us* (2021) about punk, inclusivity and belonging. She lives in Oslo with her husband and two sons, and enjoys endless reruns of *The Wire*.

NAZNEEN KHAN-ØSTREM

LONDON

Immigrant City

Translated from Norwegian by Alison McCullough

ROBINSON

ROBINSON

First published in Norway in 2019 by Kagge Forlag, as *London – Blant gangstere, rabbinere, oligarker, rebeller og andre ektefødte barn av det britiske imperiet*

This edition first published in Great Britain in 2021 by Robinson
This paperback edition published in 2023 by Robinson

3 5 7 9 10 8 6 4 2

Copyright © Nazneen Khan-Østrem, 2019
Translation copyright © Alison McCullough, 2021

This translation has been published with the financial support of NORLA.

The moral right of the author has been asserted.

IMPORTANT NOTE
Some names and identifying details have been changed to protect the privacy of individuals.

A CIP catalogue record for this book
is available from the British Library.

ISBN: 978-1-47214-571-0

Typeset in Adobe Garamond Pro by Hewer Text UK Ltd, Edinburgh
Printed and bound in Great Britain by Clays Ltd, Elcograf S.p.A.

Papers used by Robinson are from well-managed forests and other responsible sources.

Robinson
An imprint of
Little, Brown Book Group
Carmelite House
50 Victoria Embankment
London EC4Y 0DZ

An Hachette UK Company
www.hachette.co.uk

www.littlebrown.co.uk

For my parents.
For all my aunties and uncles.
For everyone who came.

Abel and Elliot
– London is yours now.

Contents

Introduction – London's global heart

My nose is flattened as I press my face against the cold car window – I want to take in everything we pass. Mum, Dad and I are making our way west, from Croydon, in south London, to Southall. It's 1973, and I am five years old. Mum has dressed me in a tartan miniskirt with a matching blouse and red, knee-high boots.

Endless streets of almost identical brick houses catch my eye. Some of the front gardens contain bags of rubbish and rusty washing machines. Some of the houses are majestic, Victorian – with Jaguars in the driveways and magnificent oak trees and roses posing stolidly in the gardens. We also pass blocks of council flats towering there like landmarks, with their rows upon rows of small, symmetrical windows; clothes hung out to dry on vinyl washing lines along the balconies. The never-ending chain of shopfronts – a nation of shopkeepers.

It is on these trips that I study London's geography. We drive past the concrete structure of Croydon's Noble Lowndes Annuities Tower, its faceted shape reminiscent of a stack of British fifty-pence pieces. We manoeuvre through the suburb of Streatham and alongside charming Clapham Common, on to Battersea Power Station with its iconic chimneys, past Victoria station, Hyde Park Corner and Wellington Arch, the Dorchester Hotel where film stars stay. We crawl around Speakers' Corner – where activists have campaigned for years – past Marble Arch, before we turn down Bayswater Road, which is all too often thick with tourists and where hundreds of amateur artists display their paintings on Sundays. We continue along Holland Park Road and on to Shepherd's Bush, past the BBC's headquarters in White City, and then merge on to the A25 motorway before arriving in Southall.

As I try to remember all the streets and bridges, the landmarks and houses, I'm also looking forward to the next few hours, in which I'll amble around after my mum as she buys the basic ingredients for an Indian curry. I'm mainly thinking about the highlight of our trip, which always comes in the form of a freshly baked golden naan bread rolled around a shish kebab from the Shahi Nan Kebab snack bar in the middle of the bridge above the railway tracks. Topped with red-hot chilli sauce. We always sat in our orange Vauxhall and devoured the treat. I remember how I would have to dampen the flames with ice-cold Coca-Cola. Once we had eaten, we always felt a little closer to heaven. This was our piece of London.

Of course, we wandered around like wide-eyed tourists, too: we visited Trafalgar Square and chased the pigeons, stood with our mouths agape before Big Ben and Westminster, strolled across Tower Bridge, shopped until we dropped on Oxford Street, sauntered around Hyde Park and through Alexandra Palace, admired the waxworks in Madame Tussauds and were dazzled by the grand illuminated advertising at Piccadilly Circus. Because all this is also London. At the same time, I discovered that another London existed – a city full of people all with unique stories of how they came to the British capital and created a new life for themselves. And in doing so, created London.

In 1948, the British Parliament passed a piece of legislation that would have wide-reaching consequences: the British Nationality Act. In practice, this meant that all citizens of the British Empire

– around 800 million people – now had the right to settle and work in Britain.[1] The following year, on 26 April 1949, one of the most decisive changes in London's history took place: the signing of the London Declaration of 1949, which marked the formation of the British Commonwealth of Nations, formerly known as the Commonwealth. Instead of being part of the British Empire, these countries were now member states that would share values and principles,[2] with the British Queen as their symbolic figurehead.[3] With the close connection this gave Commonwealth citizens to Great Britain – including through their schooling, where they learned more about the British Queen than their own history – the British Isles were transfigured into the motherland. And people came in droves: from India, Jamaica, Pakistan, Uganda and Kenya – and later from Australia, Malaysia, Sierra Leone, Tonga, Sri Lanka, Bangladesh, Barbados, Trinidad and Tobago, New Zealand, Zambia and Nigeria. When these various groups arrived in London, they settled alongside people of their own nationality, establishing distinct communities all across the city. It isn't so surprising that these new arrivals found each other, because London's geography invites such organisation – a mosaic of districts that are almost like villages, in which it is easy to live in one's own little bubble.[4]

My family were also British subjects, and my entire life has been bordered by the British zeal for expansion. We were – or you might say we became – Kenyan Asians. My grandparents had moved to India from the young nation of Afghanistan as children. They were offered positions as civil servants in Kenya, which back then was known as British East Africa. Together, they moved with their families to Nairobi, and left before the partition of India and Pakistan in 1947 – an event that would have fundamental consequences for our identity. Our roots were torn up, with all that this entails. My mother was born in Mombasa, and my father in British India – only because his mother was on holiday there and unable to travel back to Kenya because she was so heavily pregnant. When my father was a few months old, he travelled back to Nairobi to be reunited with his family; I was born at the Aga Khan Hospital there. My parents grew up in a multicultural, hierarchical environment – the Kenyans, *the natives*, were at the bottom of the social ladder; the Indians were somewhere in the middle, while the English ruled at the top. My parents attended British schools in Mombasa, where English was almost spoken as the mother tongue, interspersed with Swahili, Punjabi, Urdu and Pashto. They continued along the family's established educational path – my father became a doctor, my mother an English teacher. They were happy in Kenya.

One day in January 1970, my parents landed at Heathrow with me in their arms. One of my uncles, my father's elder brother, had already settled in London with his wife – he and my aunt lived on the same street in Willesden Green from when he emigrated from Kenya in 1960, right up until he passed away in October 2019. This was a devastating loss as it affects the very essence of who I am in terms of roots and identity. My aunt is still there and now she harbours the precious memories of who we once were. Their neighbours came from all corners of the world. Every time we found ourselves outside their house an elderly couple would come up to us to have a chat. My uncle's life might have been taken straight out of Zadie Smith's novel *White Teeth* (2000) – albeit with a slight twist. Whenever I have visited him and my aunt, I have always felt the urge to leaf through the old photo albums they kept in a sideboard in the front room – a time capsule from the 1960s. There was one image in particular that I liked to look at, a photograph from London in a newspaper clipping – it felt as if I was holding a piece of world history in my hands. In the faded picture, my uncle, always enthusiastic and unapologetic, is wearing a black suit and narrow tie. Around his neck is a traditional drum used by the Maasai people in Kenya; his hands are raised, ready to hit it, and around him stand four Kenyans with a banner that reads: *Free Jomo Kenyatta!* The British believed that Kenyatta, the Kenyan freedom fighter who would later become Kenya's prime minister, was a risk to the kingdom's safety, and had therefore imprisoned him. The photograph encapsulates everything I associate with London: a city built and shaped by people from across the world, a vision of a global metropolis, manifested in each millimetre of the tens of thousands of streets that stretch out from the city centre in all directions.[5]

But for my father, green, affluent Surrey held much greater appeal than the dirty streets of London – I was therefore unable to experience the city as my cousins eventually did. When we visited them, one of my cousins would tell me stories about the skinheads who shouted, 'Bloody Pakis!' after him; about how he and his friends weren't allowed to play at the local tennis court that was run by an Englishman. But revenge was sweet. They threw milk bottles over the fence, immediately rendering the court unusable. I ran happily among the bluebells, memorising lists of words at the public school in Godalming that my parents had decided to send me to. At least I didn't have to go to boarding school like several of my other cousins. Instead, I had to make do with the weekly visits to the capital, where I constantly longed to be just like my cousins in Willesden Green: a London kid.

In the 1970s, Britain seemed washed in grey and stricken with poverty. The optimism of the 1960s had been replaced by a sense of melancholy, and the children of the British Empire quickly came to realise that the motherland treated them with anything but love. I remember that my father always voted for the Conservatives, in the belief that the efforts of the individual would be rewarded – regardless of that individual's background. My father hoped that this would improve Britain's economic prospects. But his patience eventually ran out.

One summer day in 1976, a few months after my sister Maha-Noor was born, we made our way across the North Sea. When I later asked my father about why we moved to Norway, he explained that several of his colleagues had been there and told him how well the Scandinavian health system functioned, compared to the NHS. He was a specialist in internal medicine and cardiology, and got a job as a senior consultant, later becoming head of his department – a position he held until he retired.

For me, the move came as a rather dramatic cultural shock. In 1976, Norway was characterised by puritanism. I was devastated at the fact that there was only a single television channel, and Mum shook her head at the limited selection of products in the stores – this was before the discovery of oil transformed Norwegian society. But despite moving to Norway we remained deeply connected to London and Britain, and, from then on, I lived with my heart torn in two. My father's eldest brother, who worked as a professor in Lusaka, Zambia, had bought himself a holiday home in South Croydon, and my parents did the same.[6] Our flat became our 'cabin' and my second home – and remains so today, as my parents now divide their time between Oslo and London. We decided to become proper Scandinavians by getting ourselves a Volvo, and through the eighties I would return home from London with stacks of vinyl records and music newspapers such as the *New Musical Express*, *Melody Maker* and *Sounds*. One of my childhood friends in Guildford introduced me to the burgeoning punk scene and instantly showed me a new London: sleazy side streets and underground spaces, which gave me a new perspective on the capital – at that time simmering with rage and colliding pop cultures. On the streets of London, I found freedom. Like other children of the British Empire, I found I could navigate my way out of narrow nationalistic notions.

The melting pot that immigration created in London laid the foundations for cultures that tore down barriers, and which continue to act as magnets for people from across the world to this day. Imagine just about any street in London – you'll almost always be able to find a Turkish butcher, an Indian or Chinese restaurant, a Polish bakery, an Italian café, a travel agency run by Nigerians or a doctor's surgery run by Dr Khan or Dr Patel – and the music you hear at the places you visit will probably have roots stemming from the music the Caribbeans brought with them. Over 300 languages are spoken in London, and there are at least fifty ethnic groups that have a population of at least 10,000 individuals.[7] Almost 40 per cent of the population was born outside the UK – a third of them in EU countries, and the rest outside the EU. Children of mixed race relationships are the demographic group that is growing most rapidly – London is full of British Meghan Markles.[8]

Immigrants continue to come here – from Eastern Europe, the entire African continent and South America – all with their suitcases full of dreams. Common to all of them is that they transform London's streets: where the Indians settled into their new lives, the Somalis now live; where the West Africans once hung out, the Colombians have found a home. In New Malden live the Koreans, while the Japanese have found their home in Acton, the Australians in Earl's Court and the Americans in Chelsea. The English – the Anglo-Saxons – are of course to be found here, too, but their numbers are decreasing in many of London's boroughs. This phenomenon has been termed 'white flight', and is a concern for some, while others couldn't care less.

London's pre-eminent British institutions – those we all pose proudly in front of to take photos – are framed by a global history that has made and continues to make its mark on the city's streets and inhabitants. In 2016, the British voted to leave the EU – nobody currently knows what effect this will have on immigration. Over a million people from the EU currently live in London. Freedom of movement has been ended.[9]

London's diversity is an ongoing social experiment that has existed ever since the city was first founded, and London is therefore also a seething Petri dish for increasingly pressing and complex conflicts relating to nationalism, globalisation, identity politics and immigration. A battlefield – and a paradise.

This book is an unapologetic declaration of love for all the people who live in London, and for the city I insist on calling the centre of the world.

I've chosen to focus on the groups who have left some of the deepest traces on the city, and my view of London is of course influenced by British colonial history. I have been shaped by both the English environment of my years in Surrey, and by a familial history that extends all the way back to the Pashtuns in Afghanistan – a nation never conquered by the British (nor by the Soviet Union). Over the years, I have devoured books about London in an attempt to get closer to what I believe to be the *authentic* London, but in my view very few, if any, of these publications has ever managed to portray London's global heart in the way I feel it beating when I walk the city's streets, thinking about all the people who have given us a city that never fails to fascinate. This book is a snapshot of a restless city in a continual state of flux.

The next time you walk around London, I'd like you to expand your lens. Look up at the shopfronts, notice the cobblestones and the railway tracks – yes, even the asphalt itself – or take a second glance down a side street. Think about the name of the shop in which you're trying on clothes, or the little pharmacy you've had to seek out; the restaurant in which you're eating, or the gallery you've visited to peruse works of art. A story lies hidden there – and it is one that is always worth listening to.

Irish London – Camden, Bexleyheath, Clapham

Irish building blocks

'Keep going!' I call out to my sons. They smile at me, indulgently. Probably because they know that it's myself I'm encouraging as I walk breathlessly up the steep, narrow stone staircase in St Paul's Cathedral.

But it's worth the effort. After 528 exhausting steps we can delight in the views from one of London's greatest lookout points. The panorama is overwhelming. Roads, railway lines, bridges and pavements twist themselves around old Victorian houses, exclusive buildings, aqueducts, blocks of council flats, glass skyscrapers and countless cranes. In 1958, standing at 158 metres high, St Paul's Cathedral was the tallest building in London. Now it seems almost small. The Shard in Southwark, which was completed in 2012, is almost twice as high – it towers 310 metres above the ground. From the top of the cathedral, London's skyline looks like a veritable architectural competition of glass, steel and creative names: the Scalpel, the Gherkin, One Canada Square, the Walkie Talkie, the Razor and the Cheesegrater. There even might have been a Tulip.

It's easy to forget all the people who built this city when standing there looking out across it. All those who have hacked, shovelled, tarmacked, dug and drained. But they shouldn't be ignored, and there is one group of immigrants in particular who took on most of the physical labour that created the infrastructure I can see from the top of St Paul's: the Irish.

In the period spanning the end of the Second World War up to the early 1960s, over half a million of them made their way across the Irish Sea. After the German bombing London lay in ruins; the Irish took on the job of rebuilding the capital. They continue to do so today. The new Crossrail line, for example, was built with significant contributions from Irish tunnel workers and engineers. Several of the spectacular skyscrapers that now tower over London were designed by architects with Irish roots, and many of the buildings house hugely successful Irish businesses. Without the Irish, would London as we know it even exist?

Poverty first drove the Irish from the Emerald Isle to England in the 1200s, as beggars and travelling salesmen.[1] Then, between 1845 and 1849, the Great Famine that struck Ireland when blight caused the potato crops to fail resulted in almost a quarter of the population – around 1 million people – losing their lives. Millions made their way to the USA or Australia, or across the Irish Sea to work in Britain.

But the British regarded the Irish as vermin – they were Catholics, beggars and drunkards. In the Britain of the early 1800s, Catholicism was almost on a par with devil worship.

Young Irishmen arrived in London with rebellion on their minds, and in 1861 the Irish Republican Brotherhood made their mark on the capital's cobbled streets. In Soho and Finsbury, they formed secret groups whose members dreamed of Irish independence; they started a war that would persist on the city's streets for over a hundred years. In 1867, a group of Irishmen attempted to free Irish inmates from a prison in Clerkenwell. Six people were killed, and the incident is regarded as the first Irish terrorist attack to take place in the United Kingdom.[2] A few years later, bombs exploded at Paddington station, injuring seventy-four people; bombs were also found at

Victoria station, but luckily disarmed. Plans to blow up Nelson's Column in Trafalgar Square, along with Scotland Yard, the Tower of London and London Bridge, were discovered and thwarted.[3] The authorities asked the public to enlist as voluntary special constables – no less than 166,000 people volunteered to patrol the streets.[4]

But the fight for Irish freedom gradually saw results. In 1921, the six counties in the south of the country were granted independence. In 1937, Ireland became a republic, and later part of the Commonwealth. The British withdrew in 1949, but Northern Ireland remained under British control.

In London, the Irish settled in areas such as Cricklewood, Camden, Edgware, Brent and Kilburn. The factories in these locations needed labourers, and the neighbourhoods therefore developed into Irish villages, often subject to strict social control. Significant trading also took place between British and Irish merchants; the Irish ran shops, and were employed as bakers and tailors. Other Irishmen made their names as businesspeople. One of these was John Murphy, who in the 1930s left a small farm in Kerry, unable to read and without a single penny in his pocket. During the Second World War he worked clearing snow at London airport, which would later become Heathrow, and established his own contracting company, which grew during the building boom that followed the war. His green trucks – often a little battered-looking, and with Murphy written along their sides in white capital letters – quickly became as ubiquitous as the red telephone boxes on London's streets.

Today, the Irish are a natural part of British society. But it often takes no more than a few beers and a couple of bad jokes about potatoes to lay bare underlying tensions. There remains a generation of Irish in London who still remember the posters in shop windows that proclaimed: 'No Blacks, No Dogs, No Irish'.

*　　*　　*

One spring day, I take the train from Victoria station to Bexleyheath in south-east London. All around me, I see a city that has changed dramatically. In the 1970s, London was a chaotic, angry, grimy and aggressive city – not the sophisticated, shimmering metropolis it is today. When Conservative Prime Minister Margaret Thatcher came to power in 1979, she had big plans for London. First, she set in motion the comprehensive deregulation and privatisation of state-owned companies, and then encouraged people to buy their own properties – especially those who lived in social housing. Under her Right to Buy policy, people living in social housing were able to purchase their properties at up to a 70 per cent discount. Thatcher wanted to change London, and make it attractive to foreign investors. In just a short time everything changed, and Derek Jarman's experimental films *Jubilee* (1978) and *The Last of England* (1987) capture the remnants of the lost wastelands and pessimistic paranoia that had characterised London. On the Isle of Dogs, Canary Wharf emerged as one of Britain's biggest financial centres along with the City of London, and in 1991 the skyscraper One Canada Square, with its distinctive pyramid-shaped top and flashing light, was completed. Between 1991 and 1997, large blocks of council flats containing over 12,000 apartments were torn down.[5]

In contrast to other large cities with grand cityscapes, London's geography is not logical or symmetrical. There are so many labyrinthine alleyways here – so many backstreets, little enclaves, underpasses, parks, fields and hills – that the city inspires perpetual wandering. When I was younger, I used to sit and study the thick *London A–Z*. It's pages were faded, and many of them were dog-eared. In it I would try to mark all the streets I had driven or walked down with a red ballpoint pen. In the end, I gave up – there were simply too many of them.

At the nondescript station, Mary Ann Lucas is waiting for me. She's an older woman with a lot to say – an ardent soul who for years has documented the lives of the Irish in London. She drives me to a church hall, where a group of Irish pensioners has gathered. I take a couple of deep breaths as I enter the premises: grey linoleum, grey chairs. Rows of long tables covered in plastic tablecloths, whose designer seems to have had the sole aim of using every clashing colour under the sun in the creation of their patterns. It's almost parodically geriatric – Jarvis Cocker from Pulp would have loved it – but the public sector decor puts no dampener on the atmosphere of joie de vivre. Laughter and smiles, despite the wrinkles, wheel-chairs and grey hair. Every week, Irish pensioners meet here to play bingo or eat a meal together. Mary Ann introduces me to Kathleen, a warm and sprightly woman. She and her husband met in Woolwich in the 1950s; he worked at Ford, while she was a serving girl for a Jewish family. Kathleen wasn't alone in having such a job. Jewish families were sought-after as employers because they were regarded as kinder than the English, and often permitted the Irish women to live with them – something that provided a roof over their head, three square meals a day, and not least a respectable salary. Those unable to find a job as a nanny worked at John Lewis or Boots, or in hospital kitchens or school canteens.

'The first thing you did when you came to London was contact the priest at the nearest Catholic church,' says Kathleen. 'Not for religious reasons, but because the priest would be able to put you in touch with other Irish, and you'd learn everything you needed to know about where you could find lodgings and job opportunities. The communities that grew up around the churches were sort of like the villages back home,' she explains.

For better or worse, the church held a central role among the Irish. The priests came down hard on anyone wishing to divorce, which could result in individuals being shut out of the Irish community. The same applied to contraception, and – God forbid – pregnancy outside marriage, or abortion. Sometimes, the

Catholic Church in London was responsible for imposing inhumane living conditions. In one case, 150 Irish men were crammed into three small houses in Southwark, just because the landlord was an Irishman of 'good character' – that is, someone who would enforce proper Catholic conduct.[6] The priests didn't want the Irish staying with the English, as they believed the English had questionable morals. Éamon de Valera also spearheaded this puritanical attitude as Irish prime minister, and then as president from 1959. He was known for his strict morality, and his embracing of Catholic values.

It was especially women who found freedom from the strict Catholic regime upon leaving Ireland. The mother of my best friend in Guildford was an Irish nurse. Through the Catholic school in her village she, like many other young women across Ireland, had been offered free schooling in exchange for employment in Aneurin Bevan's dream project, the National Health Service (NHS), founded in 1948 as one of the major welfare measures to be implemented after the Second World War. I have no doubt that I wouldn't be the person I am today without my best friend, Helen. It was she who played the Sex Pistols for me for the first time, in her bedroom. The snarling vocalist frightened me a little, but I decided there and then that I too was a punk, just like Helen. I didn't know it back then, but Johnny Rotten was also the son of an Irish couple who, like thousands of others, had made their way to London.

We're interrupted as our meal is served: roast beef, boiled vegetables, and apple crumble.

As we eat, Kathleen tells me about how shame has been a recurring problem for her generation. Not everyone coped so well once they had arrived in London. The village communities the Irish came from had been close, and it was often the men who faced the greatest challenges. They were frequently discriminated against, and this only got worse when the conflict in Northern Ireland began to spill over on to London's streets. Nobody dared read an Irish newspaper in public.

If you want to understand the enormous impact the Troubles have had on the lives of the Irish in London, all you have to do is look at the figures. The presence of the British military in Northern Ireland through Operation Banner spanned a period of thirty-eight years, from 1969 to 2007.[7] Over 250,000 British soldiers served in Northern Ireland during this time, and the British Armed Forces were responsible for killing over 300 people during the conflict. Most of these individuals were civilians, but over a hundred of them were members of the Provisional Irish Republican Army, better known as the IRA. Between 1973 and 1997, the IRA took the lives of 115 people and injured over 2,000 – most of them civilians. In 1973, the IRA was also responsible for as many as thirty-six bombings in London.

Irish men were watched closely by their British colleagues, who suspected anyone Irish of being in league with the IRA. Most Irish were not especially politically engaged with the conflict – they just wanted to live safe, normal lives. They had families and careers, and regarded themselves as solid pillars of the community – not possible terrorists.

I was six years old in 1974 when two bombs exploded in Guildford – as it happened, this was where we lived at the time, and my parents were deeply shocked by the incident. The bombs went off one Saturday evening in October, when the pubs in town were full of punters. In two of them, four soldiers on leave lost their lives; an additional sixty-four people were injured for life. The IRA was behind the attack, but innocent people ended up being imprisoned for it. The British courts' handling of the suspects was a scandal beyond compare.

There is no shying away from the fact that the IRA has a lot of blood on its hands, and the years that followed the bombings in

Guildford also saw several major bomb attacks. On 20 July 1982, two IRA bombs exploded in Hyde Park and Regent's Park, respectively. Eleven British soldiers died and over forty civilians were injured. On 17 December the following year, a bomb was detonated outside Harrods. Six people died, and a hundred were injured.[8] I remember the incident well. We were in the car, on our way to South Kensington, when we were stopped by the police just by Wellington Arch. The traffic was gridlocked. I can recall the department store's famous awnings lying in tatters on the pavement. It felt too close.

On 12 October 1984, the IRA managed to strike right at the heart of British politics. Hundreds of besuited men and women adorned with pearls had made their way to the coastal town of Brighton for the Conservative Party conference, the party members thronging together at the exclusive Grand Brighton Hotel. In the middle of the night, a bomb went off; Prime Minister Margaret Thatcher was awake when it exploded. She is said to have been sitting at her desk, finalising her speech for the next day. The entire middle section of the hotel collapsed, but miraculously enough only five people died and thirty-one were injured. The IRA claimed responsibility for the attack the next day. The bomb, equipped with a timer, had been set under the bathtub in a room above Thatcher's suite three weeks earlier by IRA member Patrick Magee. He was sentenced to thirty-five years in prison, along with four other members of the organisation.

In 1998 the Good Friday Agreement was signed, which resulted in the establishment of a separate democratic assembly for Northern Ireland and the release of political prisoners, including Patrick Magee. Through the Good Friday Agreement, old wounds appeared to be healed, and Sinn Féin, the political arm of the IRA, became an acceptable party – despite the fact that its MPs do not meet in Westminster because they refuse to recognise British control over Northern Ireland or to swear allegiance to the Queen.

'Now it's time for bingo!' calls a woman from somewhere in the hall; the pensioners eagerly take out their stamps and books. They have, for the most part, been lucky. But the older Irish are over-represented in homelessness statistics and surveys of those with mental health struggles in London.[9]

I say goodbye to Kathleen and Mary Ann, leaving them both very cheerful. I'm going to Arlington House. To the forgotten Irish.

The dark streets of London

The large glass doors open automatically as I approach them. I'm surprised by how clinical the entrance feels here at Arlington House – a Victorian building that has opened its doors to the homeless since 1905. I take a seat on a minimalistic wooden bench beside a frail old lady with unkempt hair.

'The wind is biting, you have to make sure to really wrap up warm,' I tell her. But she seems far away.

Nobody who hung out on the streets of London in the 1980s could avoid making the acquaintance of drunken and homeless Irish – these individuals were part of London's urban landscape. Some of the lucky ones managed to stagger into Arlington House. When it opened, the building could house up to a thousand people, and was one of six such shelters in London. The house was financed by Victorian philanthropist Lord Rowton, who believed that working people should have a decent place to live. At the time, there was little accommodation available for workers – especially men without permanent jobs. At Arlington House, they were each given their own room containing a sink and a bed. In exchange for a small sum of money, they were also given a daily meal. With its total of 1,200 beds, Arlington House was the biggest shelter in Europe at the time.[1] George Orwell wrote warmly of the shelters, but had a few objections: 'the Rowton Houses are splendid buildings, and the only objection to them is the strict discipline, with rules against cooking, card playing, etc.'[2] Among the citizens of London, Arlington House became known as a kind of slum where the most hopeless members of society ended up, and conditions at the shelter slowly deteriorated. In the end, the building was taken over by the local authorities in Camden, who significantly reduced the number of residents, and completely renovated the building in 2006.

I sit there with the old woman, watching all the people who pass through the doors. Several of them look fairly young. Then a woman comes towards me, her steps brisk.

'Oh, how nice, I see you've met Christine! Doesn't she look great for somebody who's almost eighty?' she shouts, gesturing to the elderly woman I'm sitting next to.

Christine looks at me and smiles. Maria speaks English with a Spanish accent, and is wearing a kind of uniform consisting of black trousers and a piqué shirt with 'Arlington' printed on the left side of the chest. Around her waist she has a belt with a walkie-talkie hanging from it.

'Christine would love to tell you about what it was like moving to London in the fifties! She's my favourite customer – let's go down to the food hall,' Maria says, escorting us through some heavy double doors.

Maria's choice of words surprises me. Is Christine a *customer*? Is she not a resident? Christine trails obediently in Maria's wake as we make our way down a corridor, then into a canteen. Photographs of bland urban landscapes have been hung on the walls, I suppose in an attempt to create a cosy atmosphere, although without much success.

'Tea?' Maria asks.

She disappears. Two men in suits and a woman wearing sleek, formal clothes come in, and for a moment I'm unsure of where I am – I have the sensation that I'm in an office building for consultants, the premises wiped clean of any and all personal attributes. I know from experience that it's never good when people in generic suits turn up.

'What a lovely place! Is this where you eat your meals?'

I look at Christine and hope she doesn't notice how my voice has taken on an excessively positive register. She leans towards me, as if she wants to share something confidential.

'I only get two meals. After five there's no food to be had, and I only get five pounds a day – it's nothing! And the food is terrible.'

I feel my stomach clench.

'I don't have money for cigarettes any more, either. It was better at the other shelter in Kentish Town, but they shut it down and spread us all over the place. I feel like I'm in prison,' Christine says in a low voice.

I don't have time to respond, because Maria comes in with two cups of tea.

'This is quite a place,' I say. 'I'd imagined something completely different. It's so clean and . . .'

I pause for a moment. '. . . um, nice here.'

What I actually want to say is: Sterile. Lifeless. Inhuman. Empty. Maria lights up.

'Yes, isn't it? We take good care of all our customers here.'

That word again – *customers*. She leaves Christine and me alone, telling us that she'll be back in a little while.

'So you want to know what it was like to move from Ireland to London?' Christine asks.

I nod. I feel ill at ease. She looks so tired. She doesn't touch the cup of tea, even though I'm sure the warmth would do her good.

'I came to London with my sister. It was summer, and we'd been told that we could get work at the hotels in London, so we signed a contract with an agency that paid the fare for our journey and got us our first jobs,' says Christine.

She remembers the hard, busy days she spent working as a hotel cleaner.

'We worked all the time, my sister and me – we lived together as well. In Kentish Town. There were so many Irish there already.'

She speaks quickly, and every now and then a glint enters her old eyes.

'We cleaned fifteen rooms a day, I think it was. Not so bad. We weren't paid very well, but it was just enough.'

Christine went home to Dublin for a few months, but when she was unable to find work there she returned to London. This time, she found a place to stay in Cricklewood, in the north-west of London, where another large Irish community had settled. She never went home again.

'I didn't have the money to go to the funeral when my mother died, that was painful. It didn't matter so much for my father – he drank too much.'

All at once, Christine falls silent. It's as if she disappears into her thoughts, before her eyes suddenly light up again.

'I loved to dance!' she exclaims, and excitedly tells me about the dances at the National Club in Kilburn, where she met cheerful, friendly people. The Buffalo, just next to Arlington House, was a little rough, but the National was a place where you could get dressed up and go dancing. Perhaps even meet your future husband! Christine remembers how she loved to wear a red dress from Marks & Spencer.

'I had thick, auburn hair – not this thin white hair I've got now,' she says, explaining how she always used to put it up in a pretty style.

She never married.

The doors to the food hall swing open – it's Maria. Smiling and energetic.

'Would you like to show her your room?'

We go out into the floodlit corridor, where the glossy walls are hung with paintings. Maria explains that all the artwork has been created by the shelter's *customers*. She opens a door for me, so I can peer into a room in which a dozen buckets of paint stand on the floor. But Christine has already moved on – she's looking at one of the photographs of Arlington House from the 1980s. The contrast is striking. The food hall in which we were just sitting used to be covered in brownish-red tiles, and the tables were heavy. Simple, but cosy. The framed black-and-white photographs on the wall show men wearing flat caps and thick, threadbare suit jackets. Their faces are furrowed. Many of them developed an unfortunate relationship with alcohol, along with the associated physical and mental health problems, but the pubs were gathering places for single men who hardly had a bed to go to. Often, it would be the pubs that paid out the wages they had earned over the course of the day. This wasn't an especially sensible arrangement.

Together, we look at the framed old newspaper clippings that also hang on the wall. One of them features a photograph in which a young man stands with both his arms out to the sides to show how little space he has. His fingers touch the walls on either side – the breadth of his open arms is the actual width of the room. Two arm lengths. That's how small the rooms were before Arlington House was renovated.

We take the lift four floors up. Maria leads us to a glass door, and it strikes me that it looks like one you might find in an institution. I had imagined that Arlington House would consist of apartments between which the residents could wander freely – not such impersonal solutions as this. Maria explains that each floor has its own team to look after the residents. Nobody can enter without permission, and if anyone should need help, there is always somebody available. I follow Christine, who almost hurries down the corridor. For someone so old, she's extraordinarily quick. We come to a stop, and Christine asks us to wait a moment as she disappears into her room. Maria discreetly confesses that it isn't easy, having to constantly confront all the sad fates of the people here. Despite calling Christine a customer, Maria seems a very warm-hearted person.

Christine opens the door to the room that is hers. Newspapers lie thrown in a corner on the blue linoleum floor. I can see a small bathroom, with a shower. In another corner of the room is a bed with a duvet. Two chairs heaped with clothes stand against the wall. That's it. Nothing on the walls. No TV. No chest of drawers. A large wall lamp casts a harsh light above the bed. The room has three tiny windows.

'I promise we'll get you some furniture next week, and a fridge at least. You've only been here a couple of weeks,' says Maria.

Christine shrugs.

'I don't have any money for food, so it doesn't matter,' she says.

I can see that she's ready to drop; her face is redder than it was when we first met. I don't want to bother her any more. As Maria and I leave the room I see that Christine sits on the bed and collapses.

'Does she really only get five pounds a day?'

Maria nods, and we start to talk about the welfare cuts introduced by the Conservatives in recent years. The elderly have been hit hard. Maria feels frustrated in her role; incapable of doing much to help. They used to have more time and more money.

We take the lift up a floor – I'm now going to meet one of the residents who has lived here longest. Sean has been at Arlington House for thirty-two years. Some would probably call him a real 'Paddy' – a somewhat derogatory term for the Irish.

'He's had a stroke, so it can take a while before he manages to speak, but once he gets going he's quite funny,' Maria says before she opens the brown door.

I follow her. A man with thick black hair cautiously turns towards me in his wheelchair. His face is ruddy. A tiny TV flickers in the corner. Like Christine's room, this one has three windows, and against one wall is a bed and a small bedside table. On the walls are photographs. It's quite homely, and reminds me of a student's room. On one wall a plastic sheet with images of fruit on it has been hung up to create a kind of kitchen nook, where Sean has a microwave, a hotplate, a kettle and a small fridge. Above the counter is a shelf where there are boxes of tea, a bag of sugar, various cans of food and bags of instant mashed potato. Sean's movements are slow. He came to London from Mayo in 1965, and found a job casting concrete in Woolwich. His workdays could last between twelve and fifteen hours.

'There was no overtime, no bonuses, no unions – you could freeze to death, but nobody would have cared. And no holiday pay, all the money went to those above you. Once you were done with the job you were done, and you went on to the next one,' he says.

In Ireland, the poor often had no other choice but to hop on a boat and come to London, where Irish companies were waiting for them. Some of the companies would cover the workers' travel fares; the men would stand on the dock with a note attached to their coat so that they could be identified and collected. Many of the Irish were wary of the British authorities, and chose to live a life on the fringes of society, without opening bank accounts or registering as immigrants. Sean says that the weekends were the high point of the week that everyone looked forward to. They would all go straight to the Galtymore dance club in Cricklewood, which is where Sean met his wife.

But the heavy physical labour and stress of being a construction worker without a permanent position, along with Sean's excessive alcohol consumption, eventually began to take a toll on the marriage. Sean looks up at the wall and points to three photos. Two of them are in gold frames, and show two young girls with brown hair and red sweaters. These are his daughters. The third photo is a wedding portrait of him and his wife.

'I haven't seen my daughters in thirty years. I sent letters, but they were always returned. The post office said that they didn't have a forwarding address.'

Sean moved out of the house he and his wife owned when they divorced, and had no other option but to contact the Salvation Army, who helped him get a room at Arlington House. He didn't feel he could go to friends or family because of the shame.

'Those of us who lived here, we looked after each other. We could visit each other freely, it was nice and relaxed. Now we're completely shut in. We have to get permission for everything,' Sean says.

We sit there in silence. I can hear a clock ticking. Sean looks at the photographs of his daughters.

Sean's life echoes all the history books I've read about the Irish in London; I feel almost dizzy with sadness as I leave Arlington House. This city has a singular ability to drain people's energy and cast them into a darkness it can be hard to escape. It's as if there's a monster living on London's streets – a kind of vampire, circling poor struggling souls.

I try to shake off my gloomy thoughts and walk to Camden High Street, where garlands, balloons and banners in green, white and orange wave in the ice-cold wind. Tomorrow will be 17 March, St Patrick's Day – Ireland's national day and the feast day of Saint Patrick, Ireland's national saint. For three days, London will become an Irish province.

Some of the Irish who arrived in London came with big dreams – dreams that would earn the city its reputation as the rock music capital of the world. And Camden was the dive to which everyone was drawn.

A ballad of Camden

I can still remember the joy I felt in my stomach the first time I saw the band Madness perform on *Top of the Pops* in 1979. They played 'One Step Beyond'– their first top-ten single. The band went berserk onstage, and I was hooked. I became obsessed with music from a fairly young age: Mark Bolan from T. Rex. The Bay City Rollers. The Boomtown Rats. I loved the songs and the clothes, the energy. When I discovered punk, I also stumbled into the Jamaican genre of ska and two-tone – a combination of punk and new wave. The various bands often came from specific areas of London, and I felt an urge to go out and observe the streets and landscapes the music came from.

Madness led me straight to Camden, the neighbourhood the band were from. I wandered up and down Camden High Street, wide-eyed at the eccentric mix of tourists and gaudy market stalls, dope heads, vintage clothing stores and pubs, where skinny band-members fought for the adoration of tipsy youths who should have been anywhere but here. And still do.

I studied people to discover which badges they pinned to their coats, which shoes they shuffled around in, and not least which band T-shirts they were wearing. Everything was about belonging to the right clan – maybe the people I observed liked to listen to the Cramps or the Cure, like me? Camden High Street was lined with both record stores and clothing shops, so here I could easily get hold of both the music and the clothes I needed. Creepers, Dr Martens, fishnet tights, second-hand biker jackets, paisley shirts, studded belts, tartan trousers, cowboy shirts, Converse – everything could be had here.

If I wanted to dance, I went to Camden Palace, a central institution in the influential post-punk era of the early to mid-1980s. This was where the New Romantics, along with guiding light and host Steve Strange – who had even answered the fan letter I sent him – held their weekly club nights. Hordes of men and women, the latter decked out in ruffles, harem pants and shameless amounts of make-up, moved their bodies to the sounds of Visage, Soft Cell and the Cure, pretending they were at the Studio 54 nightclub in New York. Camden Palace offered a sanctuary from the alcoholic, unshaven punks who spat everywhere and frightened ordinary people. Anyone who remembers Madonna from this era will probably not be surprised to hear that she played her first UK concert at Camden Palace, performing 'Everybody', 'Burning Up' and 'Holiday'.[1]

I can remember the first time I was allowed to go to the club, and that incredible nervous excitement in my stomach. My older cousin, who had just moved to London from Nairobi, and his sister were my chaperones. I was wearing a white blouse with puff sleeves and ruffles all over it, a skin-tight ankle-length skirt, the obligatory fishnet tights, and shovelfuls of black eyeliner and green eyeshadow; I also sported a gravity-defying backcombed fringe. We drank soft drinks, danced, and stared shamelessly at London's clubbers as they sashayed past us.[2]

Camden was the place where the loutish cool kids hung out, so it wasn't strange that an increasing number of concert premises opened their doors here, making Camden the definitive mecca of rock music. In the 1960s, the area was already notorious due to the venue the Roundhouse, where an all-night rave was held with Soft Machine and Pink Floyd when the underground newspaper

International Times was launched. The Doors also performed here in 1968. Live music venue Dingwalls wished rockers welcome in 1973, and the club quickly became popular, especially for unruly and beer-thirsty punks with a penchant for three-chord tunes. London's prominent position in the fashion and music industries also meant that Camden became a bustling place throughout the 1970s and 1980s.

This was a time brimming with innovation and the breaking of boundaries – and the Irish. They were the very backbone of Camden's music scene. Madness can even thank an Irishman for giving them their first proper gig – the band's success is ascribed to Alo Conlon and his pub the Dublin Castle, situated just a five-minute walk from Arlington House. Suggs, Madness's vocalist, has said that the band managed to get this first gig by claiming to be a jazz band. Alo Conlon came to London in the 1950s as a stowaway on a boat from Kiltimagh, County Mayo; he worked digging tunnels in the capital, before the Dublin Castle became his home. The pub was established to give Irish people a place of refuge where they could gather after work – if they went to pubs run by Englishmen, they would be subjected to casual remarks that soon escalated into fistfights. Conlon likely knew the melancholy of his fellow countrymen all too well, and the lonely Irishmen residing at Arlington House found comfort at the bottom of a pint of Conlon's Guinness on many an occasion.

Today, Camden's identity oscillates between a tourist trap, a playground for rich bohemians, and a place where the less well-off live in public housing. In the 1980s and 1990s, the shops were almost exclusively family run – young Turkish boys used to wish me welcome whenever I came shopping for clothes here, knowing all too well that a little flirting would go a long way in making a sale. Now the shops mostly contain Pakistani boys selling London T-shirts and little red buses to youths on language exchange programmes. I have to smile when I think back to one afternoon in the 1980s when I visited one of my cousins, who at the time attended the exclusive Roedean School in Brighton. She was rather shocked to hear that I enjoyed hanging out in Camden. 'Is that not a bit rough?' she said in that nasal tone somehow acquired by everyone who goes to public school. It's no longer so rough here now, even if the streets aren't as wide and well kept as they are in Chelsea.

I saunter towards the large green railway bridge that crosses the main street, the name Camden Lock painted on it in big yellow letters, stopping for a while on the lower bridge that crosses the canal that runs through Camden. The water is dark and dirty. Regent's Canal was dug in response to the changes brought about by the Industrial Revolution – an entire network of canals was created to transport coal and other goods. Several locks had to be built.[3] One of these was Hampstead Road Lock, which became known as Camden Lock after an advertising agency was tasked with marketing the borough – the original name seemed too affected. In the old days, boats also transported imported timber here from Norway, along with bricks and glass. While the area is known locally as Camden Market this can be a little misleading, since there isn't one market, but several – including Lock Market and Stables Market, which merge into each other. I'm glad to be wearing my trainers, because the slippery cobblestones can be difficult to walk on. Had it been a warmer day, I would have walked to Primrose Hill just close by, where one of London's finest views can be found. It was from these very hills the author H. G. Wells apparently had a vision of the aliens he wrote about in his novel *The War of the Worlds* (1898). I wonder if Tom Cruise has ever been there? I am sure Wells would have thought his novel had become reality if he saw all the modern buildings in front of him.

Large-scale renovation is now underway in Camden. The Israeli billionaire Teddy Sagi has bought up the entire market area, and it is now being rehabilitated – in fact, it seems the entire city is being flushed through a sanitation system. Diggers and scaffolding stand shoulder to shoulder along parts of the canal, tearing down the past in order to create the future. Cleaner. Ever more sterile. Beside the canals once dug by the Irish, new luxury apartments are now being built.

I walk towards Camden Town Underground station – I want to find the entrance gate to the Buffalo on Kentish Road, which Christine spoke about so fondly. It turns out to be right next to the shop where I bought my first pair of Doc Martens in the mid-1980s; the boots were part of the punk uniform at the time. I replaced the black laces with red ones, to show solidarity with the anti-racist skinhead movement – although I'm not sure anyone noticed. Now Dr Martens has a huge store in the middle of Camden, where the shop assistants sport massive beards, piercings and tattoos. There's even a dedicated 'Made for Camden' collection. It's easy to feel like an old fart when you're here.

I move as close as I can to the iron gate and peer into the darkness beyond it. The gate is locked and I can't see anything, but the Buffalo must be somewhere back there in the dark. The books that document the lives of the Irish in London from the 1950s onwards feature photographs of young men, some wearing suits and ties, some more casually dressed, smiling and hopeful about the upcoming evening's events. The women in the photos are also smiling, and a little more elegant with their lacquered hairstyles and red lipstick. Some of them would arrive in their nurses' uniforms, straight from work. If they weren't at the Buffalo, they could be found at the Round Tower, the Estate, the Garryowen, the Hammersmith Palais or the most popular nightspot, the Galtymore in Cricklewood. Every weekend. An island of familiar faces in a country of strangers; a place where they could escape the isolation and loneliness for a while. I can just imagine Christine dancing there in her dress from

Marks & Spencer, her eyes glittering, excited about whose arms she might sway in that night.

The Buffalo opened in the 1930s, and the dance bands that played there had names like Mick Delahunty's Big Band and the Royal Showband. When Camden Town Tube station and the adjacent buildings were bombed in 1941, the Buffalo's Kerry-born owner Bill Fuller took the opportunity to expand the premises. He built a hall with capacity for 2,000 people, which gave him the opportunity to invite bigger stars. Country artist Jim Reeves, who always honoured his Irish ancestors, played the Buffalo in 1963, but is said to have left the venue in protest because the piano wasn't tuned to his liking. The organisers, however, ran off with the proceeds of the ticket sales before the club's owners could inform people that the concert had been cancelled. This led to an uproar, with 2,000 concertgoers running amok. The police turned out in force with horses, in an attempt to calm the crowd. The incident didn't exactly improve the Buffalo's dubious reputation.

From the old entrance to the Buffalo I can see straight into the World's End pub, where Irish labourers would go to have a drink after work.

It has long been a sore point among the Irish in London that some Irish families established hugely successful contracting firms by using 'their own'. I think of Sean and his friends at Arlington House, who have lived such tough working lives.

On the other side of the Buffalo is a door to what used to be the dance hall, with a sign that shines neon pink in the darkness – an entrance I've used countless times. Bill Fuller operated out of this building, and was instrumental in making Camden into London's rock music mecca. During the 1960s and 1970s, he opened numerous concert premises in both Ireland and the US, including the Palladium in New York, where Frank Sinatra and Jimi Hendrix played. In London, Fuller changed the Buffalo's name to the Carousel, and the place became a kind of hub for London's growing rock scene. The concert premises also functioned as a sort of practice studio for greats like the Clash and Frank Zappa. Fuller then turned the Carousel into the Electric Ballroom, partnering up with his friend Frank Murray – the manager of Thin Lizzy, a hard rock band from Dublin featuring the legendary Irish-Caribbean musician Phil Lynott.[4] Lynott himself would later share gripping stories about being a mixed race kid in Ireland, and how London became a place of freedom for him.

Thin Lizzy had already caused a stir with their version of 'Whiskey in the Jar', and the Greedies (also known as the Greedy Bastards), one of Phil Lynott's side projects, were given the honour of playing the first concert at the newly named premises on 28 July 1978. Fuller gave the band their name because they demanded 75 per cent of the ticket sales. Rock history was written that night when the Greedies ended their concert with the song 'Pretty Greedy' – an overt homage to the Sex Pistols' 'Pretty Vacant'.

In the audience that opening night was a young man with a rather dubious-looking set of teeth, who would soon reveal his own talent on the city's stages. Bad teeth have rarely hindered a career in rock, and Shane McGowan harboured his own dreams, which soon came to fruition through the Pogues. The band was formed in King's Cross, which, like Camden, was an Irish colony, and originally named themselves Pogue Mahone – a rendering of the Gaelic phrase for 'kiss my arse'. With their irreverent mix of punk and Irish folk songs, the Pogues grabbed the attention of music fans with the album *Red Roses for Me* in 1984. McGowan, who had attended public school and wasn't quite the working-class boy he made himself out to be, wrote songs about heartbreak, fighting and drinking. His melodies struck an undeniable chord with partygoers and melancholics the world over.

*   *   *

The unstoppable Irish passion for music lives on in London, and not just in Camden. All the way on the other side of the city, in Clapham and Wandsworth, young Irish have found a new base. In the basement of an office building surrounded by high-rise blocks in Battersea Park Road, every Sunday evening between 7 and 9 p.m., Kealan Duignan and his staff Niall Jackson, Melanie Simpson and Rob Cotter play Irish music on the local radio station, Wandsworth Radio. Kealan's programme is called *The Irish Jam*, and is, as Kealan declares, 'free of obituaries and country music'.

A generational shift now characterises the Irish community in London. Its younger members, who have flocked to the city since Ireland became a well-off and proactive nation, often lovingly poke fun at their older and more conservative counterparts who are obsessed with reminiscing about the old days.

I meet Kealan on a Sunday evening. His office is a small narrow room full of computers, and the studio is tiny. I look around me: a sofa, a packet of Jaffa Cakes and tea from a vending machine.

Thanks to foreign investment, EU funding and the large amounts of money the diaspora sent home, from the 1990s onwards the Irish economy began to grow at record speed. This boom became known as the Celtic Tiger, and a generation of Irish entrepreneurs thrived. The Irish could finally let somebody else do the building for them: they employed enthusiastic Poles. Ireland was full of young, well-educated people, and many of the most ambitious made their way to London. When Ireland was hit by the financial crisis, they remained in the city – like the post-war generation, the young Irish quickly found out that Ireland was not a place you went back to. But now things are different, because the young people of today are proud of their Irish heritage, and highly educated. They rarely encounter the challenges faced by the first Irish emigrants, and to them, the streets of London offer an entirely different experience.

Kealan organises showcases of Irish bands in London, but when he started his radio show, he noticed that the older members of the Irish community were sceptical. Irish music holds a special place among the older Irish, who want to hold on to what is regarded as 'original'. At the same time, conflicting values emerged between the different generations, which became all too obvious when the Irish Centre in Camden appointed a new director. Once an arena that mainly helped the less fortunate Irish, the centre now has diversified and also caters for the younger Irish; comedy and fashion shows and literature nights, because the younger Irish were beginning to drift away from the venue.

'The change was absolutely necessary. The older Irish have dominated the space there, and feel nostalgic about the era in which they came to London – and with good reason, by all means. But I do think it's time for us to show that there is a new Ireland, which among other things is about challenging some of the old Catholic values,' says Kealan. The new Ireland he describes can be seen in south London: Croydon, Battersea and Clapham. It costs little to travel between Dublin and Gatwick, and the airport is hardly thirty minutes from the city centre by train. Ryanair, which was established by three Irish businessmen in 1984, offers tickets for as little as £20.

If you take a walk around Clapham on a Friday or Saturday night, you'll see a striking number of well-dressed young Irish standing in long queues at the cocktail bars and pubs. A number of them regularly frequent the Alexandra, an Irish bastion in Clapham that specialises in showing rugby matches. Rugby is a favourite sport among almost all Irish, and for the time being Ireland seem to be doing much better than England, so the pub is packed whenever matches are played. The influx of Irish to Clapham was so noticeable that in 2013 Channel 4 produced the comedy series *London Irish*, which followed the lives of a group of twenty-something friends who liked to party. Terrorism, paedophilia, homophobia, jokes about rape and the Great Famine were all covered in the first episode, and the critics were soon raging. Interestingly, the comedy was written by Irish playwright Lisa McGee, based on her own experiences as a young person in London.

But it isn't just the older members of the community that the young Irish have to worry about – new challenges have now come to the fore in a scenario few could have imagined: Brexit. Kealan tells me that he has noticed a change in London, and casual remarks about people's ethnic backgrounds are now being cast around. The tension between the United Kingdom's cold-shouldering of the EU and Ireland's enthusiasm for Europe has led many of the Irish to return home. The *Irish Times* reported that 3,600 Irish returned home in 2016; 6,600 Irish returned to Ireland the following year; and in 2018 this figure grew to 8,600.[5] These Irish are known as 'Brexiles'. Irish with British citizenship have also begun to apply for Irish passports – they don't want to risk anything. Kealan has no intention of returning home himself just yet, and he thinks this trend is a sad one. He appreciates the attitude of Mayor of London Sadiq Khan, who insists that London is a city where everybody is welcome, regardless of ethnic background, sexual orientation or class.

The border between Ireland and Northern Ireland has also become a serious problem due to Brexit – a problem that could have major consequences. Until now, crossing the border between Ireland and Northern Ireland has been easy – both goods and people have freedom of movement, and there are no border controls. But now that the United Kingdom has chosen to leave the EU, a worry arose that border checks could be reinstated. At one point this resulted in a revival of the fight for freedom among the people of Northern Ireland – some believe that this is a clear sign that Northern Ireland must now be united with Ireland. Kealan is sick of the British who in all seriousness believe that the whole of Ireland should just become part of the UK again and then the problem would be solved – he's also tired of the fact that people continue to ask him whether he comes from 'Southern Ireland' or Northern Ireland.

'There is no "Southern Ireland" – only Ireland! And if you're asking me that kind of question, then you haven't understood the faintest thing about the Irish,' he says. 'Yesterday, I was referred to as a leprechaun by an English colleague. I know that he didn't mean anything truly offensive by it, but still . . .'

I'm surprised to hear that Kealan has had these uncomfortable experiences as an Irishman in London – I had presumed that after so many years of unrest, relations between the Irish and the English were good now. I think some of the challenge might lie in the fact that the Irish love to revel in stereotypes of themselves – something I discover on St Patrick's Day.

#IamIrish

I'm not sure what awaits me as I walk to Wellington Arch to meet up with my Irish friends, but I suspect it'll be a proper celebration – narrow-mindedly enough, after a couple of trips to Dublin, I've succumbed to the idea that the Irish like to party. It's Sunday, and time for the big St Patrick's Day parade that has been held since 2002; smaller parades and celebrations have occurred since as far back as 1713.[1] Far too many people have come out dressed up as Catholic priests, leprechauns and clowns. It seems almost reckless in the current political climate – all the national stereotypes are being emphasised here, rather than challenged. As I walk up Piccadilly to find Claire Nolan Sturley, my companion for the occasion, I once again register that far too many men have dressed up as various types of gnome. Up the street I can see an endless line of floats with dancers, Hare Krishna devotees, Boy Scouts, jugglers on stilts and a banner that proclaims '#More Blacks, More Dogs, More Irish'.

In the international spirit of London there are also several Latin American groups in the parade, including ones from Bolivia and Mexico, wearing colourful flowing clothes and sequins. Mayor of London Sadiq Khan has insisted that the Irish parade must also reflect London's openness.

I meet Claire at one of the hotels along Piccadilly. She's in her early sixties, and is London's Irish social butterfly: she knows everyone who's anyone, according to all the members of the Irish community I've met. When I tell her this, she laughs.

'If you're going to understand the Irish community in London, you have to be part of this parade,' claims Claire. She's lived in London since the 1980s, after spending several years in Australia.

Before I know what's happening an Irish flag has been shoved into my hand for me to wave. Nationalism has never been my strong suit, but Claire only smiles at me when I tell her that it feels a little false. I have at least taken a couple of trips to Dublin, I think, as we walk further up Piccadilly and I reluctantly wave the flag. We're making our way up to Piccadilly Circus, and will then head along Pall Mall towards Trafalgar Square, where the big party will take place. People stand shoulder to shoulder along our route, waving to us. I'm convinced that everybody can see that I'm not Irish, but this probably reveals more about my own prejudices than anything else. I see several people who are clearly of African or Caribbean heritage walking with signs that state '#IamIrish', and I recall Phil Lynott's fate.

The organisation Mixed Race Irish and the #IamIrish movement aim to raise awareness about Irish people of mixed race backgrounds. #IamIrish was launched in October 2016 by photographer Lorraine Maher, who is of Caribbean-Irish descent, to expand perceptions of what the Irish identity can look like.

The Irish have a bleak track record on this front. Children with mixed race backgrounds were often treated poorly by the Irish child protection and welfare services, which were mainly run by the Catholic Church. Racism and abuse were widespread. These negative attitudes were also common among the Irish in London in the 1950s and 1960s, who were not keen on Irish women having children with people from Caribbean or West African backgrounds. Some of these children ended up in the care system, where their lives with white English foster families could be extremely troubled. Claire tells me she's proud that this difficult subject has finally become part of Irish public discourse. If the Irish are emigrants, she says, then they must also be welcoming to immigrants.

We continue towards Whitehall, where the majestic offices of the Foreign, Commonwealth & Development Office and Ministry of Defence are not too far away. The ruling classes have not exactly been supportive of the Irish over the years. In a conversation with Peter Mandelson, Secretary of State for Northern Ireland, the late Margaret Thatcher is said to have asserted: 'You can't trust the Irish, they're all liars.'[2]

In Trafalgar Square, in front of the National Gallery, crowds have gathered before a stage on which rock music mixed with Irish folk songs is being played. We try to move closer to the front, but it's impossible. The sound of plastic cups crunching underfoot is deafening, and we can see endless rows of people all keen to have a good time. I wriggle my way through the crowd, making my way up to the beautiful gallery building, where I stand looking out over the square. Green hats and wigs stick up everywhere; Irish flags wave against the sky.

The Irish also occupied Trafalgar Square back in 1887 – not with music, but with shouts and protests. On 13 November that year over 10,000 people marched against unemployment, and to demand the release of William O'Brien, an Irish-born Member of Parliament who agitated for a free Ireland. Earlier that autumn, on 9 September, O'Brien had organised an even larger demonstration in Mitchelstown, Ireland, but the demonstration hadn't gone according to plan. The fray ended badly, and several people lost their lives. The demonstration in Trafalgar Square was arranged by the Irish National League and the Social Democratic Federation – the United Kingdom's first socialist party. Among those who gathered in Trafalgar Square that day were playwright George Bernard Shaw and textile designer William Morris, both of whom were political activists who supported the Irish cause. But the London police had no intention of letting the demonstration go ahead, and 2,000 policeman – along with 400 soldiers – were deployed to stop the march. The atmosphere soon turned hostile, and after bloody clashes between the demonstrators and the police, around 400 people were arrested. Around 30,000 people are said to have stood and watched the fracas, almost like a theatre performance. The incident would later become known as Bloody Sunday.[3]

From where I'm standing, I can see a group of young women and men who are rhythmically shouting: 'CHOICE!' These are activists from the London-Irish Abortion Rights Campaign. Some of the women are holding up home-made placards featuring paintings of Bernadette Devlin, the Northern Irish activist and politician who had children outside of marriage. The battle Irish women have fought to change abortion legislation has been a bloody one – quite literally. In 1867, abortion was regarded as a criminal act punishable by life in prison. In 1983, the life of the foetus was granted equal status to that of the mother, and those who performed abortions could risk up to fourteen years in prison. In 2012, Ireland's strict abortion legislation had fatal consequences for Indian dentist Savita Halappanavar when the hospital in Galway to which she was admitted refused to terminate her pregnancy, despite the risk it posed to her life. After developing blood poisoning at seventeen weeks pregnant, Halappanavar died. An abortion could have saved her life. The story led to outrage and significant public engagement, and Ireland was strongly criticised for its restrictive legislation.

But despite the strict abortion laws, Irish women managed to have several hundred thousand abortions over the years. London became the arena for a bustling, radical feminist community, which many Irish women joined; these women quickly formed a network to help their Irish sisters find doctors who could perform abortions, along with a place to recover after the procedure. In 1980, the informal Irish Women's Abortion Support Group (IWASG) was established, with the aim of formalising the collection of funds and providing accommodation, advice and lists of doctors' contact details.[4] Two years later, in 1982, the London Irish Women's Centre was opened at 59 Stoke Newington Church St, where access was limited to women only.[5]

'Some people in the neighbourhood stopped speaking to me when they found out what I was doing,' says Ann Rossiter.

I look at her, dumbfounded.

'It's true. There are many Irish women around here. They were appalled and wouldn't have anything to do with me for many years. Now they say hello, at least.'

I'm in Northfields, west London – a neighbourhood full of Irish from back when they built Heathrow airport. Ann helped Irish women to access abortions at a time when this was regarded as more shameful. She's an older woman with red hair and a big heart – a heart that has recently been operated on. Unembarrassed, she tugs down her blouse to show me the scar. Ann's husband, an Indian mathematician now retired from his position at the London School of Economics, tries in vain to get her to take it easy, but Ann has so many books and journals she wants to show me here in her cosy house in Northfields. This is clearly the home of two people who love to read and write. Ann came to London in the early 1960s to attend university. But then the unmentionable happened.

After Ann fell in love with a Nigerian law student and found herself pregnant, she had an abortion. The experience affected her deeply. The United Kingdom in the 1960s wasn't just parties and free love – it was also a period steeped in moralism and indignation. Irish author Edna O'Brien was one of the first people to dare to depict Irish women's desire – and hint at divorce and abortion – in her book *The Country Girls*, which came out in 1960. The book's publication shook Ireland to its core, and O'Brien was publicly disgraced. The book was banned. O'Brien's parents were harassed, and the priest at the author's local church burned the book in public.

'People know that Irish women travelled to London to work, but that wasn't the only reason. Most of all, it was freedom they were looking for,' Ann says.

Many Irish women felt trapped in the towns and villages in which they lived, but their emigration didn't go unnoticed. President Éamon de Valera believed the women who didn't wish to stay in Ireland, instead choosing the backstreets of London, risked falling into a moral abyss. But Leo Varadkar – Taoiseach from 2017 to 2020 – is cast from a different mould entirely. He has an Indian-Irish background, and was not only the first openly gay prime minister of Ireland, but also the first to permit a referendum on the liberalisation of Ireland's abortion law, the Eighth Amendment. On 25 May 2018, Ann cried with joy when an overwhelming majority voted to repeal the Eighth.

But Ann remains worried about a group of Irish women who pass under the radar for most people – the travellers.

'I've helped girls who belong to the travellers,' Ann explains. 'One of my recent guests was a young girl who had fallen pregnant after cheating on her husband – she risked being beaten if he found out what had happened. These girls often have many children – their families are large and many of them live under strict social control,' she says.

Irish travellers have always been part of the city landscape and are in constant conflict with local inhabitants; tensions always increase when the travellers settle in parks or large car parks. Official figures don't exist, but according to the London Gypsy and Traveller Unit, around 30,000 travellers with an Irish background live in London – descendants of the first Irish travellers to make their way to the city after the Great Famine. The men sold horses and worked as tin smelters, which earned them the unflattering nickname 'tinkers'. YouTube features numerous videos of young male Irish travellers bareknuckle fighting – a tradition among the Irish – and these are enthusiastically shared. The travellers and their fighting culture have also been immortalised in Guy Ritchie's film *Snatch* (2000), featuring Brad Pitt as 'One Punch' Mickey O'Neil.

In 2010, the Irish travellers burst into the British public consciousness through Channel 4's documentary series *Big Fat Gypsy Weddings*, which gave viewers an opportunity to see inside an extremely closed community for the first time. But the serious problems faced by the community were not examined by the programme, which instead chose to focus on the extravagant wedding dresses of women who were portrayed as spoiled and rich – a reality that isn't true for the majority of Irish travellers.

'I don't want to seem prejudiced, but the fact that many girls in this community suffer under extremely patriarchal attitudes is a real problem. Many of them are encouraged to marry extremely young, and having an abortion would cause a complete scandal. Homosexuality is also mainly frowned upon,' Ann says.

A significant proportion of women among the Irish travellers have been subjected to domestic violence. Illiteracy is widespread, and many girls are taken out of school at a young age in order to marry. They live in caravans under a strict social regime, and the suicide rate within the community is significantly higher than among the rest of the population. Due to urban renewal, the travellers are losing access to an ever-increasing number of the green spaces in which they were once able to stay. This creates an unsafe situation for the women, who lose the opportunity to seek out crisis centres when they are forced to move often. Previously, the travellers would tend to stay at a site for a much longer period of time.

On my way back into the city I take the bus, and there, hidden beneath the Westway motorway that stretches from Paddington to

North Kensington, I catch a glimpse of the caravans and mobile homes of Stable Way. I see them because I know that they are there; the caravans are surrounded by wrecked cars and other rubbish. Since it was built in 1968, between thirty and forty travelling Irish families have lived beneath the Westway, not far from the Westfield shopping centre, which stands on the former site one of London's most disadvantaged housing areas, White City. Most of the travellers make their living by manning stalls at Portobello Market. The children cycle around and catch rabbits, apparently completely unfazed by the traffic that thunders past them.

To walk around beneath the Westway is to explore concrete and brutalism, a place that is both alienating and captivating all at once. In this area in which property prices are skyrocketing, it is probably only a matter of time before the travellers are forced to move on for being a perceived stain on the city.

One of London's enduring strengths has always been that anyone can find a home here. If the travellers disappear, then a special part of the Irish heritage in the city will also be lost. And not only that – London's hospitable and open heart will become smaller, too.

My heart sinks as the bus moves on.

Jewish London –
Stamford Hill, Arsenal, Tottenham, Finchley

The myth of Kosher Nostra

'Isn't it a fantastic sight?'

Alan Dein and I are standing at the entrance to the Coronet, an old cinema that has been converted into a pub on Holloway Road in north London. As far as the eye can see there are red and white scarves and football shirts. Men with thinning hair wearing slightly too tight Arsenal jerseys and gold chains around their necks. Families with children, each wearing the shirt of their favourite player. Alan is visibly proud. I'd like to enjoy the view, but he's impatient. 'Come on, let's go to the stadium – that's where we need to be,' he says, ushering me down Holloway Road. Alan is in his fifties, with horn-rimmed glasses. When he's not attending Arsenal games he runs the show *Don't Log Off* on BBC Radio 4.

Surrounded by Arsenal fans we walk past the Islington pub, where the singing is alarmingly loud. In the 1980s, British football fans were notoriously violent, and known for their racist attitudes; they were often skinheads and members of the National Front. I see a big crowd of bald-headed white men inside the pub, and am actually a little relieved that we're not going inside. We turn on to a small side street. On a corner, a group of football fans are drinking beer.

'Look, Che Guevara is a "Gunner" too. The revolution is red!'

Alan Dein points towards the El Comandante pub, with its hanging sign featuring an image of Che. So-called 'Gunners' have taken over the pub, the street corner – yes, the entire street. We're on our way to the Emirates Stadium, which looms into view a couple of hundred metres away. Surrounded by council flats, modern apartment complexes and rows of traditional British terraced houses, the facility actually looks a little out of place. Not far away, Tottenham have built their new facility in White Hart Lane. Tottenham Hotspur Stadium can hold a couple of thousand more spectators than the Emirates, and in some people's eyes has given a tired neighbourhood a much-needed lift. In the early 2000s, oligarch Roman Abramovich is said to have considered buying Tottenham, but thought the area too dilapidated and so chose Chelsea instead. Just as well, I think, because he obviously hasn't understood the slightest thing about London if he can't appreciate a touch of grime.

'I'm sure Che would have supported Arsenal. By the way, did you know that Osama bin Laden once went to an Arsenal game? Once you've seen Arsenal play, you'll be addicted for life – I can promise you that!'

I have to laugh at Alan's boundless enthusiasm. Football fans seem to lose their grip on reality whenever their favourite team is playing. And this isn't just any game that is about to take place: Arsenal are about to play Tottenham – Gunners against Spurs. Two teams from north London. Bitter rivals. A decisive match. Arsenal have been struggling; Spurs are full of themselves. Anything could happen. I'm here because both teams have deep roots in Jewish London, and Alan is a Jewish Arsenal supporter.[1]

'I've heard rumours that Arsenal are the team of the intellectual, slightly more refined Jews, while Spurs followers are working class?'

Alan laughs loudly.

In the years between 1880 and 1919, around 250,000 Jews arrived in Britain from Eastern Europe due to the pogroms. They wanted to escape the brutal persecution, and sought refuge in Manchester, Glasgow and London. The British Jewish community, however, was not entirely enthused. They had been in the country since the 1200s, and had fought a hard-won battle to become part of the British middle class, into which they were now almost entirely assimilated. They spoke English, and apart from when they visited the synagogues, they were like most other Brits. Religion was a private matter. They were worried that the arrival of the new Jewish immigrants, the *Ostjuden* (Jews of the East), would stir up anti-Semitic attitudes, because these Jews came from the villages, belonged to the working class and spoke Yiddish.

The British organisation, the Jewish Board of Deputies, printed advertisements in Eastern European newspapers in an attempt to dissuade Eastern European Jews from coming to England, but these had little effect. The poor, homeless Jews arrived, and began working in east London in the garment industry, often under terrible conditions in sheds, stables and dilapidated industrial premises.

Looking for a way to help the newly arrived, the wealthy British Jews set in motion a grand-scale project to 'anglicise' them, including teaching them English and encouraging assimilation to try to ward off anti-Semitism. A dedicated Jewish youth organisation, the Jewish Lads' Brigade, was founded in 1895, inspired by the British Scouts movement. Their motto was *A good Jew and a good Englishman* – the emphasis being on 'Englishman'.[2]

In the early 1900s, the Jewish Committee for Dispersion encouraged Jewish families to move from overcrowded Brick Lane and Whitechapel in east London to find better properties and work elsewhere. Over the next thirty years, large groups of Jews moved north – to Holloway, Tottenham and Arsenal.

Developing an interest in sports was one of the keys to becoming part of British society. When the Jews made their homes in Tottenham, it became natural to follow the local football team. The

Jews felt they had to prove that they were part of British society. They didn't want to stand out, and one way of assimilating was through football. But this new-found interest wasn't equally well received by everyone within the community. The rabbis denounced physical activity, and especially football. '*Footbollick*. Grown men running around like *meshuga* [crazy people],' the older men are said to have exclaimed in disgust.[3] They would have preferred the boys to concentrate on staying in *schul*, synagogue. Resistance was therefore futile. In the 1930s, a third of Tottenham's 30,000 inhabitants were Jewish. Few of the Jewish boys could permit themselves to dream of having a career as a professional footballer – religious life was too important for that. But even if they couldn't play, they could at least watch.

The weekly pilgrimage to White Hart Lane on Saturdays would turn out to be a challenge for the more Orthodox Jews with football on the brain, because the matches were played early in the afternoon. In the Jewish faith, the Sabbath – which lasts from Friday afternoon to Saturday evening – is holy. A practising Jew is not permitted to travel, drive a car, use electrical equipment or write – to mention just a few of the thirty-nine rules that exist – during the Sabbath. Jews are also expected to be at home or in the synagogue during the Sabbath, not at football matches. Prior to the Second World War, the buses were operated by electricity, and using this form of transport during the Sabbath was therefore not an option for Jewish football fans. Even among the most secular Jews, going to football games before the Sabbath was over gave rise to great pangs of conscience. But the problem was solved when some smart person realised that they could take the tram – this was steam-operated, and tickets could be purchased in advance on Friday morning. This meant that eager Jewish boys could attend the matches, even if doing so might involve sneaking away before the Sabbath was technically over.

'Did you ever have to sneak out before the Sabbath was over when you were young?' I ask Alan.

'Hahaha . . . Luckily I had a liberal upbringing. We went to football matches instead of *schul*,' he says.

Arsenal was first embraced by the Jews in the 1930s, when Jewish intellectuals arrived from the Continent and were dazzled by the team's wonderful stadium and management.

Alan and I walk past the statue of popular Arsenal manager Herbert Chapman, who is standing on a plinth outside the Emirates Stadium, looking reasonably pleased with himself. In addition to being pioneering in the way he nurtured his players, he was also an enthusiastic supporter of Jewish charitable causes throughout his years as the team's manager,[4] and when he died in 1934, the *Jewish Chronicle* described Chapman as a friend of the Jewish people. Even as far back as the 1960s, Arsenal would wish their spectators a happy Yom Kippur, the holiest of all holy days for the Jews, in honour of their Jewish fans. Tottenham followed suit in 1973. Arsenal also once delayed a match for an hour, just to be sure that it wouldn't coincide with Yom Kippur, which lasts for twenty-five hours. But it is Tottenham that many football fans think of as being the most Jewish team in London. Alan and I ponder why this impression has stuck, and we can't quite figure it out. Alan tells me that Leyton Orient has a strong Jewish heritage, too.

Today, Arsenal FC is owned by the unassuming American billionaire Stan Kroenke, who isn't Jewish.

Small groups of police officers have been stationed all around the stands – I'm clearly not the only one to have thought about the chaos British football fans are capable of setting in motion.

'By the way, did you know that the Jews were originally into boxing before they became football fans?' Alan asks.

'Yes – I've heard that! But it seems hard to believe now,' I say, thinking about how boxers like Amir Khan, Frank Bruno and

Lennox Lewis have made names for themselves in recent years. They are of Pakistani and Caribbean descent.

The Jews embraced boxing as a sport because they had to protect themselves against attacks from the fascists who went around east London looking for trouble throughout the 1920s and 1930s.[5] The British Jews who had attended private schools, and found that physical exercise was good for both body and mind, also encouraged other Jewish youths to take up boxing. Jewish philanthropists started comprehensive boxing training programmes for the young men at all the Jewish youth clubs. Matches against gentiles, that is, non-Jews, were encouraged, to signal that Jewish men were capable of participating in society at large and able to protect themselves. But throughout the 1920s and 1930s, influential conservative Jews believed that boxing was bringing about a decline in morals. They didn't like how the young Jewish men seemed to prioritise a secular, anglicised lifestyle that involved visiting cafés, dancing and hanging around cinemas, rather than preserving their Jewish identity at the synagogues.

In 1929, the *Jewish Chronicle* asked 'Is Anglo-Jewry Decadent?' and stated: 'in the East End today we find young men growing up almost with a loss of moral sense. They are adherents of the cheap boxing halls ... [and] are joining, unfortunately, the hooligan element of the populace.'[6] But what some deemed a lack of morals was a way out of the ghetto for others. And those who criticised boxing overlooked the fact that strong men were actually a part of Jewish folklore. Strong men, *schtarker*, had always been part of Jewish life. In the 1920s, escape artist extraordinaire Harry Houdini was a perfect example of such a *schtarker* – they were protectors of the Jewish people.[7]

For several young Jewish men, a love of boxing led to international success. Two such men were Ted 'Kid' Lewis, born Gershon Mendeloff, and later Judah Bergman, better known as Jack 'Kid' Berg. Both Mendeloff and Bergman were born in east London to

Eastern European parents, and began boxing at the age of fourteen. Bergman exhibited his talent early on by winning the youth welter-weight championship, and went on to live an extravagant lifestyle. Although Bergman was in no way Orthodox, he would often perform a long prayer ritual in the ring before each match, but allegedly only did so to give the match an 'ethnic twist'. Regardless, he insisted on wearing Orthodox clothing before fights, and often boxed with the Star of David on his shorts. Kid Lewis, who was often referred to as the Yiddish Wonderman, went even further, sewing small leather pouches containing tiny scrolls featuring texts from the Torah into his shorts. Other Jewish boxers went the other way – they changed their names or adapted them to make them more accessible. Buchalter became Bookman, Gidanansky turned into Goldberg. But despite the success of the Jewish boxers, in the 1930s the older Jews were worried about the fragmentation of the Jewish communities, and what they regarded as religious apathy. While the boxing ring became a place where young Jewish men could prove themselves, the world of football became the arena for a more troubling incident that would bring hidden anti-Semitic attitudes in England out into the light. Jewish football supporters in London soon realised that they had more than angry rabbis to worry about.

In October 1935, it was announced that White Hart Lane had been chosen by the English Football Association (FA) as the arena for a friendly between Germany and England. This was regarded as a curious choice, because it was well known that Tottenham was the team in London with the strongest links to the Jewish community; some of the club's players were also Jewish at the time. The decision was cast in an extra harsh light because it was only a month since the Germans had introduced the Nuremberg Laws, which stripped German Jews of their citizenship and prohibited marriages between Germans and Jews. Extensive protests from Jewish organisations, unions and football groups were ignored by the FA, who claimed that it was too early to judge Hitler and that sport should be apolitical. A diplomatic shuttle service would turn out to be necessary, however, and Goebbels agreed that the German players would dress as neutrally as possible and not wear the swastika. At the same time, British newspapers were full of letters from readers who didn't appreciate the Jewish attempts being made to stop the game. One letter writer to local newspaper the *Tottenham Weekly Herald* said: 'It's going too far when the Jews try to dictate to us. It will be the Jews who cause another war between England and Germany.' Another believed that English sports fans should be able to enjoy 'their favourite pastime without interference'. Others were clearer still: 'The Jews apparently do not realise they are guests in England. They are only making things worse for themselves.'[8] When it became known that 6,000 Jewish supporters had planned to leave the match in protest, one of Spurs' oldest supporters wrote an article entitled 'England for England': 'I am in every way with them that they should walk out – but with a one-way ticket and not come back. The Spurs will always find enough English support without worrying about the "Yids" . . . It will be very nice to watch an English match with only English supporters.'

Pathé News followed some of the 10,000 German men in suits who arrived in London's West End to go sightseeing and shopping ahead of the match; 300 coaches and 800 guides were hired for the occasion. The bus drivers were given specific instructions about where to drive, and instructed not to go into east London, where the Jews lived. Nor were they permitted to answer political questions. Among the guides were German Jews, who lacking other work had accepted the job. Pathé's news reports praised the German football fans for their proper conduct: 'We must give them their due, they were an orderly crowd. There was no shouting or flag waving.'[9]

At White Hart Lane, 60,000 spectators had gathered to watch the match. A large number of them were Jewish. Eight hundred police officers were stationed at the event – an unusually high number for a football match, but the organisers were nervous and didn't want to take any risks. Anti-Nazi demonstrators lined the road all the way from the train station where the fans arrived, down to White Hart Lane. The police ripped down posters and banners stating: 'Our Goal, Peace. Hitler's Goal, War', 'Hitler Hits Below the Belt' and 'Keep Sport Clean, Fight Fascism'. All those who shouted slogans were arrested, and flyers were torn to pieces by the police. Near the football pitch, anti-Semitic groups had hung up posters with the words 'Perish Judah' – these the police left alone. The German fans were gathered in the eastern corner of the stands, and despite the agreement Goebbels had made with the British, all of them waved Nazi flags bearing the swastika. Before kick-off, the German national team raised their arms in a Nazi salute, while the English team stared at the ground. Astonishingly, the FA had given the Germans permission to raise a Nazi flag above White Hart Lane.

One Spurs supporter in particular felt his heart sink at this. Ernie Wooley was a blacksmith from Shoreditch. He decided to show his disgust, and halfway through the match climbed up on to the roof and tore the flag down. 'The Nazi flag is hated in this country,' he explained to the policeman who arrested and fined him, but just a few minutes later, the flag was waving above the stands again. At the time, nobody had any idea just how symbolic this match would turn out to be. Germany lost 0–3 to England, and after the game, during the subsequent dinner with representatives from the German and English football associations in attendance, Sir Charles Clegg, president of the English FA, rebuked the British Trades Union Congress for bringing politics into football. Clegg believed this should be the last time anything of the sort ever took place. At the end of the dinner a toast was raised to the Queen – and to Adolf Hitler.

*　　*　　*

The Jewish presence in British football has been complicated, when it comes to both the fans and the clubs. Sports journalist and author Anthony Clavane says that the Jewish traces in football's history are hard to find, because many Jews were reluctant to publicly reveal their Jewish background. The true number of players of Jewish descent is therefore difficult to quantify.

However, some players were indeed open about their identities. One such player was Mark Lazarus, who was born in 1938 in Stepney, Tower Hamlets. He became a hero among Jewish football fans, when after a brief career as a boxer he turned to football. He first played for Leyton Orient, and was later recruited by Queens Park Rangers. The high point of his career was his match-winning goal in the 1967 League Cup final, when Queens Park Rangers beat West Bromwich Albion 3–2 at Wembley.

'Leyton Orient were the team the Jews originally stood with. West Ham, in Stratford, were the dockworkers' team. They were too white, too cockney, for the Jews, who didn't feel entirely welcome among them,' Alan says.

But not everyone was equally comfortable with their Jewish roots. Micky Dulin, who played for Tottenham in the 1940s, has said that he never spoke with anybody about his Jewish background: 'It was best to keep schtum.' Former BBC sports editor and author, Mihir Bose, has claimed that a kind of unofficial apartheid existed between the Jewish supporters of the club and its English owners, and that this continued until Jewish businessman Irving Scholar bought Tottenham Hotspur FC in 1982. When Scholar took over the club, Tottenham's Jewish heritage was firmly reinforced. Because the club was heavily in debt, Scholar and businessman Paul Bobroff, who was also Jewish, decided to list the club on the stock exchange. This led the club into a catastrophic financial situation, which was finally resolved by two other Jewish businessmen – Robert Maxwell and then Alan Sugar. Today, Tottenham Hotspur is mainly owned by

British investment group ECIN, led by Daniel Levy and Joe Lewis, who also have Jewish roots.

I talk to Alan about all the Muslim footballers who are highlighted in the media – there are now a great number who have played in the English league: Mohamed Salah, Paul Pogba, Mesut Özil, Yaya Touré and Sadio Mané. And they have truly made names for themselves. In 2015–16, 2016–17 and 2017–18, the Premier League's 'Player of the Year' was Muslim: Riyad Mahrez, N'Golo Kanté and Salah, respectively. Salah continues to play an important role as a Muslim footballer.

'Where are all the newspaper articles about the Jewish football players?' I ask Alan.

He shakes his head.

'Isn't there a kind of Jewish Zlatan?'

'Well, some people like to point to David Beckham – his grandfather was Jewish. Other than that, there's nobody. The most significant was probably George Cohen, who almost scored a goal at Wembley when England won the World Cup in 1966. But he wasn't raised Jewish, so . . .'

Alan believes Jewish boys don't have the incentive to work as hard as professional footballers need to – they don't have to become footballers in order to do well in life. It's about class. Most British players come from the working class, where football is their ticket out of poverty. There's no escaping the fact that Jews have won more Nobel Prizes than football trophies.

London's Jews have taken formidable strides up the social ladder, from dilapidated housing in Hackney to large, well-maintained detached properties in Golders Green, Hendon, Finchley and Muswell Hill. Prosperous neighbourhoods that reflect the positions of Jews in the media, medicine, law and other middle-class professions. The ultra-Orthodox, however, continue to live in east London, in Hackney and the neighbourhoods of Stamford Hill and Stoke Newington.

We're now standing in front of the gates, where the enthusiasm of the crowd seems bottomless. The Tottenham fans have long since gone inside – they've been let in early in order to avoid clashes.

In the 1970s, Tottenham's opponents began to mock the team's Jewish affiliations. At first, the heckling was good-natured. From among the stands, fans could be heard shouting: 'Does your rabbi know you're here?' Gradually, the jeers became darker: 'Spurs are on their way to Auschwitz, Hitler's gonna gas 'em again', followed by sounds reminiscent of a gas leak and the increasing use of Nazi salutes. The hate continued to develop, and the team's opponents began to use the word 'Yids' to describe Tottenham's supporters.

Historians continue to debate the origins of this word, but everyone agrees that it was originally used by Oswald Mosley and the British Union of Fascists as they stormed around east London shouting: 'Take the Yids!' In an attempt to stop the hate, Spurs fans decided to claim the word for themselves and display their Jewish affiliation with pride. During the games, spectators could suddenly hear Tottenham fans shouting: 'We are the Yids! We are the Yiddos!' The traditional Jewish skullcap, the kippa, also became a common sight among the crowds in the stands. Israeli flags appeared, as did the Star of David on home-made banners. There could be no doubt: Tottenham fans were proud of their Jewish heritage. But not everyone was comfortable with the use of the word Yid, and it gradually became regarded as just as loaded and offensive as other ethnic slurs.

In 2013, use of the term attracted national attention when for the first time the Metropolitan Police decided to criminalise use of the word Yid during a match against West Ham. Three Tottenham Hotspur supporters who sang 'We are the Yids' were charged, and publicly denounced as racists.[10] But strikingly, the West Ham supporters who sang about Hitler and gas chambers were not reprimanded – not by the police, nor by the FA. As part of their bail conditions, the three Tottenham supporters were prohibited from being in the vicinity of a football pitch within four hours of the start or end of a match – and during the game itself, of course. But the charges were dropped when the prosecution found that there were no realistic reasons to believe that a prosecution would be successful. This only meant that the word Yid became even more popular among Tottenham fans.

Jewish comedian and Chelsea fan David Baddiel became tired of the use of the term, and in collaboration with the FA therefore decided to record the video *The Y-Word*, in which several British footballers condemned the use of the word Yid. Baddiel was sick of being at matches when Chelsea played Tottenham, and hearing Chelsea supporters at Stamford Bridge shouting: 'Fuck the Yids! Fuck the Jews!' while raising their right hands in salute.[11]

Around us, even more fans have arrived, roaring: 'Arsenal!' My ears begin to hurt. When the Premier League was started in 1992, on the initiative of Arsenal's David Dein and Tottenham's Irving Scholar, only eleven of the players were from overseas. Today, the league features over 300 overseas players from sixty-six countries. Over half of the clubs are owned by foreigners. Chelsea is owned by the Russian oligarch Roman Abramovich, an acquisition which prompted the *Sun* to write a column about Kosher Nostra, because Abramovich's closest employees were all Jewish. In 2007, even *The Times'* chief football correspondent Martin Samuel commented: 'To understand Abramovich, it is important to acknowledge that the strongest cultural influence on his life is not his nationality but his faith. In the early days of the Roman invasion, when the owner was a figure of some mystery, it was pointed out to those seeking a handle on the new man that his Jewish heritage was felt more strongly than his Russian roots. It is this that he shares with his inner circle.'[12]

Abramovich has taken action in the fight against anti-Semitism: in 2018, the media-shy club owner went public, encouraging fans to confront it. Chelsea have also said that they want to send fans caught using hate speech on study trips to Auschwitz in an attempt to educate them, rather than banning them for life.[13]

The match is about to begin. In the stands, the roaring of the crowd has increased in intensity. I can tell that Alan wants to go. He waves to me as he disappears inside.

I find a pub showing the football on TV nearby, where Arsenal fans have got themselves set up to watch the game. They shout and cheer. After the first half, Arsenal is two goals down. The mood is subdued, and out on the terrace the loud cheers have turned into bitter mutterings. But during the second half, things turn around. In the end, the Gunners win the game against Spurs 4–2. There will be unending cheers of joy in Arsenal tonight. And maybe Jewish supporters will throw a kippa or two skywards in unrestrained ecstasy? If so, I'm sure the rabbis will forgive them, just for this afternoon.

My rabbi in London

A group of Orthodox Jewish men are walking down the pavement towards me. They give me a wide berth, anxious not to make any physical contact. All of them are wearing long black coats; on their heads they wear black hats; and they carry paper bags filled with shopping and bouquets of flowers. More emerge from what seems to be a bakery. I check my watch – it's almost one o'clock. The Sabbath is just a few hours away. I'm on Old Hill Street in north-east London, in the neighbourhood of Stamford Hill. Few streets in London are as kosher as this one. Alan suggested that I take a good old-fashioned sightseeing trip to this street to get a glimpse of *shtetl life* – Jewish village life. Right at the heart of east London.[1]

The Orthodox Jews keep to themselves here in north London, where they have everything they need. I've observed them several times with deep curiosity in the neighbourhood of Mea Shearim when I have visited Jerusalem, and in London I've sometimes caught sight of members of their community on the Underground in Hackney, or when visiting the spectacular Alexandra Palace on its hill halfway between Turkish Wood Green and Jewish Muswell Hill, where like most families they visit the playgrounds or go for walks. If you look closely, you'll notice that the women wear wigs, *sheitel*, while others cover their heads with shawls or hats. They often shave off their own hair – a practice that becomes compulsory when they marry. The requirement to cover the head is connected to ancient customs dictating that women should show modesty, and refrain from boastful behaviour. Some Orthodox Jewish women choose to wear a scarf or shawl because they believe that wigs look too much like real hair, and so therefore defeat the object of the exercise. The men must also follow certain requirements: they always wear a hat or kippa. Some of the men also wear a large, round fur hat, a *shtreimel*, and they always wear a beard. To outsiders, all Orthodox Jewish men may appear alike, but within the ultra-Orthodox community there are many nuances to orthodoxy. And there are also many other smaller branches to Judaism – it is just as diverse as most other religions.

In the same way that Muslims have become a seamless part of London's urban landscape, the Orthodox Jews have also inhabited the capital for a long time – since as far back as the 1800s. They keep a low profile, and have a reputation for being introverted. They have their own gender-segregated religious schools, *yeshiva*, and keep their distance from the secular world, as they believe it prevents them from maintaining a close relationship to God. Ultra-Orthodox Judaism, also known as Hasidism, is a branch of Judaism that arose in Eastern Europe in the 1700s as a reaction to increasingly liberal Jewish practices, where scholars became proponents of the integration of secular life. The ultra-Orthodox regulate their daily lives by the 613 commandments of the Torah – a collective term for the five books of Moses. The commandments contain both prohibitions and commands.

It is estimated that there are around 1 million ultra-Orthodox Jews across the world, and around 20,000 of these live here in London – the largest group in Europe. Ultra-Orthodox Jews are also the group of Jews that have the most children, and in 2030 they may comprise over half of all British Jews, which today account for around 0.5 per cent of Britain's population.[2]

I go into the bakery that I just saw the men rush out of. Lining the walls are rows of steel shelving stuffed with all sizes of braided breads – challah – and on smaller shelves are plastic containers filled with Jewish biscuits. Stacks of small, croissant-like pastries known as *rugelach* fill the premises with the smell of freshly baked goods; the fresh-produce counter contains bagels filled with cream cheese and salmon, wrapped in cling film. Behind the counter, three men are rapidly adding up prices as men wearing suits choose between spelt and sweet challah. Old Hill Street has several such bakeries, and they seem to be equally busy. Next to one of the bakeries is a bookshop, which specialises in Orthodox Jewish children's books. The publishers of such books are strict about what can be shown in them – you'll find no bare legs here, and girls and boys are presented separately. There are occasional newspaper reports that, in Jewish schools, the textbooks that depict boys and girls together are censored. Across the street I see a grocery store, a kosher snack bar that must be the only one of its kind to serve fresh falafel in pitta bread, and beside this, Hoffman's Fish & Delicatessen.

Old Hill Street is not just a kosher street. The Orthodox Jews here live side by side with Kurds, Caribbeans, Sikhs, Christians, Muslims and Hindus. St Thomas's Church towers at the end of the street by Clapton Common, and right beside the church is a mosque. It is not only Jewish village life that is found here – this is a microcosm of London, of urban life. London's ability to absorb diversity can hardly be better observed anywhere else.

Old Hill, however, is not the only place where you can experience the feeling of Jewish village life. Ten minutes away by bus is the small but equally bustling community of Stamford Hill. The queue at the well-preserved J. Grodzinski & Daughters bakery is long. This kosher bakery chain has existed since as far back as 1888, and was founded by husband and wife Harris and Judith Grodzinski. In the mid-1960's, the chain became Europe's largest supplier of kosher baked goods. In the light, tidy store there is a separate sushi section, and shelves upon shelves filled with baked goods such as bagels and challah. These can also be made to order in various shapes, from keys to menorahs (seven-armed candlesticks). My bag is soon heavy with warm challah from Old Hill and rugelach from Grodzinski's bakery.

The next day, I'm on my way to Stamford Hill once again, to visit Orthodox rabbi Herschel Gluck. Dusk has fallen by the time I exit Seven Sisters Underground station in the middle of Tottenham – the train that should have taken me to Stamford Hill has been cancelled due to track maintenance, a common occurrence at the weekends. Anyone who thinks it's easy to set out on a weekend journey in London using public transport will have a surprise in store; I have to wait for a bus. I perch on the bus stop's slippery, sloping bench, which has been designed to make sure it can't be used as a bed by anyone sleeping rough. It's eight-thirty in the evening, and the character of London's streets changes when darkness envelops the city. I always move with a touch of apprehension in Tottenham, which is notorious for being a rough area. Maybe this is unfair – perhaps I've been taken in by trite newspaper headlines, I really should know better, but there is little doubt that poverty, gangs and a pervasive weapons culture have made their mark on these streets. This is also an area with one of the highest rates of teenage pregnancy in Britain. Broadwater Farm, once described as Britain's worst housing estate, is just nearby; it was on these streets that riots broke out after Mark Duggan, a young Black man, was killed by police in 2011.

From where I'm standing, I can look straight at London's little Latin American paradise: Pueblito Paisa and Wards, or Seven Sisters

Indoor Market. From the outside it looks like any old rundown building, but inside it is something else entirely: over sixty small retailers selling food from all across the Latin American world, offices offering legal services, various jewellers, and an extensive range of nail and hair salons with long waiting lists. Around a hundred locals work there. On the walls are small notes offering work and lodgings, all of them written in Spanish. The market has been dubbed 'Little Colombia' and has existed here for over a decade. But the market is currently fighting for its survival – even the UN has pledged its support in the case. I wish the market well as I step aboard the bus, which finally arrives.

I take a seat by the window and watch the neighbourhood pass by. We drive past kosher butchers, and some synagogues surrounded by high fences. The *yeshivas* (the Jewish schools) are always protected by security guards.

I don't know this area of the city very well, and so end up getting off the bus too late, in Stoke Newington – a Turkish enclave, but also a place full of hipsters and left-wing radicals. Anarchist organisation the Angry Brigade, a sort of slightly cosier version of the Red Army Faction and Red Brigades, hung out here in the 1970s. They were behind a couple of minor explosions and a demonstration during a beauty contest, but never managed to cause national outrage on the same scale as their German and Italian counterparts. Eventually, I find my way to Stamford Hill. I see an increasing number of ultra-Orthodox Jewish men, easily identified by their coats, hats and beards. The Sabbath is over. On a quiet street lined with old trees and towering Victorian houses I find the home of Rabbi Gluck; a man with a slightly unruly beard opens the door and bids me welcome. We stand in the spacious hall for a moment, and the rabbi looks at me with a friendly but searching gaze as we enter the living room. Then, with a small smile, he says:

'You are Pashtun?'

'Yes, that's right.'

'So perhaps you already know that you belong to one of Israel's ten lost tribes, and so are actually Jewish?'

'Yes. That's why I'm here.'

The rabbi chuckles loudly as he disappears into the kitchen to make some tea; I have the opportunity to take in my surroundings. Cabinets filled with books and prints of old rabbis fill the dining room. The thick curtains that hang before the large room's window have been drawn. There are no family photographs or unnecessary knick-knacks here. The rabbi returns with tea, which we drink from small porcelain cups.

We quickly hit it off – the rabbi is so funny and wise that I almost consider converting. But I have my suspicions that other rabbis would probably have been much more sceptical about meeting me.

Herschel Gluck's parents originally came from Orthodox homes in Austria, and fled to London in 1939. They first lived on the outskirts of the east of the city, but then moved to Stamford Hill to improve their quality of life – the houses were bigger, and there were more parks to enjoy. They were forced to create a home from almost nothing. Gluck's father served in the British Army during the Second World War, and joined the Jewish Brigade – a dedicated Jewish division. The rabbi disappears for a moment to find the insignia his father wore – it is blue and white, faded, and bearing the Star of David. Some members of the brigade found their way into the Israeli army (Israel Defence Force) in 1948.

The Jews were part of the British Army during both world wars – around 100,000 of them fought, and 6,000 died. Gluck's father was there when the British liberated the prisoners from Bergen-Belsen concentration camp – he was traumatised by the experience, and decided to help Jews on the Continent to find their relatives after the war was over. Back in London, Gluck's father continued to help refugees, and his mother did the same. Gluck was born in 1958, and believes that his parents' benevolence and charity, which he naturally witnessed while growing up, have shaped him.

'I was lucky to grow up in London at that time; I was surrounded by people and cultures from all around the world. I had the opportunity to study with them, to interact with them and learn how they thought about things. I went to a Jewish school and was taught to be a proud Jew by obtaining knowledge about our rich Jewish intellectual heritage. We faced a crucial task: we had to strengthen our identity and culture, which had been threatened during the Holocaust,' Gluck says.

Life as an Orthodox Jew in north London was marked by a necessary isolation. After the war, the community needed to recreate a sense of safety – they avoided interaction with people who were not Orthodox, and often experienced harassment as they walked down the street. They didn't need the outside world. They established their community in Stamford Hill, with their own bakeries, clothing stores, restaurants, butchers and schools. In several areas of London where Jews live, such as Golders Green and Hendon, there are still old people's homes solely for Holocaust survivors.

Despite this social isolation, Gluck became interested in the outside world, and has played the role of active peacemaker in several of the major international conflicts of our time – including the wars in the Balkans and the Middle East – through the Century Foundation think tank. He believes his desire to engage in these activities is due to his background, growing up with parents who themselves were refugees.

'My work abroad led to me deciding to improve relations between Jews and Muslims here in London. It seemed like a logical extension of everything I had done, and my initiative was surprisingly well received,' says Gluck.

The Muslim–Jewish Forum was established in the year 2000, and I'm both surprised and impressed by the rabbi's work.

'As religious minorities in London, we have so much in common. We both face secular forces that want to destroy our traditions, and which seek to divide us,' Gluck says.

Five years later he founded the organisation Shomrim, which means 'protectors' in Hebrew – a Jewish neighbourhood-watch organisation that patrols the streets of Hackney, Haringey and Stamford Hill. They collaborate closely with the police, and describe themselves as the 'eyes and ears' on the street. According to Gluck, police in the area were overstretched and needed help. The number of anti-Semitic attacks has increased; Eastern Europeans are often behind them.

Not far away is Green Lanes, a street that features an overwhelming number of Turkish restaurants. The area is the heart of the Turkish community in London. Conservatism rules here; gender roles are set in stone. In Elif Shafak's novel *Honour* (2012), Turkish London is described through the life of a woman and her deeply complex relationship with her sons, who will do anything to protect their mother. They are strict with her, and she has little freedom. The story highlights the forces affecting women who want to move to a new country in order to live a better life, and the hypocrisy that weighs heavily on the lives of both women and men. Gluck is genuinely worried about the changes he sees within the Turkish communities in Stamford Hill and Stoke Newington. He is apprehensive about the conservative form of Islam represented by Turkey's president, Recep Tayyip Erdoğan, and how this is affecting Turkish people here in London – where Erdoğan has ardent followers.

Rabbi Gluck often shares his experiences from his meetings with various Muslim organisations on his Facebook page, and receives many comments from Jews who are clearly confounded by him.

Gluck's openness towards Muslims is regarded as almost impossible, considering that parties on both sides consider their views on Palestine to be irreconcilable.

Israel remains a touchy subject within British politics, and criticism of Israel has recently led to an intense debate about anti-Semitism in the Labour Party. The conflict's roots go all the way back to 1982, when the Labour Committee on Palestine, which later became Labour Friends of Palestine and the Middle East, was founded to promote what the organisation regarded as justice in the Middle East. The Friends of Palestine comprise a large group within the Labour Party, and former Labour leader Jeremy Corbyn was a central figure. At the same time, another decisive change took place when Margaret Thatcher came to power. She was enthusiastic about British Jews' entrepreneurship, and in 1979 five of her ministers were Jewish. The Conservative Party was also considerably more Israel-friendly. Over the years, discussions about what constitutes criticism of Israel and what constitutes anti-Semitism in British politics have become increasingly complex – especially within Labour. In October 2020, the Equality and Human Rights Commission (EHRC) published a damning report on anti-Semitism, which led to Jeremy Corbyn being temporarily suspended before he was allowed to return by Labour's new leader, Keir Starmer. However, the Labour whip will remain withheld until Corbyn apologises, which he has not done.

One evening before my meeting with Gluck, I visited the JW3 cultural centre, located on Finchley Road in West Hampstead. The modern building is surrounded by a several-metre-high metal fence you would have to be Tom Cruise to climb over. The security guard, a young Black man who was checking everyone who wished to visit the premises, gently corrected me when I tried to take photos.

'They don't like people taking photos of the outside,' he said to me.

'Why not?'

'They're afraid somebody will attack the place,' he said.

JW3 is named after the postcode and neighbourhood NW3, and is modelled on the Jewish Community Center (JCC) in Manhattan. The organisation aims to give London's Jewish population a more modern cultural institution, without the usual emphasis on traditional Jewish symbols such as menorahs or Torah scrolls. On the evening I was there, a comedy night with stand-up comedians had been arranged. A rabbi, a priest and an imam each gave a monologue, before the room was invited to take part in a discussion about religion and humour. The performance reminded me of comedy film *The Infidel* from 2010, written by British Jew David Baddiel and starring Iranian Muslim Omid Djalili in the main role as Mahmud Nasir, a relatively modern Muslim man who finds himself having to act like a believer so that his son can marry the woman of his dreams, whose family is deeply conservative. In a bizarre twist, it turns out that Nasir is adopted, and . . . Jewish. This discovery leads to cultural and religious chaos, in which all the prejudices and stereotypes Jews and Muslims hold about each other collide. I cried with laughter when I watched it.

The clerics before me in JW3 were at times tremendously funny, but would hardly be taking Baddiel or Djalili's job any time soon. Since I had identified myself as a Muslim during the discussion, Rabbi Lee Wax, who was part of the line-up, came up to me after the show and said: 'Thank God you came, I was so afraid that there would only be Jews here tonight.' Mamadou Bocoum, the young imam of Senegalese descent who participated in the performance, turned out to be an especially progressive man employed by the state to reform former terrorists. 'We have to change the way Muslims interpret Islam. Our interpretations are stuck in ancient notions that don't have anything to do with today's modern society,' he said. We quickly hit it off over the doughnuts that were handed out to celebrate Hanukkah, the festival of lights that lasts for eight days. The festival is celebrated with a special event in Trafalgar Square every year, where young Orthodox men dance unrestrainedly and everyone who wants to can eat doughnuts, which are handed out for free.

The tense relationship between parts of the Jewish community and the groups of the political establishment, and any ambitious attempts to be modern, are luckily nowhere to be felt in the little Shaarei Mazel Tov synagogue in Stoke Newington, which I visit on the weekend after my visit to the rabbi. Gluck, who led the synagogue for twenty-five years before he retired, has invited me to participate in the Saturday morning service.

Women are not permitted to enter through the main entrance of the synagogue, and I therefore have to use a special door at the side. A steep stone staircase leads me up to the gallery. Around thirty or so women from several generations are sitting together. Some have covered their heads, while others have not. On the floor below, I hear children's laughter. A group of boys are wildly running around as Rabbi Citron stands on a platform, the *bimah*, in front of the Torah scrolls and prays. Other men move to stand beside him, and carry the scrolls back to the *genizah* where they are stored, covered by a painstakingly made curtain. A couple of the boys sit down at a table and begin to read, but most of them continue to make a racket. Unlike other religious rituals I have witnessed, there is little that seems sacred about this service. While the rabbi sings or prays, two women walk back and forth setting out food on the table at the back of the premises in preparation for *kiddush*, the blessing that will take place afterwards. They carry out hummus and small cakes along with *laffa* (flatbreads), small plates of pickled vegetables and bottles of soft drinks. When the service is over, we gather and the rabbi performs the ritual blessing. I speak with Rabbi Gluck again. He emphasises that the congregation is liberal, and that they welcome everyone who is interested in Orthodox Judaism. The synagogue is especially popular among converts, and the congregation partly consists of Chilean and Iranian Jews. I'm lucky to have met Gluck – otherwise I might never have been granted access to an ultra-Orthodox synagogue.

'You don't think I would have managed to sneak in?' I ask Gluck.

Before he can answer, an older woman standing beside me snorts:

'You would have given yourself away because you're carrying a handbag! Orthodox Jews aren't allowed to carry anything during the Sabbath,' she laughs.

She shows me a metal chain she's wearing around her waist, to which she has attached her house keys. I'm not entirely sure whether to laugh at her comment, or whether it was intended to chide me. But one thing is certain: being an ultra-Orthodox Jew is an exercise in both limitations and creativity.

The rabbis and a group of men from the congregation are sitting around a table, sharing reflections on life and death. These discussions around existential questions are what fascinate me about Judaism. There appears to be no set answer, regardless of what the men ask the rabbis about. I remember something Gluck said to me at our previous meeting: 'Jews are always searching.' I wonder again whether Judaism might be something for me. Is it possible for a Muslim to become a Jew? I know that it happens, but not very often. I'm jolted out of my thoughts when one of the boys almost crashes into me. Nobody tells them to quieten down.

As I'm preparing to leave the synagogue, I stand with Rabbi Gluck for a moment, watching the lively boys.

'Do they play football?' I ask.

'No, no. Absolutely not. They concentrate on their schoolwork. Not ball games,' Rabbi Gluck says.

I suspected that might be the case.

An Orthodox charm offensive

'Give me a man hug!' A young Orthodox Jew is overpowered by a group of eager Englishmen. It's obvious that they are slightly rougher types.

'I'm not used to this, you'll have to teach me how it's done,' chuckles the Jewish man in his classic black coat and hat. Everyone laughs.

This is the kind of situation that can arise when strangers from different backgrounds suddenly try to find out whether they can live together as neighbours. Personal boundaries might be challenged for the greater good.

The number of Orthodox Jews in London is growing rapidly. The families are large, and can consist of up to seven or eight children. There is often little money to go around, since the men study full-time. To survive, they depend on the women contributing by working, often as teachers at the Jewish schools. But with big broods of children it can be hard to make life work financially.

Despairing at the situation, the Orthodox Jews have begun to look outside of London in their search for alternative homes. Borehamwood in Hertfordshire is one of the small towns in which they have settled; another is Canvey Island in Essex, which is linked to the mainland by a sandbank, just outside London where the Thames meets the North Sea. Canvey Island has around 40,000 inhabitants, and with house prices below £200,000 is an attractive option. But Britain's most anti-immigration party, UKIP, is one of the most popular political parties here. The majority of the inhabitants voted for Brexit, and the area seems to be home to a large number of guys who look like former gangsters, the kind you most often see in films, with thick Essex accents, tattoos and gold chains. Nevertheless, Canvey Island's political and cultural landscape hasn't scared off the Orthodox Jews, and the locals have shown an extraordinary interest in the Orthodox community, initiating 'get-to-know-you' meetings.

It all started when local businessman Chris Fenwick happened upon two Orthodox men strolling around Canvey Island town centre. Fenwick was curious, and asked what they were doing there. To Fenwick's surprise, the men said they wanted to move to Canvey Island. Fenwick – who since the 1970s has been the manager for Dr Feelgood, one of England's most popular pub-rock bands – wasn't afraid of a challenge or two, and decided to invite a delegation of fifteen Orthodox Jews to the town to talk with fifteen representatives from the local population, so they could gain an increased understanding of each other's lifestyles.

'We will eat, we will drink, we will make music and we will make conversation,' said Fenwick as he showed the BBC camera crew that was there to observe the unusual meeting around the conference premises.[1]

The Orthodox guests also brought their families along on the trip, so they could explore the area. The positive aspects of life by the beach soon became clear when the Orthodox children, who were used to playing in small apartments, began to run around with huge smiles on their faces. But the locals were still taken aback by how the Orthodox women withdrew to a separate part of the beach, and avoided speaking with the residents. The Orthodox girls went into the water fully clothed, while the local women sat unashamedly in swimsuits at the water's edge.

The women also discussed more serious matters. The suntanned, blonde, brash and smiling women from the local community wondered whether the Jewish children would want to play in the same places as the local children? The pale, covered Orthodox women shook their heads, and explained that this would never happen. The community's segregation by gender became a topic that bothered the local women.

The ultra-Orthodox communities are marked by strict dividing lines between men and women. But is it the case that the diaspora's need to uphold norms and traditions stems from fear? A fear that something original and genuine will be lost? Maybe this is why diaspora communities are like time capsules, fictive spaces where dreams and memories are canned and preserved, until they sometimes become almost unrecognisable from their origins. For Orthodox Jews, this preservation is even more important. They're protecting a cultural heritage that is rare, and which has been threatened. They are both new and old in this country.

Late one Friday afternoon I'm sitting on a train, making my way out to one of London's suburbs. The train is full of commuters, many of them nodding off after a long week at work. I've been invited to the meal that opens the Sabbath by Dina and Naftali Brawer, both of whom are rabbis. They have four children, and live in the small parish of Elstree and Borehamwood, a half-hour train ride from King's Cross station. The area is now home to the largest Jewish community in England.

Dina Brawer is Britain's first female Orthodox rabbi. In contrast to the women dressed in black in Stamford Hill, Dina is wearing a burgundy skirt and high heels. Her hair is covered by a scarf. I'm looking forward to experiencing this moment with them.

'Please don't turn off the light when you're done!' Dina shouts after me as I go into the bathroom to wash my hands before dinner.

In order to get around the strict rules regarding the use of electricity, all the lights and electrical appliances in the house are connected to a device that controls when everything should be off or on. Dina can't turn on the light herself if I switch it off – the device ensures that the lights will automatically be turned off at night during the Sabbath, so she can't use any of the switches. Before the meal, it is time for prayer. Dina's three sons come down from the first floor and into the dining room. The table is covered with a linen tablecloth, and lit with flickering candles. After a short prayer and song, Dina and her husband kiss their sons on the forehead and bless them. We sit down and break the bread, challah, and begin the meal, which consists of small Middle Eastern dishes, chicken and apple cake. Dina is originally from Morocco.

'The Sabbath means a lot to Jewish families. We come together and find peace. Nothing can disturb us. We can talk about important things that have happened during the week – I think Jewish families develop a strong sense of solidarity from this weekly tradition,' Dina explains.

She and her husband Naftali have lived in London for over twenty years. They are the driving force behind a more liberal variant of Orthodox Judaism, and have for example invited people to informal meetings to discuss Judaism – at cafés, instead of in the synagogues.

Dina's father was a rabbi in the community where she grew up, and she attended a Chabad school, where she met other Jewish children from different cultural backgrounds. She then moved to Israel to continue her education. It was only after she met her husband in New York that she began to feel uneasy at only being a rabbi's wife.

'I felt uncomfortable being so passive. Orthodox Jewish women are just as interested in politics, society and religious questions as men. I wanted to do more than make the preparations for the Sabbath and our holy days,' she says.

Like more conservative Islamic practices, where women for example cannot lead prayer, there are strict rules regarding what women can and cannot do within Judaism. Later, Dina encountered Kolech, the first Orthodox Jewish feminist organisation in Israel.[2] Inspired by them, she became an ambassador for the Jewish Feminist Orthodox Alliance (JOFA) in Britain. I tell Dina about my trips to Jerusalem, where I also discovered the Women of the Wall movement, which since 1988 has fought for the right to pray at the Western Wall (Wailing Wall), also known as the Kotel.[3] These women are not especially popular in Israel, and clashes with the ultra-Orthodox men often arise. A small area that permits men and women to pray together was established at the Western Wall in 2014, but the feminists want the right to pray in the main area. Dina supports the women. But life as an Orthodox woman can be challenging.

In 2015, shockwaves spread through the British Jewish community. In *The Times* newspaper, readers were presented with a photograph of a covered woman and her husband. The image was not of a Muslim couple, as most readers likely imagined, but an Orthodox Jewish couple. The woman had a white veil covering her face. The article was titled 'How I escaped my arranged marriage'.[4] Up until this point, such stories had only been shared within the Jewish community, in secret. Emily Green, as the woman was named, spoke to the newspaper about life as an Orthodox Jew – without a television, mobile phone or ordinary books. She could hardly speak or write English. Nor could her husband, who was chosen for her when she was twenty years old, speak English – he had spent a long period studying in Israel, and devoted his entire life to religious study. At the age of thirty, by which time Green had become the mother of four children, she declared she was unable to take any more. She didn't want her children to be brought up the way she had been raised. But the reactions from within the community were merciless. Emily Green had to obtain the help of the police, who issued restraining orders against both her husband and her parents, who were harassing her daily. In the end, she managed to get her children out of their Orthodox school and into an ordinary Jewish, state-run school. Her family hired lawyers in an attempt to prevent Emily from seeing her children – they were afraid her unorthodox lifestyle would ruin them. Fortunately, the courts chose to grant custody of the children to Emily. Others, however, have not been so lucky.

Dina and Naftali know families in which such events have taken place, and where the parents have been traumatised. They are terrified of the outside world. They worry their children don't have the tools or knowledge to understand the secular world they will encounter, Dina explains.

'Community is fantastic, but if you suddenly feel uncomfortable there, that community becomes a prison,' Naftali says. 'London gives you the opportunity to live life the way you want to live it – if you are strong enough.'

To help others who want to leave the Orthodox community, Emily Green started the organisation GesherEU. She has received many enquiries from both men and women who have been denied the opportunity to see their children. Divorce is not the only challenge the Orthodox community is struggling with – sometimes, it's young people who want to escape. They cut all ties, and have to start over with weak proficiency in English and little education. The culture shock can be alarming. The short film *samuel-613* (2015) by Billy Lumby explores the life of a twenty-three-year-old Orthodox man who decides to leave the community. He moves into council housing, devours bacon, experiments with drugs and alcohol, and sits in front of a computer 24/7 to absorb the world he has never known. He creates himself a profile on a dating website, which leads to a terribly unsuccessful date. To acquire as much knowledge as possible, Lumby himself walked around Stamford Hill wearing a kippa. When Lumby was asked which parish he belonged to, he answered: 'I'm between rabbis.'[5]

After the meal with Dina and Naftali, I take a taxi to the nearest Underground station to make my way back into London. My thoughts turn to several recent Netflix series that have shed light on the Orthodox communities, such as *Shtisel* and *Unorthodox*, as well as the movie *Disobedience* (2017), which stars Rachel Weisz as the main character who discovers that she is gay. Modernity is forcing its way in.

I take a closer look at the driver of the taxi. He's a young Afghan man, and as we drive down the dark roads, past fields upon fields, he explains how frustrating it can be that trains are often delayed or cancelled in the evening – he then has to drive passengers to Luton airport close by. He tells me that one night he had some passengers who were taking a flight early the next morning – he only just managed to drop them off in time because the motorway was blocked by police cars.

'Illegal immigrants. They ran across the motorway in the dark, but there's a lot of traffic and someone got hurt. Sometimes they're reported by drivers who see them, and then the police come out with dogs, to catch them.'

Our journey continues, and we approach Edgware station. Suddenly he begins to speak again.

'I picked up two friends like that. Two buddies who had fled Afghanistan. They made it to Pakistan, and then on to Calais in a lorry, where they stayed for a long time. They suddenly called me one day, and said that they were going to hide in a lorry and come to London. I said they were crazy. But after a couple of weeks they called me, in the middle of the night! "Come and get us, we're in Bournemouth," they said. Now they're washing dishes in a Pakistani restaurant and are learning English. I'm so glad that they're here,' he says, as he pulls up in front of the station.

Once again, I'm reminded of all the fates that London contains. Not everybody is as lucky as this driver's friends. There are so many battles that are fought here. According to the Home Office, there are over 200,000 illegal immigrants in Britain. Some of their stories find their way into crime series, novels and newspapers, or movies like *Dirty Pretty Things* (2002), in which desperate souls sell their organs to obtain fake passports, but the vast majority of them live and suffer in silence.

Everybody wants to come to London – the city where dreams either come true, or become nightmares.

Italian London – Soho, Clerkenwell, Bethnal Green

My Italian home

Is it possible to fall so deeply in love with an eatery that you want to move in? I've hardly been here five minutes, but already feel defence-less against all the friendliness that surrounds me in the E. Pellicci Italian café on Bethnal Green Road in east London. A man in his forties with an apron tied around his waist comes across to me with a greasy menu and a playful grin.

'I'm Nevio! What can I get you, darling?'

Before I can answer two women come in through the door and Nevio embraces them, congratulating them in turn with a kiss on the cheek. They beam at the warm reception, reciprocating the wet kisses.

'They just got new grandkids!' Nevio explains.

The tables are so close together that I can hardly understand how it's possible for him to manoeuvre around them and serve his guests.

'I'll have the cannelloni with ricotta and spinach, please,' I say to Nevio.

'Great choice!' he exclaims, and asks me whether I'm from London.

But our conversation doesn't get very far – Nevio is interrupted by a younger woman who is also serving the customers. This is his sister, Anna. The walls of the premises feature beautiful walnut art deco carvings. The furniture is well used and the floor worn, but this doesn't matter in the slightest – almost sitting on each other's laps, the diners don't seem to care a jot about the restaurant's unpretentious interior. Older men who look like they've worked hard their entire lives; ageing women wearing just a little too much make-up; young friends in flannel shirts and oversized sweaters. The portion sizes of the dishes Nevio carries out to them are generous, and the scent of tomato sauce generously seasoned with basil mingles with the smell of fried eggs and baked beans. The insistent sound of the coffee grinder means that the register of most people's voices is at least a decibel too loud. Here, a conversation can only be conducted if you shout and articulate, or if you whisper straight into your companion's ear.

E. Pellicci is a lavish manifestation of the long-term presence of Italians in London. The young Priamo Pellicci came to London in 1900, searching for a better life. When he arrived in the city he started working at this café, which at the time was owned by an Englishman. When the owner announced he was closing down the business, Priamo and his wife Elide decided to seize the opportunity to take it over. Priamo then named the café E. Pellicci in Elide's honour, and the combined offering of full English breakfasts and 'penne Pellicci' at low prices turned out to be a great success. When Priamo died in 1931, Elide continued to run the business with her children's help. When she passed away, E. Pellicci was taken over by her son Nevio, and his wife Maria. Nevio died in 2008, but Maria continues to run the restaurant with the son named after her husband, Nevio Jr – the waiter who just took my order. Her daughter Anna also helps her, along with their seventy-year-old cousin Tony – who was actually only supposed to spend a week in England on a language exchange programme sometime in the 1960s, but is still here. Young, cheerful, twenty-year-old Maria is this generation's Tony – she too came to London from Rome to learn English. My cannelloni arrives covered in a thick, delicious-looking bechamel sauce, which is golden on top.

E. Pellicci is the very embodiment of the good old-fashioned cliché of working-class London: broad accents, friendly teasing and a relaxed atmosphere. London's legendary gangsters of the 1960s, the Hoxton-born Kray twins Ronnie and Reggie, used to hang out here – reportedly because their mother didn't have time to make breakfast. It was much more important to iron the shirts of the well-dressed gangsters, who at the time were some of the biggest movers and shakers in organised crime in the capital. In this sense, E. Pellicci is a museum – a time capsule from another age – while simultaneously something else, too.

'OK, darling, can I tempt you with dessert?'

Nevio has returned to my table.

'Apple crumble with custard, please,' I answer.

'My kind of girl!' Nevio says.

Tales of community have always been a part of the great story of London's East End. Here, people care about each other. The area of Bethnal Green in Tower Hamlets is undeniably the very incarnation of this myth – perhaps because people here have always had to lean on one another: the area has traditionally been among London's most poor. Cows, pigs and people once lived side by side in these streets; the unsanitary conditions were absolutely terrible. Back then, each of the neighbourhood's houses was filled with several families who lived together in order to make ends meet, and in the 1800s the Jews sought refuge from the pogroms of Eastern Europe here. In an attempt to improve the standard of living, one of the world's first public housing estates, Boundary Estate, was built here in the year 1900. The only problem was that the area's original inhabitants – who really needed the new properties – were pushed out to what at the time was a rather miserable Dalston. The residents who moved in instead were nurses, policemen and lower-ranking civil servants.

Boundary Estate still exists, and is strikingly beautiful with its red-brick buildings and bay windows. At the centre of the estate is a small pavilion, Arnold Circus. A third of the 500 properties are now privately owned, while the rest are reserved for the less privileged.

During the Second World War, large areas of Bethnal Green were bombed. The new housing constructed after the war was poor quality, and attracted people of limited means. Poor Bangladeshi immigrants moved to Hackney and Bethnal Green in the 1970s; they live in the council flats just behind Bethnal Green Street. The main road is lined with shops selling cheap kitchen utensils, mobile-phone cases and inexpensive clothing – a dream for some, but more of a nightmare for those who fear the presence of Islam in Europe. Rarely have I observed so many women covered from head to toe in a single area of London. The clothing stores that stand shoulder to shoulder along Bethnal Green Street offer beautiful traditional outfits like shalwar kameez, featuring intricate golden embroidery. A glimpse of what exists beneath the full-length abayas.

Anna takes a seat at my table to rest for a moment. It's a little calmer in the café now. They're only open until four o'clock in the afternoon, and no alcohol is served on the premises. I ask Anna whether she socialises with the people from Bangladesh who live in the area. Over half of Bethnal Green's inhabitants are Muslims, and there are eight mosques here. It was from this area that three young girls were lured away to become IS brides; one of them, Shamima Begum, frequently features in the media as she is currently trapped in the al-Jor camp in Syria, and fighting to return to the UK.

Anna says that they don't socialise privately, but the area's atmosphere is always good-natured. The Bangladeshis are just as family-oriented as the Italians, she says. Rather than religious conflicts, the biggest problems faced by residents of the area are curious investors and market liberal politicians. But unlike nearby Hackney, Bethnal Green has experienced just a slow trickle of suited men with pound signs in their eyes. Still, the changes in the area are obvious: a former smoke-filled sports pub has now become a classy cocktail bar, and to quote a British comedian I remember watching on TV once: 'You can get a pizza served on a dustbin lid – or a plank, if you want – while you study the black-and-white photos of the bald working-class men who used to hang out there.'

'Our family moved here because it was the cheapest place they could find when they came to London. We're lucky, because we actually own the building that houses the restaurant. If we were renting, we wouldn't be able to manage financially,' Anna says.

After a busy day, E. Pellicci is about to close. The last guests are on their way out the door, but people continue to pop in to say hello or share news from their lives. Nevio Jr has gone to collect his daughters from nursery school. I'm still here because I haven't yet managed to move after my improbably large portion of apple crumble swimming in custard – and I'm still enraptured by all the conversations about love, illness, football and all the other things that make up life here in east London.

'Our café offers a sense of community in a city where people increasingly feel like strangers to each other. The neighbourhood is disintegrating. We used to say hello to each other on the street, but now people stare at the ground and avoid one another. Here in the restaurant, though, you can't do that. If you come alone, we'll seat you at a table with someone else. Only if that's OK, of course . . . but everyone always ends up talking to each other anyway. It's completely voluntary – but at the same time so rewarding!' Anna says.

She's right. The anonymity and sterile surroundings offered by the chain cafés is the complete opposite of what E. Pellicci gives you: the feeling of being at home among your very best friends. When I tell her that I want to move in, Anna laughs. The café is unique, because there is actually no other restaurant in London that has been run by a single family for such a long time. Reluctantly, I wish E. Pellicci goodbye.

'Would you like a little cake to take with you, perhaps?' Anna asks as I prepare to leave.

Before I can answer she's given me a large piece of cake wrapped in tinfoil, along with a big hug. If I lived nearby, I would without a doubt be one of those customers who always stay until closing time.

Cunning charlatans and comedians

There would be no London without the Italians. Not only did they give Londoners a taste for good coffee (which the Italians got from the Ethiopians and Arabs, of course) and *la dolce vita* – the good life – but they laid the city's very foundations. The remnants of the city wall, built by the Romans, can still be seen in several areas of London: at Tower Hill, at the Museum of London, and at the Barbican.[1] And at the centre of the City of London lies Lombard Street, which was one of the Romans' main thoroughfares back when the city was called Londinium. This was where a group of northern Italian merchants sold their wares, and ever since then Italian traders have strutted around London's streets on the lookout for good deals. In the 1600s, Italian artists and intellectuals could also be found among the London elite, and the Italians who came to London from Lombardy, Piedmont and the villages around Lake Como in the early 1700s were often craftsmen – framers and glaziers were much in demand. Mosaic artists likewise came from Italy to lay tiles in several of Britain's most beautiful buildings: St Paul's Cathedral, Brompton Oratory in Kensington, the National Gallery and Tate Britain.

Italian street urchins were also a common sight on London's streets in the 1800s. Barefoot and in rags, they hung around on the pavements where they played with trained monkeys and mice as they begged. They might also play a simple organ that ground out popular melodies by opera composers Gioachino Rossini and Vincenzo Bellini. At one point, there is said to have been over 800 Italian street urchins in London, and rumour has it that in more affluent areas they would play badly on purpose – they were then often paid to shut up.

But suspicious journalists soon found out that these children hadn't always found their way to the streets of London on their own – that they were often victims of human trafficking. The journalists discovered that padrones lured the young boys in Italy, promising poor parents that their sons would have a better life in London and that they would return home with money after three years in the city. In London, the boys were housed together in cramped, dirty lodgings and forced to buy the organ they played from the padrone, who they had to pay back using the money they earned by begging. They became slaves to debt who never earned enough – neither to buy themselves free, nor to return home again. The British reacted with shock at these revelations, but did little to change the deplorable situation. The Italians were lampooned in the newspapers, the cartoon caricatures depicting them as sly, hunched figures with big noses – they were Catholics, after all. In 1874, the Italian ambassador in London decided to take up arms against what he referred to as the white slave trade. He demanded that the Italian padrones be exposed, but the British didn't believe there were sufficient grounds for taking any legal action in the matter. In 1889, Italy adopted a law that would prevent children being used as casual workers, but the human trafficking continued.[2]

I've taken the Tube to Holborn, and start to walk along Rosebery Avenue, a wide road on which I'm surrounded by pink baroque buildings and tall trees. It leads to what in the 1800s was described as 'a wretched neighbourhood', but there is nothing rundown about Clerkenwell now. The area reputedly has more architects' offices than any other area of London. I'm heading to St Peter's Italian Church, on Saffron Hill. In the 1800s, Saffron Hill was known as an area for both Irish and Italian immigrants; the Italians settled here when they emigrated from Italy due to political unrest or destitution. At this time, London's 'Little Italy' was centred on Clerkenwell Road, Farringdon Road, Leather Lane, Saffron Hill and Hatton Gardens – a labyrinth of overpopulated narrow streets, foul-smelling alleyways, barefooted children in rags and cramped, filthy courtyards.[3] Medical journal the *Lancet* warned that the conditions in which the Italians lived represented a serious health risk. In the same buildings there are now restaurants with white tablecloths, where tattooed chefs serve organic sandwiches – and ice cream, of course. The ice cream on sale here, however, is of an entirely different quality than that sold by the Italians on these streets several hundred years ago. But it is precisely here that the ice-cream industry in London had its humble beginnings. Blocks of ice from Regent's Canal were hauled through the city before industrious Italians scraped off flakes of it, filling small cups which they sold for a shilling. Apparently, there were hundreds of ice-cream sellers in London in the early 1900s, and Carlo Gatti and Battista Bolla's ice-cream shop on Holborn Hill was the most popular. Gatti, who was originally from the Italian part of Switzerland, became the city's most successful ice-cream trader, and a pioneer in the refrigeration industry. He imported blocks of ice from Norway, which were used to store food at the city's finest eateries.

I can easily imagine the hot and eager residents of London hunting for ice as I walk past the spacious warehouses that once housed small-scale businesses. Hopeful Italian immigrants arrived here having crossed mountains on foot and slept under an open sky on their way to their new lives. At first there were few women among the Italians, but as the community grew, mothers, sisters and wives also made the journey. To supplement their incomes they made pasta and sewed lace for the aristocratic women of the city, or clothes for the Catholic priests. The older women often played the role of fortune tellers, and set themselves up with tarot cards and caged parrots. Should they manage to reel in an impressionable soul it would be the parrot – which, according to legend, had psychic powers – that would select which card the customer would be given, thereby sealing the fate that awaited them.[4]

There is disappointingly little of these kinds of curiosities to be seen as I stroll towards Grenville Road and on to Hatton Gardens, London's mythical jewellery district. Diamond giant De Beers has its headquarters here. The area's Jewish heritage is also apparent, and a small, dusty establishment offering cash in exchange for jewellery catches my attention as an older, Orthodox Jew unlocks the door and lets himself in. A shabby curtain hides what awaits inside the premises, and just a few pieces of jewellery can be glimpsed behind the sign: D. Shem-Tov, Dealers in Antiques and Fine Diamonds. There is little here to indicate that I'm in London's 'Little Italy'. In New York, 'Little Italy' is a tourist trap: ice cream, cakes, aprons, and signs that say things like 'Mafia parking only' and 'If you taka my space, I breaka you face'.

As I approach the church, I see Terroni's delicatessen. The enterprising Luigi Terroni opened a small shop here in 1878, to supply his countrymen with the food they missed from home. Beneath the black awnings are some small tables and chairs, but the clouds are just a little too dark and the wind too cold for anyone to be sitting there. Next to the shop is Casa Italiana San Vincenzo Pallotti, a clubhouse for Italian immigrants, whose owners have chosen to paint the clubhouse's sign in Italy's national colours. St Peter's Italian Church is right next door – the building towers above the others in the street. In a niche, a statuette of Jesus looks longingly towards the sky.

Outside Casa Pallotti waits Pietro Molle, who I have arranged to meet. The older Italian waves at me. We position ourselves under Terroni's awnings, alongside the other pensioners seeking refuge from the rain. Water drips from the edge of the little roof above us and on to the patent leather handbag of an older woman, but she doesn't seem to notice – she's apparently in a good mood. As the rain becomes more and more insistent our little group draws closer, huddling under the awning. Pietro tells me that he came to London in 1968. Today, he runs the charitable organisation St Peter's Project in collaboration with the church. He describes the problems Italy experienced with heroin addiction in the 1980s and 1990s – Italy had an astonishing number of heroin users during these decades. Many of them fled Italy following the introduction of legislation that forced them to register with the police if they were to receive treatment. Pietro says that having a drug problem came with significant shame. AIDS was also spreading among the young Italians, and in the 1980s Minister of Health Carlo Donat-Cattin referred to organisations that existed to help homosexuals as 'perverted'.[5] In London, the young Italians were able to find help and comfort from organisations who cared for them without judgement.

The door we have been waiting at suddenly opens, and the animated pensioners form a queue to head inside. The women tread carefully, taking one step at a time as they move up the steep narrow staircase. The paint on the walls has started to flake off; the handrail is worn smooth. At the first landing is an old wooden door, with a stained-glass window set into the top of it. It features an emblem in red, white and green: St Peter's Italian Catholic Social Club. Here, older Italians can meet over a glass of wine or lunch, as they are doing today. I look around at the plastic flowers and chalky walls. There's a din coming from the kitchen, along with the reverberating sound of shrill female voices. In the kitchen, six older women are chattering enthusiastically in Italian. A woman takes my hand in a firm grip and shows me the dining hall, which is decorated with red napkins and white tablecloths. She asks me to take a look at the menu.

'Doesn't it look wonderful?'

Maria tells me that she only arrived in London fairly recently.

'I moved here to be with my grandchildren,' she explains.

When both her daughters settled in London, Maria and her husband didn't want to stay behind in Italy, alone.

'What about the rest of the family, and the comfort of living in the city where you grew up?' I ask, surprised.

Maria shakes her head.

'That doesn't matter to me. My grandchildren are everything. I pick them up from school, and we spend time together. I don't miss Italy – the only thing I find a little difficult is the language.'

She wipes her hands on her white apron before she takes my hand in hers again.

'You have to speak with some of the other ladies – come on, let me introduce you' – and before I can gather my wits I find myself sitting at a table, surrounded by five Italian women who are all talking over each other.

When these women tell me about their lives, they all agree on one thing: in London, they found freedom from expectations. Just as the Irish women did.

'Families in Italian villages do so much meddling in each other's lives, and the girls in particular are always criticised. When I came to London with my friend as a nursing student, I could do whatever I wanted without my neighbours judging me. It was such a wonderful feeling! I met my husband on the very day I moved here. He was Spanish, and we stayed together until he died ten years ago,' says Ada, an eighty-year-old woman with immaculate skin and glossy black hair.

The other women around the table speak of demanding working lives with long days in the meat industry in the north of London. The

Italian women who came to London often had no education, so if they wanted to work, their options were limited. Many worked in factories.

'Come and eat!' shouts a woman before we are able to talk any further.

Everyone quickly gets up. Red plastic chairs scrape against the parquet and shuffling old feet move as quickly as they can.

The Italians left this area of London as they became more affluent, moving from Clerkenwell and into the smart terraced houses with small gardens that the British authorities were eager for everyone to acquire. Now they live in High Barnet and Islington, in the north of the city. They still look after each other. In the village of Shenley in Hertfordshire, north of London, is a special nursing home for Italians: Villa Scalabrini. The twenty-five-acre site is constructed like a small village, where residents each have their own apartment and a fixed staff of nurses and doctors around them. The property is operated and owned by several Italian foundations and businesspeople.[6]

The Italians have always been good at looking after one another. An Italian hospital was founded in Bloomsbury as early as 1884 by businessman Giovanni Ortelli, who was concerned to see his countrymen struggling due to language difficulties when they were admitted to hospital. The Ospedale Italiano therefore mainly accepted Italian patients. In the 1930s, British fascists maintained close ties with their Italian counterparts, and in 1933 the British Union of Fascists donated over £1,000 to fund a bed in the hospital as a symbolic gift to Benito Mussolini. Mussolini sent a telegram to the Union to say thank you, believing that their contribution was 'proof of the friendly camaraderie that unites the country's two people'. Today, Great Ormond Street Hospital has acquired the premises, and named them the Italian Building. The funds obtained from this acquisition laid the foundations for a British-Italian charitable organisation that helps those of Italian heritage who need financial support in the event of major surgical procedures.

The friendliness among the older Italians in the hall reminds me of the atmosphere at E. Pellicci, and that among the Irish in Bexleyheath. Community. Shared experiences. Freedom. I can relate to the challenges the older Italians have faced. Starting with a blank slate in an unknown country is tough – not just materially, but also emotionally. Habitual ways of communicating suddenly become meaningless; nuances in tone are misunderstood and have to be explained. Communities dissolve. But at the same time, the opportunities that open up are almost inconceivable. Barriers vanish. Boundaries can be ignored. It is precisely this freedom that these families have grabbed on to, and which they are attempting to use to their advantage.

I leave the cheerful Italian pensioners and go into the church to rest my head after all the lively discussions. As I step through the doors, I'm struck by the silence of the church's interior. Just a few candles have been lit. A woman sits alone on one of the pews, her hair covered, seemingly in prayer.

The idea of St Peter's Italian Church came about in 1845, at the request of priest and future saint Vincent Pallotti.[7] With him was socialist and journalist Giuseppe Mazzini, who had fled Italy for London due to his political standpoint. Together, they wished to create a meeting place for the Italians who had made London their home, and a large-scale fundraiser was launched all across Europe in order to finance the church. The aim was to build a church with space for 3,000 people, but the priests didn't manage to scrape together enough money to erect the magnificent building they had envisaged. Today, the church is able to house around 1,000 people. Beautiful, majestic marble columns and crystal chandeliers fill the building, in stark contrast to the dark wooden benches. Lining the walls are small shelves, upon which stand candles and plastic flowers. The church opened on 16 April 1863 to the sound of Joseph Haydn's *Missa Cellensis*, in a grand ceremony at which over fifty priests were present, and is still a gathering place of great importance to the Italians. When Nevio Pellicci senior's funeral was held here, the church was packed. Younger Italians who have recently moved to London come to mass at the church hoping to make friends, and to experience the sense of community their fragmented working lives – now threatened by Brexit – are unable to give them.

Outside Terroni's, there is now a queue of people waiting to eat lunch. In London, all the coffee and sandwich shops are filled with workers between 12 p.m. and 1 p.m. When I worked in London, this hour had a fixed ritual: go out to buy coffee and some kind of ciabatta, usually from Costa Coffee, the UK's outstanding largest coffee chain, founded by Bruno and Sergio Costa in the late 1970s. The Costas were so dissatisfied with the state of coffee in the capital that they decided to grind their own. In no time at all, Italians from all across London were flocking to the little café at Vauxhall Bridge to enjoy a real, homebrewed espresso. These days, branches of Costa Coffee can be found everywhere.[8]

'People will always eat, so you will never go hungry,' said the parents of the young Italians who left to find work in London in the early 1900s. These were wise words from the older Italians, and their young offspring quickly became highly sought-after as workers. They were loyal and industrious, and soon found themselves employed at fashionable hotels and restaurants like the Savoy, the Dorchester and the Ivy in London's West End. The Italian waiting staff were known among guests for being exceptionally pleasant, but in reality their friendly smiles hid a sad story. Without fixed contracts regarding their salary, tips were the only income they had – they were rarely permanently employed at the restaurants in which they worked. The figures speak for themselves: in 1911 there were over 1,600 waiting staff, 900 cooks, 1,000 hotel workers, 1,400 bakers and 500 café owners of Italian descent in the United Kingdom.[9]

In the early hours of the morning, after working their long shifts, the young Italian girls walked back to Clerkenwell, protected by the young boys who worked at the same establishments. The boys had more freedom than the girls. Should an accident happen, a girl had to make a choice: either marry at once, or be sent home to relatives in Italy. But if she was sent home, she would never be able to return. The British warned against the sex appeal of Italian men, but to little effect – the number of marriages between the Italians and the British was exceptionally high. In 1851, of the 94 marriages that took place involving Italian men, 74 of them were with British women. By 1881, this figure had significantly increased. Of the 217 marriages that were entered into with Italians, half were between Italians and British individuals.[10]

Gradually, the Italians in Clerkenwell discovered that other opportunities existed for them outside of 'Little Italy'. Some glimpsed excellent opportunities in a London that was becoming ever more cosmopolitan. In Soho, husband and wife Lou and Caterina Polledri found happiness and success.

A heathen dive

Narrow alleyways. Rainbow flags. Small shops with back rooms open only to those in the know. A veritable fairground filled with people who don't want to play by the rules, but instead follow their innermost, darkest drives. Neon lights and sex shops. Soho can feel like the devil's playground. And it is precisely this feeling of something unseemly that always creeps up on me as I enter Bar Italia on Frith Street in Soho. Perhaps because of the roguish smiles the tie-wearing baristas flash me as they hand me the small cup of coffee. Bar Italia is a tiny oasis in Soho, where flashing lights, homeless people and tourists otherwise fill the streets twenty-four hours a day. This café bar, with its green neon lettering above the entrance, plays a special role in the story of Italian immigrants in London, because it was in Soho and at Bar Italia that the British became continental in their habits.

In the 1930s, husband and wife Lou and Caterina Polledri from Piacenza in northern Italy dreamed of opening a proper café bar. Years later, through friends, they learned that there were premises vacant on Frith Street which they could rent, and they borrowed £50 for this purpose from a local businessman. Bar Italia opened in the winter of 1949. Two American actors, Bud Abbott and Lou Costello, were invited to grace the café with their presence at its grand opening. They cycled up and down Frith Street, advertising the café and handing out drinks. A competition was held to see who could drink the most coffee.

'I don't think I'd organise that kind of competition today – it's like competing to see who can drink the most vodka,' says Anthony Polledri with a laugh.

Anthony is Lou and Caterina's grandson. He's invited me to the restaurant Little Italy Soho, which is next door to Bar Italia – in the café, there are too many people who pop in to greet him for us to be able to speak undisturbed. Following the success of the café bar, the Polledri family decided to expand by opening this restaurant in 1995. The interior and menu are sleek. Anthony has an understated charm and is casually dressed, albeit with an expensive watch on his wrist. Bar Italia immediately became popular, especially among the Italian immigrant population who used the café as a kind of information centre, and because the premises stayed open late into the night.

Anthony and his brother began hanging out at the café at weekends from when they were fairly small, and so the boys were introduced to Soho at a young age. Although not everything here was equally suited to the minds of young children.

Soho has been a seductive siren for hundreds of years, luring in eccentric characters and providing spaces for indecent activity ever since the 1600s. In 1750 Madam Jane Goadby, inspired by the time she spent in Paris, opened one of the area's first luxury bordellos in Berwick Street. As was the custom in France, all the girls who worked for her had to wear silk and lace, and were subjected to weekly medical examinations.[1]

Today, Regent Street – one of the streets that borders on Soho – is most known for being where the fashionable Liberty department store and Hamley's toyshop are located, but throughout the 1800s Regent Street was most known for its sex workers. Shaftesbury Avenue, Charing Cross Road, Leicester Square, Dean Street and

Greek Street were invaded by prostitutes. And where there are whores, there are guaranteed to be gangsters, fugitives, drug dealers, alcoholics, playboys, pimps, and young people seeking excitement. During the 1950s and 1960s, several nightclubs opened their doors here. Police officers, criminals, artists, theatre types, journalists, lesbians and gays all had their own establishments, and since the small venues were not exactly legal, corruption was widespread among the London police.

'The streets had a completely different atmosphere when I was young. I remember it as being almost like in that American Mafia film, *A Bronx Tale*. Maltese gang members hung out on every street corner, people wearing string vests and gold chains, and every other building housed a porn shop,' says Anthony.

He remembers the gangsters with a distant fondness, speaking of nicknames, elegant suits and great cars.

'But I saw them do unmentionable things that frightened me. My brother and I kept our distance, but the gangsters often came in and drank coffee at our place, so I got to see several sides of them. I soon realised that people in Soho had it tough because of drugs, so I was never tempted to become like them, no matter how much money they had. When I was young, this restaurant we're sitting in didn't exist – it was a gambling club run by the Maltese gangs. I had a good friend, a young Maltese guy, he was around twenty-three years old and ran a sex shop. One day, he came driving down the street right here, in his silver Porsche with tartan seats. He staggered out of the car, no shoes on his feet, desperate, looking for a hit. It made me so sad to see him that way. He had all the money he could wish for, but he was in a terrible state. That was a defining moment for me, and I decided there and then to never be like that. I've actually never touched a thing,' Anthony says.

Anthony believes that being surrounded by people who didn't exactly live by society's norms has shaped him.

'I wouldn't exactly say that I became tolerant, but it gave me an education, if I can put it that way. My life philosophy is this: you should try to understand why people behave the way they do, and why their culture is the way it is. When I go on holiday, I try to seek out the local culture, rather than cultivate my own. Honestly, do I really want to watch *EastEnders* when I'm on holiday? Eat a full English breakfast there? Do I really want to walk around in a football shirt? No – I don't. The backstreets, and where people actually live – *that's* what's interesting. I think this mindset comes from having grown up in Soho.'

From where we're sitting, Anthony and I have a view of the street. Looking out of the window, we can see Ronnie Scott's Jazz Club, where greats like Chet Baker and Ella Fitzgerald once performed – the venue is still one of London's premier jazz clubs, and remains true to style with small lamps on all the tables. In the 1950s, Bar Italia became the perfect hub, because London was in the process of becoming the capital everyone with ambitions within popular culture flocked to. This was where they hung out, hopeful and with melodies humming away in the backs of their minds as they drank espresso and helped to bring London back to life after the grey post-war period. In the 1960s, the mod culture appeared, with young men in Italian suits riding around on Vespa scooters and drinking espressos at Bar Italia. They still constitute an active subculture in London, but the Bar Italia Scooter Club was recently dissolved due to disagreements about Brexit.[2]

In the 1950s, Soho also became expressly known for its erotic cinemas and Raymond's Revue Bar, owned by the flamboyant Paul Raymond, who from a young age understood that putting naked women on a stage would put money in the till.[3] The authorities that regulated what could be shown on British stages had decided that naked persons must not move on stage. Paul Raymond's solution was to present his models like statues – in other words, they were not permitted to move. It was also ensured that the women who posed in this way did not have breasts that were too large, as this might embarrass the punters. When Paul Raymond established Raymond's Revue Bar in 1958, he found he could get around the regulations by making the club 'members only'. This was a smart move. Over the course of two years the club acquired 45,000 members, and became popular among celebrities. The Beatles, Peter Sellers and Frank Sinatra were all regular guests. The club lit up Soho's streets, and the sign proclaiming the club's status as the 'World Centre of Erotic Entertainment' was impossible to ignore. In 1964, Raymond moved into publishing, launching the soft-porn magazines *Mayfair* and *Razzle*. He became a millionaire, and was the king of Soho. He also ran several erotic cinemas in the district. For many, it was a sad day when the lights of the iconic sign for Raymond's Revue Bar in Walker's Court were finally switched off for good.

The environment in Soho became considerably rougher through-out the 1970s and 1980s. The number of erotic cinemas and shops selling pornography escalated. Numerous erotic films were created on premises above the cafés, and young women who worked in Soho's café bars were recruited to act in them. Most of the porn shops had two rooms: in the front, all the legal material was on display, while behind a curtain it was possible to find the illegal films and magazines. The police began to crack down on these dealers, and in the early 1980s, after the close relationship between the police force and criminals dissolved, the sex industry gradually began to disappear from Soho. Politicians didn't want Soho to be so seedy. These days it's Old Compton Street that keeps Soho's traditions alive – a street to which you don't bring your children, unless you want to introduce them to the many facets of sexuality. But look closer, and you'll also notice that certain doors in Soho feature Post-it notes, which upon closer inspection offer all kinds of things. The police have clamped down hard on human trafficking in Soho over the past decade, and the area's sex workers have been subjected to much criticism.

I have always loved wandering around Soho. It always feels as if something exciting is happening, right under my nose. In the middle of Soho is mysterious Chinatown, which also houses its share of gangsters. One time I was there, one of the side streets had been closed off, apparently because of some sort of Mafia murder. Somebody had run amok with a sub-machine gun in a restaurant. I never found out whether this was true, but the rumour supports the myth of Chinatown as a mysterious, impenetrable place. The first Chinese came to London as far back as 200 years ago, to Limehouse in east London, but most of those who live here today fled to London when the communists came to power in 1949. Like the Italians before them, they came to Soho to open restaurants, calling the area the 'Imperial City'. Dean Street and Gerrard Street were filled with red lanterns and small shops, where everything from Chinese baked goods to health-promoting herbs can still be purchased. It isn't rare to bump into processions of dancing lions and dragons twisting their way through the crowds of riotous tourists. It has also been a place where the immigration police have been active, and several raids have occurred, scarring several restaurants. Rents have also been increasing. Since COVID-19 hit the capital, the busy streets here have fallen dead, and Chinatown's future appears threatened.

I spent much of my time walking these streets when I was young in the 1980s. Punk was one of London's trailblazing scenes, and made its mark on street fashion with bondage trousers, fishnet stockings and footwear only people associated with sex clubs actually walked around in. My parents were shocked when I came home with black fishnet tights and shoes that had clearly not been purchased at Clarks. Pop culture proliferated here.

In 1986, the film *Absolute Beginners*, based on the book of the same name by Colin MacInnes, was launched to wild enthusiasm from the British press.[4] It was directed by Julien Temple, the man behind the celebrated Sex Pistols mockumentary, *The Great Rock "n" Roll Swindle* (1980). *Absolute Beginners'* backdrop is a London in flux, just before pop culture made itself known on the city's streets, and the Notting Hill race riots are part of the story. The film had all the elements necessary to guarantee its success: the popular actor Patsy Kensit played one of the leads, while David Bowie played one of the central roles, and also wrote the theme song, which became a hit. He is probably mostly remembered for dancing on a massive typewriter. The Kinks' frontman Ray Davies and soul singer Sade Adu also contributed to the soundtrack. Bar Italia was naturally part of the tale, and Anthony and his brother were extras. British pop culture meant the world to me in those days, and when Anthony tells me about the film shoot I realise that I clearly should have spent more time hanging out at Bar Italia and in Soho in general. The fact that one of London's most legendary punk clubs, the Roxy, was started here in Soho was no accident. Anyone could afford to rent premises here back then.

One of the waiters waves at us and points to his watch. Anthony nods. He has a meeting soon. The family doesn't rest, even if they almost certainly don't have any financial worries. With property prices as they are here, my guess is that the Polledri family are likely not struggling financially.

'There's my father, Nino!'

The man who waves to us is well dressed, with thinning hair.

'He experienced some dramatic years during the Second World War. We had to take down the sign outside our shop to hide the fact that we were Italians. Other Italian places were vandalised, just because Italians owned them,' Anthony says.

I look at him, confused.

On 10 June 1940, Italian Prime Minister Benito Mussolini stepped out on to a balcony in Rome to cries of joy from thousands of supporters.[5] With his hands hooked into his wide leather belt, he stepped forward and began the speech that marked the beginning of one of the darkest periods in British-Italian immigration history. Benito Mussolini declared war on the British and the French.[6] In 1939, 70,000 Germans and Austrians who found themselves on British soil had been branded enemies; certain factions among the British politicians believed they represented a threat, and considered them possible spies. After Mussolini picked a side, the discussion attained renewed relevance. During an intense debate as to what should be done about the Italians and Germans resident in Britain, Winston Churchill exclaimed: 'Be damned over it. Collar the lot!'

Most of the Italians in Soho had British citizenship, and were therefore British. They loved both Britain and Italy. Nevertheless, arrest warrants were issued for all Italian men aged between sixteen and sixty who had lived in Britain for less than twenty years. At the same time, MI5 was granted extended licence to arrest anyone who might be suspected of being a fifth columnist. The consequences were severe: Italian families found that their close neighbours and customers turned against them. In several places, the windows of Italian cafés and shops were dirtied or broken. Twenty years of hard work, destroyed in twenty minutes.

Soho was hit especially hard. Over the years, the Italians had founded clubs to drink coffee, play billiards and do business. Most of these were politically neutral, but among the hard-working Italians there were both anarchists and fascists. The anarchists had flocked to the area in the 1900s with a burning passion for workers' rights, and established the catering workers' union. In the 1930s, there were so many Italians in Soho that the area was referred to as an Italian district. A large number of those who lived in Soho sympathised with Mussolini. The London Fascio had been founded in 1921 in Noel Street, and constituted Mussolini's largest fan base outside Italy.[7] Mussolini was keen on London himself, and wanted to turn the city into a first-class fascist colony. The local Catholic church in Soho supported him wholeheartedly, and the owner of Italian restaurant Quo Vadis, Peppino Leoni, was an ardent supporter of the fascist regime at home. For others, however, the question of their loyalty was more diffuse. The Italian London Club, for example, was directly financed by the Italian authorities – that is, the fascists – and although the club's members didn't sympathise with the regime, they were still regarded as suspicious. The fact that they maintained close ties with the authorities in their homeland was more for practical reasons, such as the payment of taxes or the distribution of deceased family members' estates. In the midst of all this, there were also passionate anti-fascists and Italian-Jewish refugees. Some of them enlisted in the British Army.

Four-thousand Italian men were identified as potential enemies of the kingdom by the British authorities. Anthony tells me that his grandfather was interned, and that his grandmother had to continue the running of the café alone. The men were sent to internment camps spread all across Britain. They were not told where they were being taken, and when they arrived at the camps, nor were they given any information about what was going to happen to them. The British powers that be regarded the interned Italians as a nuisance, and wanted to send them out of the country. Out of sight, out of mind. Some wise soul figured out that the prisoners could be transported to the fishing village of St John's, a former British colony in Newfoundland in Canada. It was necessary to act quickly.

On 30 June 1940, interned men from various camps were sent to the docks in Liverpool and ushered aboard an old cruise ship, the SS *Arandora Star*.[8] The ship, launched in 1927 to transport first-class passengers on holiday, had been converted into a prison ship. It was painted grey, and its distinctive feature, a large scarlet band that gave the ship its nickname 'the wedding cake', was also covered. All internal signs of luxury were removed. On 1 July 1940, one month after

Mussolini's declaration of war, the SS *Arandora Star* departed the docks in Liverpool with Italian and German prisoners of war on board, a total of 1,500 passengers – double the number of people the ship was actually designed for. Of those on board, 734 were Italians. The men believed they were being taken to the Isle of Man and, contrary to international law, the Red Cross flag was not raised when the ship set out from port. Nor did the SS *Arandora Star* have an escort, despite this being mandatory for non-military ships during the war.

At dawn, at 06:15 on Monday 2 July, the ship was detected off the coast of Ireland by German U-boat captain Günther Prien. Unaware of the vessel's civil status, he fired a torpedo that hit the SS *Arandora Star*. The oldest Italians were crammed below deck, unable to get to the lifeboats. In the existing eyewitness testimonies, survivors describe the oil and flames on the sea, the fight to reach the lifeboats, the helplessness, how the captain of the ship had shouted that it was every man for himself, and the sight of friends drowning right in front of them. Over 800 passengers died; 446 of these were Italians, 241 of them from London.

The tragic incident hardly registered with the British authorities. The nonchalance exhibited towards families who had no idea where their fathers or sons had gone caused an outcry among the Italians in Britain. When the authorities finally made public the lists of the dead, mourning mothers, sisters and spouses gathered in front of the Italian embassy where the lists had been read out. They never received an official apology from the British authorities – not a single telephone call. Some never found out what had happened to their men. During August 1940, 213 bodies were found along the Irish coast – in all likelihood those who had perished when the SS *Arandora Star* was sunk.

But the Italians who survived were not set free by the British. They were put aboard another ship to Canada, and again came under fire. Upon their arrival, they were treated as prisoners of war, but the Canadian guards quickly realised that the men were not Nazis, but rather terrified, starving Italians, and released them. The incident remains an aching wound among British-Italians. Almost every Italian family with members resident in Britain during the war years remembers a grandfather or uncle who never came home. Anthony's father was lucky. He was interned, but able to return home shortly afterwards.

Anthony says that he bears no grudge against the British.

'It was war – they had to do it, to defend the country,' he says. 'But it was a tough time for the entire family.'

I'm stunned that Anthony isn't more bitter, because I certainly feel provoked when I think about how eager the British were to make use of the Italians after the Second World War when they needed workers. In 1949 the British established the Official Italian Scheme, because access to Latvians, Ukrainians and Estonians from the war camps was beginning to dry up. The British and the Italians established five emigration centres in Milan, Genoa, Messina, Turin and Naples, where those who wished to travel to England were subjected to physical and mental examinations. All communist sympathisers had to be weeded out, and southern Italians were denied passage regardless because they were viewed as suspect. Those who were selected entered into contracts lasting three to four years, with no possibility to complain about their working conditions. They were quite literally guest workers, without rights. If they complained, this would lead to immediate deportation.[9]

Three men in their fifties come in through the main door, all of them wearing suits. Nino goes over to greet them. I get no sense of dodgy dealings in New Jersey or offers I can't refuse – just a hug from Anthony as I make my way out. I disappear on to Soho's streets, in search of a glorious time.

Gangsters and Brexit

'I've stood here every year. Hammering away, setting things up. Ever since I was quite young. Although I'm not sure whether the next generations will do the same, I have to admit,' says Peter Capella. His blue piqué shirt and shorts are flecked with paint.

I'm back at St Peter's Italian Church. It's a sleepy Saturday in July. Peter, who in his day job is an architect, is standing in a little side street, Back Hill, beside the church. Boring flatbed trucks have to be transformed into representations of stories from the Bible. Lengths of ruched velour have been neatly stapled around a statue of the Virgin Mary: Our Lady of Mount Carmel. She is patroness of the Carmelite order – a Catholic order founded by hermits from Mount Carmel in Palestine – and holds a special place in the hearts of Catholics the world over. Tomorrow is a special day, on which she will be celebrated.

Every year, on the Sunday that falls closest to 16 July, Italians hold a procession to pay tribute to Our Lady of Mount Carmel. The Italians in London have arranged this parade every year since 1896, with the sole exception of the years of the Second World War. This was the first public Catholic event to take place in England after the Reformation, when Henry VIII of England broke with the Catholic Church by divorcing his wife Catherine of Aragon, and marrying Ann Boleyn, without the Pope's blessing.

An older man comes over to us – he's English, and grew up in Clerkenwell. He's been a part of the Italian community here ever since he was small, and with his gold chains and teasing disposition he reminds me of a British East End gangster. Bill has had many Italian girlfriends, he confides in me with a wink. As I stand there with Bill and Peter, it occurs to me that the Italians in the US have always been part of American pop culture. There's an entire succession of Italian-American actors: Al Pacino, Robert De Niro, Ray Liotta, Sylvester Stallone, James Gandolfini . . . But what about the Brits? I can't think of a single Italian-British actor who comes close to any of the Italian-Americans. The most famous Italian actors in Britain I can think of on the spot are Hammer horror film legend Christopher Lee, and Tom Conti, who seduced everyone in the film *Shirley Valentine*. The Italians have obviously not been immortalised in the same way here in Britain – and what about the Italian Mafia in London? I challenge the group of men standing with Bill and Peter.

'Oh, of course! Back in the day. We ran the dog track. The Jews controlled the horseracing,' says the bus driver, Roberto.

Roberto is an older man with thick gold chains, astonishingly defined muscles and a strong East End accent. Greyhound racing was big during the post-war period. Back then, there were over seventy dog tracks in the UK; thirty-three of these were in London. The last of them, Wimbledon Greyhound Stadium, closed its doors as recently as March 2017, and with that, a hundred years of sporting history came to an end.[1] A couple of older men and women come across to us – they're curious as to what we're talking about. Everyone spontaneously shares stories about incidents in which they have been referred to as 'Mafia' at some point or other in their lives. Even if British film hasn't iconised British-Italian mobsters, London has had its share of Italian gangster families. Charles 'Darby' Sabini was born here in Saffron Hill in 1888, and led the notorious Sabini family, which with its over a hundred members was well known for its dunning and blackmailing activities. Sabini was interned during the Second World War, but released after having been held captive for a year. The Sabini family collaborated with the Messina brothers, who were originally from Sicily and ran a prostitution ring. It's said that the gang was originally formed by the two families so they could defend themselves against the harassment they were subjected to by English gangs, who came to Saffron Hill to bother the Italian girls and act tough around vulnerable, recently arrived immigrants. Sheer survival tactics.

In July 2017, an obituary appeared in the British newspapers to more than a few raised eyebrows. A British-Italian Mafia boss had passed away, at ninety-four years old.[2] Even arch-conservative newspaper *The Times* gave column inches to Bert Rossi – officially Umberto Rossi – who was born to poor Italian parents in Clerkenwell in 1922. A Christmas turkey is said to be the first thing he stole, and thereafter followed a life on the fringes of the law. In the 1950s, Rossi ended up in prison after stabbing a rival. While in prison, he met Ronnie Kray. It's said that at one point the two were about to go at it, each armed with a knitting needle, but the fight was averted. As fate would have it, Rossi instead became the Kray brothers' advisor. Rossi was known for his impeccable style, and in the 1960s he acted as a link between the American and British Mafia. In the US, he was also an active intermediary between the various gangster families, and therefore highly respected at home in London. Rossi lived in Clerkenwell for his entire life. At his funeral, music from the films *Once Upon a Time in America* and *The Godfather* filled the church.

'I'll tell you one thing – when I was young, we were beaten up just because we were Italians. People didn't like us,' says Roberto. 'But then we'd beat up other people for revenge.'

He chuckles. The men suddenly begin a hot-tempered discussion about what it's politically correct or not politically correct to say about people. If the term 'Mafia' is offensive, shouldn't the names applied to other groups also be problematic? Not everybody agrees. Bus driver Roberto feels discouraged at the attitudes among today's youth. He admits, with an almost proud grin, that he's called Black boys the n-word – but that was when he was angry at them for misbehaving on the bus.

'You're not allowed to say anything any more. We used to take the mickey out of everybody, and everybody took the mickey out of us – we were never offended! We just gave as good as we got.'

The atmosphere becomes tense. People start to move away, returning to their tasks. Peter stays standing beside me, and sighs. He's much younger than Roberto. We start to talk about the church to lighten the irritable mood. It turns out that Peter is both one of the initiators behind and the designer of the *Arandora Star* Memorial inside the church. We go in to take a look. The memorial was erected in 2012; I look at all the names from London on it. So many lives that were taken far too soon. We stand there together in silence. Then Peter suddenly turns to me, and flashes me a wide smile. The grief has gone – from his face, at least.

'Tomorrow!' he says. 'There'll be plenty going on here then – you have that to look forward to.'

The next day, I hear the pounding music long before I arrive at the church. Parts of Rosebery Avenue and Clerkenwell Road have been closed off and Italian flags wave in the air. Down from the church, the street is crowded. I wriggle past stalls selling 'Pimms and Bellinis', lemon biscotti, pizzas, pasta dishes, hams, and ciabattas filled with aubergine and grilled pepper. It's a far smaller version of the St Patrick's Day celebrations, but then there are far fewer Italians in London than there are Irish. In this city, immigrants are not modest

– they celebrate themselves, putting on national celebrations that everyone can take part in.

In one side street, Eyre Street Hill, I see a large garage door labelled Chiappa Organ Builders Ltd. This is where the Italian Chiappa family built its first unique organ in 1877. If you've been to a British fairground you're guaranteed to have seen and heard them. They are often gilded, and painted with flowers.

It's almost three o'clock in the afternoon, and people are beginning to head up Back Hill to Clerkenwell Road. Beside the entrance to the church, young people in long linen tunics restlessly shift their weight from foot to foot – it's so crowded it's almost impossible to move up there. Children have always played a central role in the procession. The girls are dressed in white and wearing veils; the boys in suits. Along the road stand classic Italian cars: Fiats, Ferraris and Lancias decorated with roses, their flags at the ready. I also see Bill, who is wearing a long white robe and carrying a cross. He waves cheerily to me, and despite the ecclesiastical get-up he still looks like a sly old fox. Small groups representing Italian organisations gather; the entire area in front of the church is filled with expectation. Then a small gasp fills the air as the priests emerge from the church in their white robes. Around me I hear the expectant whispering of those in attendance: large families, couples, young and old, nuns, monks – from all countries. I stand beside some elderly ladies who have found themselves a place to rest at the bus stop along the road. One of them is incessantly kissing her cross, obviously deeply moved at what is taking place. Silence settles over the crowd as one of the priests walks down the street. In a dramatic gesture, he releases a white dove towards the sky. A fraction of a second later, huge volumes of confetti explode into the air, followed by clapping and excited cheers. The old ladies beside me have tears in their eyes and on their cheeks.

The procession isn't just a religious celebration. Every step is taken in remembrance of all those who came to London with dreams of a better life: Podesta, Milordini, Dondi, Pozzilli, Cattini, Viazzani, Comitti, Menozzi-Zanetti, Cavaciutu, Nastri – the list of Italian families is endless. Life wasn't easy for those who emigrated from their villages in the 1800s, nor for those who started their restaurants and cafés in the years before the Second World War – and certainly not for the Italian men who were suspected during the war years. Some also had to pay with their lives. I stand there and watch the procession disappear down Rosebery Avenue. The tall trees on either side frame the parade. The cross is held high.

Nor is life likely to be easy for the new waiter at E. Pellicci's, nor the other young Italians who grind the coffee in Costa. Everyone I speak to in London tells me that Brexit has lit a fire under attitudes they thought belonged to bygone days.

What will life be like for the Italians in London going forward? I ponder this with my Italian friend, Leonardo. I've brought him along to Pellicci's and, squeezed in between two women, we eat pasta and drink coffee. Nevio teases me about my new gentleman friend. Leonardo is an author, and a correspondent for British and Italian newspapers. He's also a good example of why English women swoon before Italian men. He distances himself from everything that touches on Italian nostalgia or nationalism. Leonardo has lived alternately in London and his home city of Rome for over twenty years, and is worried about the trends he's witnessed. He reminds me that Italy has lived through difficult times under Berlusconi. Young Italians face many challenges in Italy. Unemployment is high, and social conventions prevent both women and men from reaching their full potential. That's why they come to London.

As Leonardo sees it, young Italians are in a real bind. Italy is a tough place to live, but those who move to London are abused by the retail chains, which offer terrible salaries.

'I'm sure you've noticed that all the people working in the coffee chains are foreigners, and often young Italians,' Leonardo says, giving me a weary look through his glasses. According to Leonardo, these employees often have a high level of education from Italy that they are unable to make use of in London, and which they struggle to get recognised in the city. Many Italians with British citizenship voted in favour of Brexit, deeply sceptical of the EU, and Leonardo thinks it isn't improbable that Italy will also leave the bloc. There are over 3 million EU citizens in Britain – almost 7 per cent of the labour force. Should they disappear, this will cause significant problems within British industry, the welfare sector and the health service. And if immigration declines, the cosmopolitan diversity that characterises London will likewise vanish. London's streets will no longer be filled with stories about Italian families like the Pelliccis, who established their unique restaurants, nor processions celebrating saints – in themselves small, seemingly insignificant events, but still enough to change London completely.

Caribbean London –
Notting Hill, Brixton

Caribbean occupation

August in London, and the thermometer shows a temperature of over 30°C. On St Mark's Road near Ladbroke Grove, floats and buses roll past. Everybody is happy when the Notting Hill Carnival is on, with its sequins, war masks, warpaint, feathers and glittering glass beads. People sit on window ledges, enjoying the music that booms from the cars, houses and small stages. A throng of people as far as I can see. Bunting featuring flags from Jamaica, Trinidad and Tobago, and the other Caribbean islands, in addition to a few solitary Union Jacks, has been hung between the lamp posts and on the buildings. The smell of fried chicken is pervasive.

On the evening before the annual carnival is due to take place I walk along Portobello Road, towards the Tabernacle community centre. I end up in Powis Square, with its shabby playground surrounded by tall, terraced houses containing sought-after apartments. In the 1920s, the same buildings were overcrowded slums – without bathrooms, hot water or electricity. Brian Jones is said to have been living in an apartment here when the Rolling Stones formed in 1962. Back then, luxurious sports cars could be seen parked along the grubby streets, and moans and groans emanated from bedroom windows.

I have always been fascinated by Notting Hill. On the surface, everything is so idyllic: fashionable houses, climbing ivy, neat flower beds with vintage cars parked alongside them. But I know better. A certain calm and refinement usually reign supreme in Notting Hill, but during the last weekend and Monday of August each year the area is transformed from a pastel-coloured cream puff into a dripping cocktail of deep-fried chicken and rum.

Only a tiny percentage of the residents here live the way people do in the films *Notting Hill, Four Weddings and a Funeral, Bridget Jones's Diary* and *Sliding Doors*. Films that present retouched versions of London, in which people on low incomes are able to live carefree lives in beautiful surroundings. Urban fairy tales.

The music leads me to a brick building with a towering cupola. A party tent, bunting featuring Caribbean flags and a bar have been set up in the lush courtyard. The Tabernacle was originally a church, but the parish's poor financial situation meant that the local authorities ended up taking over the building. They turned it into a community centre, with practice rooms for musicians. The Rolling Stones, Pink Floyd and Joe Strummer have all practised here.

It was in 1965 that a chaotic parade first wandered through Notting Hill, back when poor bohemians, hippies and other revolutionary souls walked the streets.[1] Over the course of fifty years, Notting Hill Carnival has grown to become the largest in Europe. Between one and 2 million people gather here in the neighbourhoods of west London to dance, eat and show off their painstakingly crafted costumes in endless parades that are in no way inferior to the chaotic festivities that can be observed in Brazil, or during Mardi Gras in New Orleans.

A group of young men appear, carrying oil drums. They're on their way to a truck parked in front of the iron gates. It is from these shiny drums that the carnival's unmistakable steelpan rhythms will fill the streets – the steel bands are the very pulse of the parades, and the Tabernacle has its own local band, the Mangrove Steelband. During the carnival, the true soul of Notting

Hill comes to the fore, lured out by the ecstatic dancing and the sounds of the steelpans.

Notting Hill is brimming with stories. You don't have to look very far to discover a motley district, full of deep wounds left by brawls and broken dreams. Notting Hill and Brixton were the areas of London where people from the Caribbean first settled when they arrived in the capital in 1945. Brixton was dubbed 'Little Jamaica', while Notting Hill became home to those from the smaller Caribbean islands: Barbados, Trinidad and Tobago and Saint Lucia. Their suitcases were filled with flowered dresses and stylish suits, their hearts and minds with dreams.

An old warship puts in at Tilbury docks on 22 June 1948,[2] and a television crew is on site to document the ship's arrival. Over 400 men and women are aboard, the majority from the Caribbean islands. The men are wearing suits and ties, while the women are dressed in elegant coats and hats. All of them are ready to start a new life at the heart of the British Empire. Fathers carry sleeping babies in their arms, tired after the long journey. Other tiny tots toddle along, a little bewildered by all the commotion. The TV reporter begins to look for a specific person, someone who has attracted attention even before setting foot on British soil. When the reporter finds the well-dressed man with the thin moustache, one of those world-history-making moments occurs. With a careful smile, the young man looks into the camera and begins to tap out a rhythm on the steel railing as he sings:

> London is the place for me
> London this lovely city
> You can go to France or America,
> India, Asia or Australia
> But you must come back to London city

Lord Kitchener, or Aldwyn Roberts, as was his real name, was already well known for his calypso music, and he had spent the journey to London thinking up a new song in order to impress everyone upon his arrival. The song 'London Is the Place for Me' became the very soundtrack to the Caribbeans' early days in London.

The arrival of Lord Kitchener and the other passengers aboard SS *Windrush* was no ordinary event in the history of the British Empire – never before had so many people crossed the Atlantic simultaneously to seek their fortunes in what they regarded as the motherland. People from the Caribbean had the right to settle in Britain following the establishment of the British Nationality Act in 1948 – legislation that granted them British citizenship. The Second World War had exhausted Britain. The country had to be rebuilt, and there was political consensus that the solution was to recruit workers from the colonies. The immigration authorities transported the new arrivals to Paddington station by train, before they were escorted to Clapham in south London. In Clapham, the immigrants slept in underground bunkers – the bomb shelters that had been used during the war. They were given food vouchers, and the men were directed to the employment office in Coldharbour Lane in Brixton to collect their work permits. The British took a somewhat relaxed approach to the registration process, so many of the recent arrivals were provided with no documentation of their right to reside in the country; children were registered on their parents' Caribbean or British passports. This would come to have catastrophic consequences in the future.

The men were allocated work at factories and in the construction industry, and over the years that followed many more Caribbeans flocked to London. By 1958, ten years after SS *Windrush* had docked at Tilbury, around 7,000 Caribbeans had settled in the neighbourhoods of Notting Hill and adjacent Notting Dale, which were already crammed with poor Irish, Greek, Spanish, Jewish and British residents. Racists dubbed the area 'Brown Town'. Some Caribbeans had made the journey randomly, while others had responded to advertisements British employers had printed in the local newspapers. London Transport and the National Health Service had both made extensive use of ads in the biggest newspapers in Barbados, Trinidad and Jamaica. During those first few years, the Caribbeans were paid scant attention by most Brits – they quickly disappeared into the vast urban darkness that exists in any capital city. But for the Caribbeans, their first encounter with London came as a shock. They were spat on and shouted at. Back in their homeland, they had believed London's streets would be paved with gold. But in London, the Caribbeans soon discovered that the British were in fact just ordinary people, and that many of them were poor.

The *Windrush* generation arrived in London against a historical backdrop in which Black people had always been categorised as inferior. The British undertook their imperialistic project with zeal. Throughout their childhoods, the people of the Caribbean were schooled in English and learned about British history, but were taught nothing about their own heritage – they were regarded as barbarians, who would have to be civilised through Christian culture.

Even though thousands of Caribbeans had fought alongside English soldiers during both the First and Second World Wars, there was significant scepticism on both sides when the Caribbean immigrants encountered the white working class of Notting Hill. The white families, who were often unemployed, lived in cramped conditions and felt slighted by the British authorities. They made it clear that the Caribbeans were not welcome. Rumours circulated that Black families received more social assistance and were prioritised on waiting lists for council housing.

As the Caribbeans were arriving in London, the city was also going through a major housing crisis. The majority of new homes were being built outside the city, and in the capital's inner districts people were fighting over properties. The general standard was appalling. In many buildings that offered rooms for rent, the Caribbeans often encountered notices stating: 'No Blacks, No Dogs, No Irish', or 'Europeans Only'. The spacious Victorian properties in Notting Hill, which in the 1900s had belonged to a sophisticated upper class, were now abandoned, taken over by cynical landlords. These slum-like properties were rented out to desperate Caribbean families, and quickly became overcrowded. Large families often lived in just one room, with mould-infested carpeting and decaying furniture. Many families had to share a kitchen – no more than a hotplate in the hall – and something that was supposed to pass for a bathroom. Paradoxically, this overcrowding also offered certain benefits: families could look after each other's children, enabling mothers to work, and mealtimes could be shared.

At this time, Notting Hill was somewhat isolated, and notorious among London's residents – in an essay collection, author Wyndham Lewis referred to the district as 'Rotting Hill'.[3] It certainly didn't help matters that British fascist Oswald Mosley and his new organisation the Union Movement had a huge body of followers in Notting Hill at this time. Their slogan 'Keep Britain White' struck a chord among the area's unemployed white youth. They also often surrounded hostels in west London where Black men were known to reside, which led to several bloody brawls.

In 1956, author Sam Selvon published his novel *The Lonely Londoners*. The book offers an insight into the lives of the Caribbean immigrants, and became a sensation among Britain's literati. Selvon, who was an Indian from Trinidad with Scottish ancestors, managed to do what nobody had ever done before: to capture in prose the multicultural London that was in the process of taking shape. His novel depicts just how much of a magnet – and nightmare – London was for the stepchildren of empire. Damnation, emptiness, frustration, exclusion and crushed dreams are described through a lively cast of characters, with Selvon simultaneously incorporating

Caribbean slang into British literature for the first time. The book follows the life of well-to-do Moses Aloetta, who has lived in London for over ten years without achieving all that much. His days are spent at Waterloo station meeting recent Caribbean immigrants who wish to try their luck in London, and helping them find the employment office and a place to live. But just two years after the novel was published, blood would be running in Notting Hill's streets.

Late in the evening on 30 August 1958, Caribbean–Swedish couple Raymond and Majbritt Morrison are on their way home after a day out in the city. At Latimer Road Tube station, the couple get into a heated argument. When a group of white men attempt to intervene, the dispute develops into a physical scuffle. The men assume that Raymond is a pimp, and Majbritt attempts to defend her husband. The episode is witnessed by a group of Teddy boys wearing long suit jackets, skin-tight trousers and a generous help-ing of hair pomade, inspired by Tony Curtis and Elvis. In addition to being dandies, they also have another hobby – hunting down Caribbean men. The next day, Majbritt Morrison is subjected to racial slurs by young white men in the neighbourhood. Some of them throw milk bottles at her as she walks down the street. Rumours spread, and that evening between three and four hundred white youths storm a Caribbean area in Bromley Road, attacking the buildings and running around with placards proclaiming: 'We'll get the blacks', 'Down with niggers' and 'We'll kill the blacks'. The unrest also spreads to adjacent areas like Kensal Rise, Latimer Road and Harrow Road, a little further west. Chaos ensues, and during the riots police end up arresting 140 people. Notting Hill is almost in a state of emergency, and the Caribbean community is terrified.[4]

The English working class and the Caribbean immigrants live in completely different realities, despite the fact that they have much in common. Both groups are poor and economically disadvantaged.

At the same time, rumblings from the independence movements in the colonies are growing ever louder, especially in Kenya, where the Mau Mau guerrillas are gaining strength. The children of empire want freedom. And in Notting Hill, the Caribbeans have likewise had enough of the racism and harassment. A new age is dawning.

Notting Hill before Hugh and Julia

I walk behind the float that the young men are using to transport the steelpans to All Saints Road, where the stage on which the band will play is situated. They're about to run through one last rehearsal. Here, I meet up with the director of the Tabernacle, Matthew Phillip. The streets are already teeming with people, the crowd restless with expectation. We're standing in front of a Caribbean restaurant called the Rum Kitchen, which has several hundred types of rum on the menu. The premises used to contain the Mangrove, a popular restaurant that served as a base for London's Caribbean activists during the 1960s.

Matthew tells me that he started playing the steelpan with his father, at a young age. Matthew's father moved to London from Trinidad in the 1950s, and settled here after meeting Matthew's mother, an Irishwoman. When they attempted to find a place to live together, they quickly experienced the infamous rejections of landlords.

'All they were missing was the dog,' Matthew laughs.

After living in London for a time, Matthew's father started to get involved in the local political movements. Several organisations that were formed also welcomed recently arrived immigrants from the Indian subcontinent – after all, they were also subjected to hate attacks, just as the Caribbeans were.

We move towards a large grill that is occupying the corner of All Saints Road, the smell of spiced chicken filling the air. The street's small designer boutiques have hung signs in their windows, informing customers that they will be closed for the long weekend. Depending on your perspective, Notting Hill Carnival makes the area into either a battlefield or a fantastic celebration. At several locations in the district plywood boards have been installed to protect properties and shop windows.

In 1955, a young woman arrives in London. Claudia Jones is originally from Trinidad, but moved with her family to the US at a young age.[1] Due to her political activism and membership of the American Communist Party, however, she has now been deported. In Notting Hill, she is distressed to see the conditions under which her fellow citizens live, and immediately joins the British Communist Party. She tries to organise and unite the British Caribbeans – who she believes spend too much time bickering about internal divisions – and decides to arrange a carnival like those held in Trinidad. And in January 1958, she books St Pancras Town Hall for 30 January.

Jones has a large circle of acquaintances: many in her social circle are artists, dancers and musicians. When the first carnival kicks off, over 1,000 people turn up to take part and support her ambitions to unite the people of the Caribbean in the capital. In connection with the carnival, Jones also arranges the first beauty contest for Black women in Britain, the Carnival Queen Beauty Contest – an extraordinarily radical act at the time. Fay Craig, the woman who won the competition, had very dark skin, and broke with the prevailing conventions as to what was regarded as beautiful. Sadly, Claudia Jones would never experience just how big the carnival would become over the years. She died of a heart attack in December 1964.

Recently, the origins of the carnival have become the subject of heated discussions: who founded the carnival, and when did it really start?

'Claudia was a key figure, but she wasn't the person who created the carnival as we know it today. It was a young social worker named Rhaune Laslett who decided to do that as she continued Claudia's work. Claudia actually staged cabarets, not a carnival,' Matthew explains.

We have managed to find a place where it's possible to hear each other as the Mangrove Steelband rehearse. Rhaune Laslett was a nurse and social worker who lived in Notting Hill, and who wanted to find something fun to do with the many vulnerable children in the local community. Rhaune herself was born in east London, to a Native American mother and a Russian father. In 1966, she and John Hopkins – one of London's most well-known hippies – founded the London Free School. Strictly speaking, the school was little more than a motley gathering of beatniks with dreams of freedom. That same year, Laslett invited everybody in the local area to participate in an event inspired by English village fêtes. She borrowed costumes from Madame Tussauds, and convinced a local hairdresser to do people's hair and make-up for free. The Fire Brigade loaned her a float, and steelpan musician Russell Henderson, who was originally from Trinidad, was recruited to play. A thousand people participated that first year, and the carnival's success ensured it became an annual event.

The comprehensive book *Carnival – A Photographic and Testimonial History of the Notting Hill Carnival*, published by Margaret Busby, Britain's first black female publisher, contains photographs from that first parade of happy children, clowns and wizards. Year by year, the nature of the carnival changes. The hippies grow scarcer, while the number of Caribbean participants increases. When Laslett had to step down from her role in organising the carnival due to illness, it was the Caribbeans who took over.

During the 1960s, while the carnival increased in scope, the political landscape was also changing dramatically. 'If you want a nigger for a neighbour, vote Labour,' said Conservative politician Peter Griffiths during an election in October 1964. When confronted about the rhyme's offensiveness, Griffiths insisted that it was a 'manifestation of popular feeling'.

'I was surrounded by active people from a really young age, and it was impossible not to be affected by the racial antagonism out on the streets. At school, everything was fine. The police, on the other hand . . . I was stopped and searched from when I was eight years old. My parents divorced, and I often spent weekends with my dad. When he dropped me off at my mum's house, they might stop us to check whether I was acting as a drug mule for my father. It goes without saying that things like that affect you,' Matthew says.

He speaks in a low voice and rarely smiles, but his eyes are warm and friendly.

'But there was one street that was always safe. This one – All Saints Road. We would run here if we saw the police or Teddy boys. We were always protected here,' Matthew says, pointing towards the Rum Kitchen, which is chock-full of people.

Matthew's father began to frequent the Mangrove, where the fight against racism became a central point of focus. The owner, Frank Crichlow, was a known activist within the local community, and had apparently irritated the local police. Over the course of just a single year, the police raided Crichlow's restaurant as many as twelve times because they suspected the place was a drug den. Ironically enough, Frank Crichlow was popular in the neighbourhood because he was one of the very few people fighting *against* the dealing of drugs. Law student Darcus Howe worked at the Mangrove at the time. Like Crichlow, and Matthew's father, Howe was also from Trinidad, and in 1970 he and his friends organised a demonstration in collaboration with the Black Power movement. On 9 August, 150 people took to the streets to demand that the police get their 'hands off the Mangrove'. The police turned out in force with 700 officers, and hit back hard. The organisers were accused of having planned riots, and nine people were arrested, Darcus Howe among them.[2] The court case attracted significant media attention, and the detainees were known as the Mangrove Nine. Howe insisted that the jury should feature only Black members. His request was denied, but two Black jury members were appointed. The investigation concluded that the Metropolitan Police had acted in a racist manner, and the accused were acquitted. The Mangrove's radical and important history was highlighted in Steve McQueen's movie *Mangrove*, part of the anthology film series *Small Axe*.

Matthew himself never had much time to be politically active. His band rehearsals took up all his time during his youth. Now Matthew lives in Hastings – he doesn't want his children to grow up in London. It's too threatening.

'Notting Hill has always been a neighbourhood with huge contrasts. Many of the buildings here contain lots of tiny flats, where people on welfare live. These flats are wall-to-wall with luxurious properties, where the cast-iron gleams and the tiles are perfect. Luckily, some of the rich residents here are committed to being part of the local community, and send their children to the state schools.'

The neighbourhood borders on districts like Knightsbridge and Holland Park, both known for their wealth. Ladbroke Grove, Westbourne Park and North Kensington, which lie further west, are not so well-off. It is in North Kensington that Grenfell Tower stands, that deepest of all wounds on London's streets: the block of council flats that went up in flames in 2017. Over seventy people lost their lives in the blaze because the building had not been adequately fire-proofed. The tower block is visible in all its horror from the streets of Notting Hill, and remains a symbol of the pervasive financial divides in the capital. The 151 families who were living in Grenfell

Tower at the time of the fire are still without permanent homes. When some of them were rehoused in the expensive residences nearby, the wealthy were outraged. They, after all, had *worked hard* for their success. The iconic Trellick Tower, designed by Hungarian-born Ernő Goldfinger, is also located in North Kensington. Like many other social housing projects, the building is no longer regarded as a repository of sadness, but rather praised by architectural afficionados.[3]

The sound of the steelpans gets louder, the young people playing them deep in concentration.

The steelpans link deepest urban London to the history of British slavery. The painful history of steelpan music goes all the way back to the 1700s, when enslaved persons were transported to the Caribbean islands. The enslaved took their drums with them, which they played to remember their homeland. In 1877, the British banned the use of the drums in Trinidad, because they believed the rhythms encouraged rebellion. The drums were then replaced by bamboo pipes, and a new type of instrument was created – the tamboo bamboo – but these too were prohibited by the English. The local population therefore began to search for other objects with which they could make music. At the dumps they found empty tin cans they could use to create rhythms. After the Second World War the American military had left behind large numbers of oil drums, which the locals discovered could be used as musical drums – the large surfaces of the oil drums could be polished to create different tones, and the musical genre of steelpan was born.[4]

The area around the Mangrove Steelband has become crowded. In an effort to avoid all the friendly attempts to get me to dance, I stand with my back pressed to the wall behind me. People shake their rear ends, and I wish I had a time machine that could take me back to the 1960s to see whether the festivities were equally unrestrained back then. This era in London's history glitters in my mind. Back then, the Mangrove wouldn't have been the only club on the street – I could have strolled from one dim dive to the next, each of them filled with the rich and famous singing and dancing close together. Throughout the 1960s and 1970s, Notting Hill had a dubious reputation, and was regarded by many as the birthplace of questionable glamour and poverty of Babylonian proportions. The combination of glamour and sex attracted free souls, who mingled with the pimps and whores at the nightclubs. The bars were often run by Caribbean men because they were denied entry to clubs elsewhere in London, where discrimination was rife. Caribbean men in lavish outfits were deemed troublemakers or pimps, although at a pinch they might be granted admittance in the company of a white woman. Notting Hill also housed countless bordellos during these decades.

When I was young, my parents always used to describe the district as a kind of den of iniquity to be avoided at all costs. Should the traffic be rerouted, and our car end up on the streets of Notting Hill when we were on our way to Willesden Green, I would stare out of the window enraptured, while my parents were more shocked. I remember how I wanted to get to know the Caribbean children I saw on the streets; how fascinated I was by the men and women I saw leaning against the walls of the houses.

If you look at a map of London, you'll discover that from the heart of Soho to Shepherd's Bush Green on the southern edge of Notting Hill, there is a single stretch that turns from Oxford Street into Bayswater Road, and then Holland Park Avenue. Back then, this strip acted like one long journey of wild entertainment the Emperor Nero would have approved of.

The stretch from Piccadilly Circus to Marble Arch was known for its luxury bordellos. From Marble Arch, all you had to do was cross the road to Hyde Park to find the sex workers, who engaged in dodgy dealings with a fixed clientele from Bayswater Road, where a hostel for military personnel was located. All this sexual activity appears to have been so astonishing that even American sexologist Dr Alfred Kinsey was shocked by the number of prostitutes he observed upon visiting London in 1955. On the stretch leading up to Marble Arch, he reportedly counted over 1,000 sex workers.[5]

A lot of strange things went on in Notting Hill, and the London Free School attracted deviant types. One such person was Michael de Freitas, also known as Michael Abdul Malik, who was originally from Trinidad. After a landmark meeting with African-American civil rights activist Malcolm X, de Freitas took the name Michael X and became active in the Black Liberation Army, which had established a dedicated group in London. Michael X then founded the Black House collective in Holloway, north London, which was financed by a young idealistic millionaire with good contacts – including John Lennon. Lennon was so impressed by Michael X's idealism that he and Yoko Ono filled a bag with their own hair, which they auctioned off to fans in order to raise funds for the Black House – there's a famous film clip of Michael X with Lennon and Ono in which they show the hair, and the couple is interviewed about having cut it off.[6] But then everything went seriously wrong. A businessman was lured to the house and upon entering was attacked by Michael X and a group of his followers. The man was forced to wear a dog collar, and blackmailed for money. The case naturally attracted a great deal of media attention, and made Michael X into a cause célèbre. A few months later, the Black House burned down under mysterious circumstances, and Michael X was charged with extortion. His friendship with John Lennon bore fruit, however, and Lennon paid his bail. Michael X fled to Trinidad, and in 1972 established a new Black House collective just outside Port of Spain. Again, the house burned down. When the police searched the ruins, they found two dismembered bodies – one of them turned out to be the daughter of a famous Trinidadian politician. Michael X was sentenced to death, and despite tenacious campaigns by international activists such as

Angela Davis, and a lawyer paid for by John Lennon, Michael was hanged in 1975.[7] That same year, over 150,000 people took part in the Notting Hill Carnival.

In the year that followed Michael X's death, the political situation came to a head: both the National Front and the police were harassing Black youths in Notting Hill on a daily basis. Slogans like 'Keep Britain White' and 'Niggers Out' were scrawled across the walls of countless buildings. Despite trying to hit back with their own graffiti – 'Nazi Filth Out' – the children of the first *Windrush* generation grew up knowing that although they were born in London and British citizens, they would constantly be pushed to the bottom of the social ladder.

In the lead-up to the carnival in 1976, several local white inhabitants had tried to stop the celebration from going ahead. In TV debates, activist Darcus Howe raged against the racism he believed was being committed against the local community. As many as 1,400 police officers were stationed on the streets during the festivities, and the police attempted to change the carnival's route once it was underway – to massive resistance. White police officers stood along the pavements, nervous and stiff, as members of the Caribbean community and other carnival-goers danced in the streets, sporting their lavish costumes. Gradually, the atmosphere began to turn irritable.

Westway is an area beneath one of the largest road junctions in west London, and was a popular gathering point for carnival-goers. A situation flared up here when police tried to arrest a man they claimed was a pickpocket. A group of youths had witnessed the incident, and attacked the police because they believed the suspect was innocent. With that, it was war. Armed with truncheons, the police stormed the carnival from all sides. Armed with rocks, the young people attacked the police, who protected themselves using milk crates and dustbin lids. Over 125 police officers were injured. The riots were also observed by a gang of punks, the young musician Joe Strummer among them; later, Strummer would describe how he and the other members of the Clash had been present when hordes of police officers attacked the carnival. The song became the Clash's first single, 'White Riot'. It was during these riots that photographer Rocco Macauley took the image that was used on the back of the sleeve of the band's legendary album *The Clash* in 1977.

This confrontation entrenched the hostile attitudes between the Caribbean youths and the police. But at the same time, the riots represented something greater. Black youths in London had shown that they would no longer remain passive in the face of police harassment. The feeling of pride among the Caribbean community increased, but among others the carnival became regarded as an event to be avoided.

Over the years that have passed since then, Notting Hill Carnival has become a national celebration that everybody wants to take part in, although one thing hasn't changed: the carnival's relationship with the police. It is still fragile, despite the fact that uniformed police officers have danced alongside carnival-goers in recent years.

Matthew disappears into the crowd around the Mangrove Steelband. The dark, insistent rhythms fill me, along with the sounds of all the police sirens, trains, buses and people in this city. Notting Hill in August is like a street musical with no director but hundreds of composers, and every time I walk down a street I can hear the sound of unknown rhythms forcing themselves into the known.

An uncompromising tribute to the pasts of the people from the Caribbean, and the unmistakable sounds of London, which you can never escape – and would never wish to.

A new life

One Friday evening, I meet my friend Debbie at Bounds Green station in north London. In the 1990s Debbie was a true popstar, playing guitar in the band Echobelly – with the charismatic Indian-born Sonya Madan as their lead singer, they stormed the charts with hits such as 'Great Things'.

We're going to visit Debbie's mother, Mitsy, who is one of the many thousands of Caribbean women who belong to the *Windrush* generation. British literature has its narratives about the years during which several hundred thousand Caribbeans arrived in the UK. Feelings of isolation and otherness dominate these stories, and all too often it has been only men who have shared their thoughts on this time. Women, however, seem to have experienced the period differently, and that's why I'm interested to hear about Mitsy's life.

Debbie's mother is a confident woman in her early seventies, with short grey hair. She's standing at the stove when we come in. The hallway of the house is narrow, and to get to the kitchen we pass two sitting rooms. This is exactly how I remember the houses of my aunts and uncles – the stairs that lead up to the first floor are carpeted, and astonishingly steep. The kitchen looks just as a kitchen belonging to an older lady should, with overstuffed cupboards and knick-knacks all over the place. Postcards and photographs from Jamaica have been attached to the fridge using cheery-looking magnets.

Debbie's mother came to London from Jamaica in 1959. In collaboration with the Royal College of Nursing, the British health authorities had printed advertisements in Jamaican newspapers, inviting new recruits to the UK to become nurses. If the Caribbean women accepted a three-year contract, all costs associated with their training in addition to all their living expenses would be covered. A total of 40,000 women from the Caribbean obtained jobs in the NHS in the years following the Second World War.[1] Mitsy got a job in Redhill in Surrey, south of London.

'I remember when the boat got to Southampton and I saw all the brick houses, I just didn't understand, because in Jamaica only prisons are built out of bricks. So the first thing I thought was: "My God, so many prisons!" I was picked up at Victoria station and taken to the hospital, where I was given accommodation in a house for female nurses. There were both Caribbean and British women there, it was a nice community. None of us cared about where we were all from. I remember the British nurses were envious of our dresses because they were so colourful,' Mitsy says.

After spending a year in Redhill, Mitsy wanted to become a nurse with the Royal Marines. She dreamed of seeing the world, but succumbing to pressure from her family she turned down the job and moved to London, where she met her husband. Someone she prefers not to talk about too much.

'I had a lovely English boy for a boyfriend, but all my friends teased me and told me I was doomed to marry a man who just wanted to eat fish and chips all the time. That was an unbearable thought for us! Jamaican food is far more exciting than English food,' she laughs. Mitsy tells me that she had few uncomfortable experiences when she moved here. The men struggled more. They were the ones who were refused housing and subjected to racism. 'I think it's because the English girls fell for our men. It created a lot of jealousy,' she chuckles.

I notice several photographs of Debbie on the walls: in one of them she's pictured in a double-breasted tweed suit and posing with a guitar, back when she played in Echobelly. Mitsy sits down at the table for a moment, her hands wet.

'You know, when I first came to London, I thought it was so strange that the bread was just thrown on the doorstep without any paper around it,' she says, wrinkling her nose. 'I mean, it's so unhygienic – it's fine for milk bottles, but bread?'

She gets up and flips the meat patties that are sizzling in the frying pan, before chopping up some broccoli with quick movements. She hands me a glass of a deep red juice – I take a sip. The drink is ice-cold, and has a sharp hint of ginger. I've never tasted it before. Debbie explains that it's a Caribbean thirst-quencher called sorrel.

'We mostly drink it at Christmas. And actually, there should be loads of rum in it, too! Would you like some?' she asks.

Mitsy has fond memories of those early years in London. The challenges she experienced with her husband were normal for people just starting out, she thinks, but there were certain aspects of their lives that were different from those of the English people they knew: the fundraising parties, the care they had for each other and the music. She says that every time a Caribbean family needed to save money for a car or a house, they would arrange blues dances. The parties were held in people's living rooms. Everybody who came had to pay a small entrance fee, as well as for drinks. The money the hosts collected would then be used to put down a deposit. In this way, close bonds of friendship were forged, and Caribbean music boomed from the Blue Spot – a combined radio and record player every home had at the time – the sounds seeping out of the windows and on to London's streets.

Because while the *Windrush* generation was settling in London, the music industry in Jamaica had also begun to flourish. Since most Caribbeans were poor, and didn't have the money to go to nightclubs to listen to music, nor to own their own radio, Caribbean DJs began to play music on mobile sound systems. These could easily be moved from district to district to play music for dances, and it wasn't long before the DJs began producing their own music. At first, this took the form of variants of American rhythm and blues, which then developed into ska, which later became rocksteady. The parties were quickly adopted among the Caribbeans in London, who did what they could to maintain a sense of cultural proximity to their homeland.

Throughout the 1960s, young Caribbean men in London would hold court for their fellow countrymen with their own sound systems. The parties were arranged in cellars or empty sports halls at schools, where many of the Caribbean men worked as caretakers during the day. For many Caribbean couples who worked hard all week, the gatherings were something to look forward to, and the weekend parties became the place to meet like-minded people, eat a good goat curry and listen to the latest music from home. London became a workshop for youth cultures that spread like wildfire, and with the Caribbeans' constant introduction of new forms of music, new genres were always appearing. Mitsy looks happy as we chat about the parties. She serves up the food as she reminisces. The meat patties are tasty, with lots of onion and pepper. Mitsy sets down her cutlery for a moment and thinks. She looks at me.

'You know, white women came to the parties to hang out with our men. But never white men. It didn't matter to me – I had English girlfriends. We hung out together. The mood was always good. No fistfights,' she says, her voice joyful.

In the post-war period, relationships between immigrant men and white English women were taboo and complex. Couples struggled to find housing, and if a woman had a Black boyfriend, she was regarded as 'loose'. But Mitsy tells me that she still thinks people are far more prejudiced nowadays than when she first moved to London.

'I had no problems with English men. They were always pleasant. We lived side by side in relative harmony. Well, some police officers were nasty to me once, I have to say, but I gave them a piece of my mind. I'd say things got harder when the Indians from Uganda came. You remember when Idi Amin threw them out? And then when the Pakistanis wanted to work here – the Pakistanis didn't want to have anything to do with us. I remember watching the news after there had been a fight between these so-called English Teddy boys and some Pakistani men. When the reporter asked why the Teddy boys hadn't attacked the Caribbean men, one of them answered: "Because they're like us – the Pakistanis are not!" '

This isn't the first time I've heard this from within the Caribbean community, and I wonder whether Mitsy can explain the ways in which the Indians and Pakistanis seemed different. Mitsy says that the Pakistani and Indian women stayed at home, and always looked down whenever she tried to catch their eye to get to know them.

'I think we were just too different, culturally. They didn't drink, and they didn't go to parties. The women from those countries didn't mix with the white people, either, so it was clear that they wanted to preserve their lifestyle from Pakistan. A shame, if you ask me,' she says with a little sigh.

Mitsy has touched on a significant difference between the Caribbeans and immigrants from the Indian subcontinent. The Caribbean immigrants regarded London as their home, while those from India and Pakistan generally didn't initially intend to stay here. Their intention was to go home, sooner or later, and they therefore didn't see the same need to integrate. Religion often set them apart, too. The Pakistani men who initially came to the UK were often single, and practising Muslims. The local mosque, rather than the pub, became a second home for them. Many of the women from the Indian subcontinent were also used to their safe lives back home, where they did the washing, looked after the children and cooked the meals, separate from the men who mostly worked in the fields. Upon arriving in England, they suddenly found themselves surrounded by men on the streets and in public spaces, and many found it uncomfortable. For lots of these women, the home they were used to seemed safer, but others got an education and became active in their communities. And there has always been a wealthy contingent of an educated elite from the subcontinent in London.

Debbie has taken out a photo album. As we flick through it, I see photographs of Mitsy in the 1960s, in her stiff white nurse's uniform and standing with her colleagues in front of the brick building of the hospital. The images warm the cockles of my heart – they remind me so much of my own years in England. The photographs are square and matt with white borders. Some of the slightly later ones are of the family, two adults and two children, all of them dressed in 1970s colours. Debbie's brother is a dancer now. The siblings mainly grew up with their mum, but their dad was around. Debbie describes him as someone who invited his friends over to play dominoes when her mum went to work – with all the fun and games you might suspect this would entail. Not exactly an ideal babysitter. Debbie was raised on reggae, ska and rocksteady, but ended up becoming a punk.

It's easy to imagine Mitsy as an energetic and competent woman during her first years here in London, and I can also easily imagine how hard she fought to feed her children while her husband struggled to find work. It's thanks to her that they are able to enjoy dinners together, here in this house – the family were able to afford to buy a property early on because of her stable income. Others were not so lucky. During the 1960s the job market shrank, resulting in the growth of a Caribbean lower class. Caribbean men often found they had to make do with work they were overqualified for. Nor was it unusual for their British colleagues to strike if the Caribbeans were promoted. The British refused to have a 'darkie' for a boss.

Mitsy worked hard to ensure her children had the stability that would enable them to do well at school.

'I noticed that both of them rebelled. They were not grateful, the way I was. They saw themselves as British, with all the rights that come along with that. They didn't make do with crumbs, the way we did. That's something that makes me very proud. Because that was something we did far too much when we came here,' Mitsy says.

I hear the front door open, and then an older Caribbean man strolls into the kitchen as if this is the most natural thing in the world. He's an old family friend, just returned from Kingston. A number of the Caribbeans who are tired of life in London have chosen to spend their retirement in Jamaica, and when I think of London's bitter winter winds I can understand this all too well.

Debbie and I go into the living room next to the kitchen, leaving her mum and her friend to chat. We look at the photos of Debbie from back when she was in Echobelly. 'I probably did sort of rebel against everything Caribbean. I embraced punk. Dad laughed when I played him the Sex Pistols,' Debbie remembers. She's DJing later tonight and has to go pick up her vinyl, so we thank Mitsy for dinner.

As we walk back to the Underground station, I feel a connection to Mitsy's life story. Like Mitsy, my dad also worked for the NHS, as a doctor. My parents had friends from different backgrounds, both white Brits and others from the Indian subcontinent. But the social conventions were marked by the discreet charm of the middle class, and there were certainly no gatherings of people dancing to seductive rhythms – just nice dinner parties at spacious properties in Surrey with their own tennis courts. I remember them well: older British physicians who wore tweed and spoke in nasal voices; white tablecloths, silverware, crystal glasses and fine china.

Our parents dreamed that we would go far. But for Debbie and me it was punk that changed our lives, and there were two larger-than-life figures in particular that had a huge influence on us. For me, it was the British-Pakistani author Hanif Kureishi. For Debbie, it was DJ Don Letts. Letts's parents were from Jamaica, and in the 1970s he transformed the musical tastes of white punks.

Without Don Letts, the Clash would never have sounded the way they did.

The sound of rebellion

'Stop saying that you *used to be* a punk. Once a punk, always a punk!'

Don Letts looks at me sternly. I try to protest, sitting there on a sofa in Letts's shed, his so-called man cave. But Letts is unshakeable. His trademark dreadlocks are tucked into a cap that moves every time he touches it. We're in north-west London, in Kensal Rise, where Letts lives with his wife and four children. On the wall hangs a photograph of a young Letts with Bob Marley. I get up and go across to look at it.

'Oh my God, you both look so handsome here!' I say.

Because they do. Shamelessly handsome. Don Letts laughs. He's still strikingly attractive.

'I think it's because I'm half Indian,' he says.

'Oh?'

'Oh yeah, take a look at this!'

He shows me a small passport photo of his mother, which he keeps in his wallet. His face takes on a soft expression.

'I knew it!' I say. 'I saw you in a documentary, walking around London with your son, and there was something about his features that made me suspect there might be something there.'

Letts chuckles.

Indian immigrants didn't just travel to Southern and East Africa during the British colonial period – they also travelled to the

Caribbean as migrant workers. Love was in the air; many Indian women married Caribbean men. Letts tells me that he grew up with a mother who made curry and rotis for him, but other than the food he feels no connection to his Indian heritage. He speaks quickly, without pausing.

'I don't feel the influence of the Indian side. We were Caribbeans. Period. I was raised that way. We were poor when I was young, and lived in Kennington. I mean *really* poor. Our house didn't have a bathroom, or an indoor toilet. In the summer we washed in a zinc bucket in the garden, and in the winter we went to a public baths. This was London in the 1960s. Everybody I knew lived that way, so I didn't think anything of it. You just did the best you could. My parents didn't go on holiday. I can't even remember anyone ever talking about taking a holiday. My parents were brought in to rebuild London, and if I'm being honest, I have to say that they were treated like shit. My parents tried to adapt to this country by forgetting who they were, denying their roots and attempting to become as much like the white Englishmen who lived here as they could. It didn't work. My generation believed that people had to accept us for who and what we are. Me and my friends were influenced by the American civil rights movement. It was tough for a while, we had to go through a whole load of trouble with the National Front and the police. Now there's a certain balance. You can't deny who you are. It doesn't work in the long run. Our differences are an asset we have to use for something constructive!' Letts says, almost without taking a breath.

Letts is wearing the kind of camouflage jacket only people from London can really pull off. He takes a long drag on his spliff. The man cave is tastefully decorated and there's a lot of vinyl here, along with vintage art and various electronic gadgets.

I'm feeling quite starstruck, because other than Sex Pistols vocalist Johnny Rotten and Clash frontman Joe Strummer, I can't think of a greater hero to us children of punk than Don Letts. In 1975, Letts ran the Acme Attractions store in the King's Road in Chelsea, where he sold clothes and played reggae all day long. The King's Road was also where the legendary shop Sex had its premises, where Vivienne Westwood and Malcolm McLaren sold their punk fashion. Acme quickly became a popular place to hang out for up-and-coming rock stars like Chrissie Hynde, Patti Smith and the Sex Pistols. Letts's accountant, a young man with Polish roots, started the punk club the Roxy on Neal Street, where Letts was asked to DJ. It was here that Letts became a close friend of the Clash, and it was also here that he turned the punks to reggae.

In the 1960s, a wave of reggae music released by record label Trojan had flooded the British mainland. Jamaica was granted independence in 1962, and in the wake of this freedom the Caribbeans returned to what they believed were their true roots. One of the movements that gained popularity was the Rastafarian faith, which regarded Haile Selassie, the Emperor of Ethiopia, as God – Jah. Bob Marley, the Rastafarians' most influential voice, spread the music to the masses, and reggae became one of Jamaica's greatest exports, with ripple effects that made it all the way to the streets of London. These included smoking cannabis and dreads – the perfect acts of rebellion for Caribbean youths who didn't want to go to church every Sunday.

If you went down to the neighbourhood of Kennington in the 1970s, you would find a Rastafarian collective at St Agnes Place. In 1969, the old Victorian houses were occupied by a community made up of people looking for an alternative lifestyle: fifty or so followers of Rastafarianism, who established one of London's most visited Rastafarian temples there. Bob Marley also stayed there every time he came to London throughout the 1970s. But with the Rastafarian community came widespread cannabis use, which according to the police led to large-scale drug dealing in the area. In the 1970s and 1980s, everybody in London talked about the Yardie gangs. Yardie – originally a term from Jamaican patois – eventually became a designation for organised criminals in London who had ties to Trenchtown in Kingston, Jamaica. In awe, I would watch them where they hung out on the streets of north-west London, especially in Harlesden. They were immortalised in Victor Headley's novel *Yardie* from 1992, and later in Idris Elba's film version in 2019 – rich and violent.

Letts thinks the link between punk and reggae is obvious. He stands in the middle of his man cave, addressing me like a teacher.

'Think about it. Reggae was created through a kind of punk-rock attitude. It's music made by people who didn't have a penny to their name, they just wanted to express themselves. They made their problems into their assets. But because we live in a world where white culture dominates – let's just agree on that – nobody realised that we've actually been punks the whole time. We've had to utilise our problems. I'd say the same thing happened with hip-hop. Black punk. Those who see punk as a kind of white thing that happened in the seventies in London – that's just lazy journalism! I'm sorry. I'm know I whining, but I'm passionate about making sure people understand this.'

He walks restlessly around the room before sitting down at the desk where his computer sits, then gets straight back up again to smoke a little more. I envy Letts. He grew up in a London I've always wanted to experience: the Notting Hill riots, punk and the Black Power movement. I was born too late, and had to create my own identity, where I combined my love of punk with being an Asian kid. I think Letts will understand, so I tell him about how I had wanted to look like punk queen Siouxsie Sioux, and how my cousins in Willesden Green were constantly having a go at me. They thought I should listen to soul, not punk.

'I totally understand what you went through! You should have seen me in Brixton! People fell about laughing at my style. But I loved it. I was no conformist, but nor was I acting consciously. That was just the way I was. I made it into something positive, something I could use. I loved Led Zeppelin and the Rolling Stones, and then other Caribbeans would wag their fingers at me and say: "That's the white man's music!" I realised early on that I didn't want to be defined by the colour of my skin,' Letts says.

In the 1980s, the children of the Caribbean immigrants became adolescents, and started to develop their own identity. They were not Caribbeans, but London kids. Not all Caribbean youths wanted to embrace Marley's message of going back to their roots; nor did they share Letts's fascination with punk and reggae. Some simply wanted a soundtrack to their lives that was about love and partying. They turned instead to the US, where rhythm 'n' blues and soul dominated the Black music scene. Caribbean musicians in London were inspired by the tender rhythms of Marvin Gaye and mixed them with reggae – suddenly the genre 'lovers rock' was born and exported to Jamaica with great success. Finally, the Caribbeans in London were able to send something back to their homeland. Punk or lovers rock – the vast Caribbean contribution to London's music scene became clear for all to see. But young Black men still found that they were not allowed into the clubs whenever they wanted to go out dancing.

This discriminatory treatment led the young Caribbeans to arrange their own parties. Where and when was communicated through the grapevine, or on the many pirate radio stations that began to pop up. In the 1980s, pirate radio brought about a revolution within the British music scene. I would sit glued to my radio late at night, searching for the sound of the deep soul rhythms introduced by enthusiastic DJs like Trevor Nelson and Ronnie Herel.[1] Letts avoided much of the discrimination at the clubs because he was a DJ himself, as well as a punk. Letts didn't just play reggae at his club nights – he also played a lot of ska at the punk clubs in London, and it was at these clubs that the doors were opened on to a profusion of Caribbean music genres that merged with new musical styles.

'The multicultural mix that characterises London is indisputably what gives the city its energy, its creativity, style and fashion. Food, too. Before the immigrants arrived, English food was awful! Of course, it took me a little while to figure out what it meant to be Black and British, but it's something that's always evolving, it isn't possible to limit it or pigeonhole it. I'd say that it was Soul II Soul who changed the notion of what it is to be British and Black.'

I'm not surprised to hear Letts mention this band. As the punk scene slowly ebbed away, the Black music scene in London continued to flourish. The Soul II Soul collective probably captured this period better than anyone else – in 1989 they had their breakthrough with the song 'Keep on Movin'', and the following year the band had a roaring international success with 'Back to Life'. Soul II Soul represented a victory for the Black music scene in the UK, and they were ultimately a culmination of all the Caribbean rhythms that had made their mark on London's streets ever since the Southern Syncopated Orchestra arrived in the city in 1919. Letts and I enthusiastically babble away to each other about these years, about the freedom from the desperation our parents' generation struggled with. An entirely new sound has now emerged in London, for which punk is an underlying premise.

'Punk celebrated individuality. It seems to me that's changed. Now, collective notions about identity are what limit people. I can't stand this debate about who started what within culture. It's divisive. London has been hit by an epidemic where Black people are killing Black people. We should talk more about that. When I was young, I wasn't afraid of being murdered by another Black man. I knew who the enemy was. Now, I have no idea. I feel we've lost a lot of what we created in the 1980s, the community. I'm naive enough to believe that music can still be a tool for social change but unfortunately, for today's youth, music doesn't have the same value. Grime is the only exciting thing to have come out of London in a really long time. I thought it was a bit macho at first, but now I have respect for the artists. The music has a direct link to Jamaican sound systems. That makes me proud. Jamaica was colonised for hundreds of years, but now Jamaica has culturally colonised the entire world. If you look at a map, Jamaica is just this tiny island, but its impact has been colossal. Style, language, music, attitudes – it's crazy. Jamaica has captured the hearts and minds of white youths all over the world. Reggae is enormous in Croatia, Finland, France – everywhere. They wear dreads. They live for reggae. But I have to admit it's pretty funny when they come up to me and speak English with a thick Jamaican accent – and I answer them in perfect English. Many young Jamaicans aren't interested in all the spiritual stuff or Bob Marley. Not really. And by the way, there aren't even any Black people at blues concerts any more! Have you noticed that? Man, I'm ranting!'

He shakes his head.

Letts sits down at the desk and lights another spliff.

'Come on – ask me another question!'

I ponder for a moment, because I want to know about everything – what it was like meeting Bob Marley; life as a DJ; the Clash; the music videos with Eddy Grant and Elvis Costello and his time with Big Audio Dynamite. But perhaps most of all I want to know what it was like hanging out with John Lydon and Malcolm McLaren during the years when punk was actually still living and breathing, and not a social phenomenon kept alive by older men who like to reminisce. After all, it wasn't exactly usual for Caribbeans to hang out with English punks at the time.

'You're right. It was just me and three other brothers who hung out at the punk clubs back then. Let me put it this way: I became the person they needed to complete the cast of the musical *Hair*, the funky Black guy, you know? But I quickly turned the whole thing on its head, and showed them that I had at least just as much to contribute, so to speak. I made it pretty clear that I didn't dance for anybody and that nobody was doing me any favours. I didn't stand there with my cap in my hand, acting all grateful. Fuck that. I had an education. I'm not trying to be funny now. But I was well aware of my background, what I represented. A lot of that knowledge came to me directly through music that changed my life.'

I understand what Letts is referring to all too well. A London without music is impossible. A London without punk and the Caribbeans is unthinkable. It never fails to astonish me that there are people who question the value of immigration. Letts is a hybrid, and the very incarnation of London. He can't be defined through crude perceptions of identity and culture, and he has an uncompromising recklessness that is infectious. His thirst for freedom is recognisable.

I'm filled with an incomprehensible energy as I leave Letts's house and head out on to London's streets. My thoughts swirl as I take the Underground south to Brixton, the neighbourhood that borders on Kennington, where Letts was born.

'Little Jamaica'

As I walk up the steps from Brixton Underground station, an all-too-familiar, freezing-cold breeze tugs at me. Everybody who arrives in Brixton by Tube feels its grasp. Brixton is probably the neighbourhood in London that I have visited most often throughout my life. The streets here are bursting with rebellion, energy, music, tenacity and community.

A sea of people greets me at the top of the stairs where the melancholic artwork *Brixton Blue*, by Grenada-born Denzil Forrester, hangs over our heads. It features Winston Rose, a friend of Forrester's who died while under police restraint in 1981. Starbucks, the very symbol of urban renewal, has opened a branch right next to the station, and the area is always dense with young people shouting into their mobile phones. Just outside the café, a young man is trying to hand out leaflets against police violence, and a florist is enthusiastically calling out for customers. A young man with dirty hair tries to scrounge some money off me. Two men in linen tunics are selling essential oils and handing out brochures about Islam, while simultaneously trying to drown out two evangelical Christian women who are waving their Bibles a few metres further down the street.

Brixton can sometimes feel like too much to handle. When waiting for friends here, I've sometimes wanted to do nothing but clamp my hands over my ears and close my eyes. But today, I manage to sort through all these sensory impressions and enjoy them. I look at the pedestrian crossing that traverses the busy Brixton Road, and feel a sharp pang of melancholy. Bouquets of flowers have been set in front of a mural of David Bowie as Ziggy Stardust. Brixton is Bowie's birthplace, and when he died in 2016 this wall spontaneously became a place visited by fans from all over the world who came to pay their respects and grieve. In the song 'London By Ta Ta' from 1969, Bowie sings about the Caribbean immigrants who flocked to London. Bowie himself was born in 1947, the year before SS *Windrush* docked. The track bears witness to how Bowie must have noticed the ways in which Brixton was changed by the coming of the Caribbeans. The entire main road seethes with people.

Brixton was the district to which recently arrived Jamaicans made their way in the 1950s. Media interest in them was huge. At the time, Pathé newsreels showed Caribbeans working as carpenters or bricklayers, often while wearing suits. They also presented Caribbean families at home, in simple but attractive living rooms. Some of the news stories show stylish Caribbean couples walking along Brixton's streets. Some of the selected couples are Caribbean–British, despite the fact that mixed marriages were frowned upon at the time. It's almost enough to make me suspect the BBC of producing journalism with ideological undertones.

We're shown Brixton's several popular markets, such as Brixton Market and the Granville Arcade, where Caribbean immigrants can find the foods they miss from home. At this point in time, Brixton is a middle-class area with ambition. If we're to believe the news coverage, there are few traces of 'the Jamaica problem' here. But just as Notting Hill became marked by unrest, so too did Brixton's streets gradually become less idyllic.

In 1968, Conservative MP Enoch Powell gives a rousing speech in Birmingham, which causes a political storm. He thunders against the immigrants he believes have no desire to integrate, referring to the Roman poet Virgil and his epic poem, *The Aeneid*: 'As I look ahead, I am filled with foreboding. Like the Roman, I seem to see the River Tiber foaming with much blood.'[1] The 'Rivers of Blood' speech shakes the political establishment, and Powell is dismissed from the shadow cabinet by Conservative Party leader Edward Heath. But even if Powell's speech is not well received among the political elite, it nevertheless attains a deeper resonance among voters. In 1970, the Conservatives win the election. In a national survey, 82 per cent of respondents state that they support Powell's stance. In another opinion poll, 74 per cent believe him to be 'generally right'.

It's as if a dam bursts. One year after the election, the Immigration Act is introduced – a significant tightening of the previous immigration legislation from 1968. All citizens of the Commonwealth who were previously able to live in Britain indefinitely now lose this right; Commonwealth citizens may only be granted permanent residency after having lived and worked in Britain for five years. Those who can point to a personal or hereditary link remain unaffected.

These legislative changes come into effect while the UK is in the grip of a class war, with militant union strategies bringing about extensive strikes in the public sector. In parallel with this, Britain falls into a serious financial crisis, in which inflation is increasing due to war in the Middle East. Unemployment is sky-high. The conflict in Northern Ireland is also draining the country's funds. The nation is wounded; the streets are strewn with rubbish and factories stand empty. Even the hospitals are in decline. In 1973, the situation reaches a low point when due to the oil crisis the authorities attempt to introduce a three-day working week in order to save electricity. It's as if somebody has drained the nation of all colour, and the country only exists in fifty shades of grey. These changes hit the immigrant population especially hard. They have been dependent on construction and industry – two sectors that are now collapsing.

After several years of strikes and an abysmal economic situation, the British want to try something new. The Conservatives start to realise that they can utilise the unrest, and behind closed doors a very special woman decides that Britain needs a revolution. In 1979, after five years of a Labour government, the Conservatives return to power – this time with Margaret Thatcher as prime minister. The Iron Lady. A new era begins. One which has dramatic consequences for London – and not least for the city's Caribbean inhabitants. The relationship between the Metropolitan Police and London's Black population is far from harmonious, and an incident that takes place two years into Thatcher's term tears this festering abscess wide open.

On 18 January 1981, a fire breaks out at a residential property in New Cross in south-east London, where thirty or so Black youths have got together for a birthday party. The flames blaze up the stairs to the first floor, where the guests have gathered. The fire claims thirteen lives, the deceased all aged between fourteen and twenty-two.[2] The neighbourhood collapses in grief, but the flames have hardly been put out when sparks begin to fly between Black and white residents. The National Front is extremely active in this part of the city, and there have been several confrontations between young Black youths and marching skinheads. Could the fire have been started deliberately? According to witnesses, a white car was observed leaving the scene, and the fire was thought to have started in the bottom of a stairwell – something that provides reasonable grounds to suspect arson. The police are criticised for not investigating the case more thoroughly. On 20 March, 20,000 people march through London's streets holding placards stating: 'Thirteen Dead and Nothing Said' and 'No Police Cover-Up'. The demonstration unfolds peacefully, but the *Sun* newspaper still runs the following front-page headline: 'Day the Blacks Ran Riot in London'.

While the police fail to take crimes committed against London's Black community and other people of colour seriously, they spend a disproportionate amount of energy chasing down young Black men in what they claim is a legitimate fight against the dealing of drugs. Crime in Brixton has reached unmanageable proportions, and the Metropolitan Police undertake large-scale raids using a much-feared law as their greatest weapon in the fight to eradicate drugs. This is the Sus – 'suspected person' – law, and the police use it with zeal. The law was originally introduced in 1824 to enable the police to stop and search anyone they believed appeared to have the intention of committing a criminal act.

The problem is that the statistics speak for themselves. In 1980, in the Borough of Lambeth with its 270,000 inhabitants, over 30,000 crimes are registered. Over a third of these are registered in Brixton. In April 1981, the Metropolitan Police decide to initiate 'Operation Swamp 81': 120 plainclothes police officers take to the streets, and 943 individuals are stopped and searched. In Brixton, 82 people are arrested. Almost all of them are Black. Anger spreads among the residents of Brixton. On 10 April, five years after the Notting Hill riots, events take place that will change Brixton's streets and British politics forever.

It's 11 April, 1981. I'm a teenager, in London, sitting in front of the television. Stunned. On the screen are burning tyres, burning cars, burning buildings. My political awareness is just starting to take shape, and I've already had several heated discussions with my father, who is an enthusiastic Thatcherite. Come to think of it, it's probably my dad's fault that I'm so politically engaged – he's always been interested in politics. But where he sees layabouts and poorly maintained houses as we drive around London, I see other things. I've become aware of the injustices that exist in the city. That's why I'm currently devouring all the newspaper reports and TV coverage

I can about the Caribbean man in Brixton who ran from a police officer.

There are several versions of the story, but the one that gets through to me is that, the day before, Michael Bailey was stopped by a policeman who discovered that Michael was bleeding from a stab wound, and therefore wanted to help him. Bailey, however, thought he was about to be arrested, so twisted free from the policeman's grasp – and ran. The police stopped him again on Atlantic Road, but this time they didn't let him get away. Instead, they helped him into a family's apartment to call for a taxi, and it was here that the misunderstanding arose. As the taxi arrived to take Bailey to the hospital, a police car also pulled up because the police believed it would be much faster to drive Bailey to the hospital in a police car. But the neighbours and others who witnessed the scene thought that the police car had arrived to arrest Bailey. They became furious, and tried to stop the police from taking Bailey away. One of the youths who was present cried: 'Look, they're killing him!' With that, all hell broke loose. Instead of remaining with the police, Bailey was attended to by a group of youths, who took him to the hospital. He died there due to the loss of blood. Rumours spread that the police were responsible for his death, and the rage increased in scope.

On the television, the news is broadcast all day long. I watch furious people screaming at the police, who stand lined up shoulder to shoulder, equipped with riot shields. Milk bottles filled with petrol and old rags fly through the air, ablaze; people of all ages storm through broken shop windows. As they stagger out again some of them are carrying televisions; others clutch piles of clothes they have ripped from the displays and shelves of the department stores.

The flames, the aggression and the smashed windows are seared into British memory, and for many people Brixton became synonymous with chaos, violence and organised crime. For others, the district became London's most important battlefield in the fight against racism and police brutality. More than 5,000 people are said to have been involved in the riots, which lasted for three days. Almost 300 people were injured; cars and buildings were burned and razed to the ground. Hundreds were arrested.

I decide I have to go there – but of course say nothing to my parents about where I'm headed. Instead, I say that I'm just going to visit the Tate Gallery. Luckily, we're on holiday in London during this week of April, and staying in Pimlico, just four stops from Brixton on the Victoria line. But it's a completely different world. In Pimlico, the rich live in huge apartments with views of the Thames. Three days after the riots, on 14 April, I take the Underground to Brixton. I want to see the area with my own eyes. Brixton has suddenly become a place with a unique history, a place that is willing to riot and rebel. I rush up the dirty staircase from the Underground station, and then I'm standing there – in the middle of Brixton Road. I look around me at the busy street, registering many homeless people and a lot of rubbish. I see broken windows. Chaos. I don't stay there long – I daren't. I run back down the stairs, and go back to my family. But my curiosity has been aroused for a lifetime.

In the wake of the riots, the events in Brixton become a national affair. Margaret Thatcher is furious, and on 13 April, in an interview with the *News at Ten* on ITN, she condemns the rioters in no uncertain terms: 'I think there is probably deep disaffection among the problems. Whatever the problems, nothing, but nothing, justifies what happened on Saturday and Sunday night.'[3]

Despite the fact that poverty is highlighted as one of the most important causes of the riots, Thatcher refuses to allocate increased funds to inner-city areas to calm the unrest, instead stating that 'money cannot buy trust and racial harmony'. A committee is appointed to investigate the cause of the riots. In November that year, Lord Scarman submits a report that takes issue with the methods employed by the police; social and economic factors are also mentioned as issues that must be addressed. But nobody seems to be interested. Brixton is granted no extra funding, and in 1985 there are more riots. An older, Caribbean woman is shot by mistake while police are searching for her son, a known gang member. She doesn't die, but rumours begin to circulate about her alleged death. Fifty people are injured, 200 arrested, and a dozen or so cars are set alight. The streets of Brixton remain a war zone.

It is during these years that I discover the Jamaican poet Linton Kwesi Johnson. He lives in Brixton, and is a close friend of activist Darcus Howe – he's spent several years working closely with Howe in the British Black Panther movement. During the 1980s, Kwesi Johnson's sharp dub poetry travels far beyond the Caribbean community with the poems 'Di great insoreckshan', 'Sonnys Lettah' and 'Inglan is a Bitch' – furious, painful reflections on life as a young Caribbean man in London. At school, the Caribbeans have only ever been taught about white poets, but in Kwesi Johnson they now have a role model – here is somebody with the same background as them. Linton Kwesi Johnson becomes a voice for everybody frustrated at the racism on London's streets, and a wake-up call for those who don't experience racism themselves.

In the 1980s, politicians are forced to implement measures to solve the social problems in Brixton, and funding for urban renewal is finally injected into the area. The dilapidated Brixton Market and Granville Arcade are refurbished, and the Underground station is transformed beyond all recognition. There is less litter on the streets, chain stores open branches in the area, and countless organisations get involved to help tackle poverty. Brixton becomes renowned because of the riots, and celebrities and role models with African roots drop by the area, to be seen and to show their solidarity. Basketball player Michael Jordan visits the area in 1985; Nelson Mandela specifically asks to visit the neighbourhood when in

London in 1996. A new Brixton develops, in which the district's Caribbean roots are recognised. Street names are changed – Bob Marley Way and Marcus Garvey Way appear – and the area is filled with murals paying tribute to Caribbean and African heroes. But in parallel with this increased financial assistance and influx of supporters, Brixton changes. Old ideals are put to the test. The community dissolves.

Just as parts of Harlem in New York have become gentrified, with a corresponding increase in property prices, Brixton is now in the midst of a similar process – although not without protest. On Brixton's streets, the class war and identity politics continue unabated. And there is still no other neighbourhood in London where Caribbean culture is so evident on the streets, over seventy years after the arrival of the *Windrush* generation.

I've come to Brixton to meet the rapper Ty, a Brixton native who has just released his single 'Brixton Baby' to launch his new album.[4] I realise that I'm going to arrive far too early – in London, I find it impossible to be on time. The completely erratic public transport means that I'm always either too late or way too early for agreed meet-ups in the city. But I can spend the extra time wandering the streets.

I stroll towards pedestrianised Electric Avenue and quickly catch sight of them, just as I always have done over the years: three musicians, two men and a woman, standing in front of glass windows where advertisements for frozen peas and onion rings frame them. Each of them is deep in concentration, playing a steelpan drum. They're not well dressed – their clothes are pilled and shapeless. I continue down Brixton Road, elated. It's as if I'm high – I never get tired of being here. Maybe it's because the neighbourhood encapsulates everything I love about music, style and food. Or perhaps it's because I have so many fond memories of spending time here in my younger days.

I turn on to Electric Avenue, just round the corner from where the street musicians are playing. One of Brixton's several markets is located here. The shops and stalls are packed close together. It isn't exactly London's wealthy who shop here, but once upon a time Brixton was actually a place where the well-to-do gathered.

Looking at old photographs and illustrations of Electric Avenue, I've been surprised at the beauty of the buildings and by how exclusive the shops were. This shopping street was the first in London to have electric lighting – hence the name – and was often referred to as south London's very own Oxford Street. Today, nothing remains of all the cast iron and elegant superstructures. In the once so attractive shops, butchers now stand shoulder to shoulder, most of them owned by Pakistani and Turkish families who have been here for years. The area is thick with the odour of recently slaughtered chicken; bloodstains cover the worn green linoleum. Meat lies in plastic tubs, and the greengrocers are overflowing with sweet potatoes and plantain, a key ingredient in Caribbean and West African cooking. The shops sell plastic cutlery, bedding and T-shirts at laughably low prices, and the market stalls seem to sell wares with no overarching theme.

On one street corner is a meeting place for the city's Caribbean population: fast-food shop Healthy Choice, which sells jerk chicken. Jerk is a special mix of spices that includes nutmeg, pimiento, brown sugar and thyme. Behind the counter, two Caribbean women with plastic gloves on their hands and white nets covering their hair are quickly serving customers. From early in the morning, people of all ages sit at the worn Formica tables in these barren premises, munching on fatty chicken legs or boiled white fish. And it is here, in the fast-food place, that everything becomes so clear to me: there are no white people in the café, neither here nor in any of the other Caribbean restaurants or bakeries. But white people *are* here in the area – they're just not where the Caribbeans are.

Beside the market stalls, my eyes are drawn to the roofs of the houses. The words 'Electric Avenue', displayed on top of the row of buildings, are also a tribute to artist Eddy Grant. Traces of Brixton's musical heritage are visible everywhere on the streets. Grant became a central figure on the British music scene in the 1960s when he formed the band the Equals – the first pop-rock band to have both Black and white members. In 1983, Grant had an international hit with 'Electric Avenue', and the song, which opens with the line 'Down in the street there is violence', was directly inspired by the riots. With pomp and ceremony, the sign was switched on by Eddy Grant in 2016 as part of a campaign to market Brixton as one of London's cultural enclaves. But it didn't take long before the lights in one of the letters stopped working, and I just can't shake the thought that this was in the true spirit of Brixton, where everything is a little rough around the edges.

Brixton Market is located right next to Atlantic Road, and I notice that the entrances to closed-down stores such as Budget Carpets and Continental Grocers are adorned with posters campaigning to 'Save Brixton Arches' and 'Stop the Evictions!' Below the railway tracks, family run shops have always existed in the arched premises that give Brixton its character. Now the owners, Network Rail, have decided to renovate. The opposition to this is visible everywhere. Stickers on lamp posts encourage people to boycott the rail company; the locals want to confront urban renewal that doesn't take the neighbourhood's original residents into account. Some of the shop owners are still clinging on. I find colourful African fabrics sold by the metre, and Caribbean bakeries selling the world's softest coconut cakes.

I realise that I'm filled with nostalgia as I walk towards Windrush Square. Where there was once a little café on Coldharbour Lane, which used to be full of photographs of jazz artists, second-hand books, deep leather chairs from the seventies, little tables and good cakes, there is now a minimalistic shop selling expensive bars of soap. I feel the irritation bubbling up within me. Brixton reminds me of a homeless person desperately trying to appear presentable, who despite the designer clothes and newly cut hair will always have fingernails lined with dirt.

I've agreed to meet Ty at the Black Cultural Archives (BCA) in Windrush Square. The centre was founded by a group led by historian and photographer Len Garrison. It used to be located in Coldharbour Lane, in dilapidated premises. Throughout his life, Garrison had been keen to document the lives of the Black population in Britain, and was eager to create a place where these stories could be shown to the coming generations. His dream was realised in 2014, when the centre opened. Clusters of young people in school uniform are hanging around outside – they've clearly just been on a tour. To look at them, you'd think they had just been subjected to torture.

I step into the centre's café, and after a couple of minutes, Ty – or Ben Chijioke, as is his real name – comes in. We sit down at one of the tables. All the café's patterned tablecloths are covered in thick, transparent plastic, which I suspect has been done on purpose to give the place a consciously retro air – there can hardly be an immigrant who grew up in seventies London without having the experience of sitting on a plastic-covered sofa. Ty's parents are Nigerian, but Ty has lived in Brixton his entire life. He has mixed feelings about the changes that are now taking place in the neighbourhood.

'I think we have to get involved, and not just criticise the trend. After all, Brixton Village was ours before, but we didn't manage to do anything with it. Now others have come in and given the place a renewed energy. It's up to us to take advantage of that, and not just sulk,' Ty says, looking at me through glasses with thick black frames. He is the very incarnation of a cool rapper: broad-shouldered, tough.

In 2004, Ty was nominated for a Mercury Prize for his album *Upwards*; he can also boast having collaborated with American group

De La Soul. He hasn't made music for several years, but now he's full of enthusiasm for his art again. Paying tribute to Brixton was a natural step, he explains.

'So far the trend here isn't as bad as in Shoreditch. The people who started Pop Brixton, with small privately owned restaurants and shops, have a real desire to make the place a resource for the locals. I'm happy that younger designers from here have established themselves there. But it also leaves a weird taste in my mouth. It's as if there has to be a certain aesthetic before our lifestyle becomes palatable to white youths. For me, it's almost as if an attempt is being made to colonise Brixton, to make it into a kind of playground for white middle-class young people,' says Ty.

He leans back, stretches.

'Listen, Nazneen,' he says, leaning towards me again. 'White kids almost never come here to visit the centre. I know that because I live here, I know what's going on. They come to Brixton at the weekends because it's cool. It's tropical and exotic. They can walk around here with lions and tigers that don't bite. We no longer have teeth. That's the way things are now, Nazneen.'

Ty has a world view I recognise from young, Black activists. Everything centres on race. I wonder why those of us who are brown find ourselves in this complicated terrain. In the 1980s, we were all allies. I no longer see that alliance so clearly. Black used to be a political term that encapsulated anybody with Asian or African heritage.

Ty wonders what kind of relationship I have to Brixton, and I don't need to be asked twice. I prattle on and on about Brixton in the old days. *My* old days. About the first time I came here after the riots, and my love for the neighbourhood through my interest in music. I talk about squats, collectives I visited with people who were looking for some kind of revolution. In the mid-1990s, the offices of alternative fashion magazines like *2nd Generation* were here – an attempt to create a 'coloured' version of fashion magazine *The Face*. London's young Asians were in the process of finding themselves. My Brixton was synonymous with concerts at Brixton Academy and just as many after-parties – I staggered around, high on all the music. My feet were always tired, but in the coolest trainers – otherwise you weren't part of the in-crowd. Brixton was where everybody went to party – to the Dogstar, or the Bugbar, a tiny crypt under St Matthew's Church in the middle of Brixton, or the Fridge, one of the biggest clubs playing electronica. But partying here also involved the struggle to find a taxi that could drive me to Victoria station, where I would get the train to Croydon. The safest alternative – but the taxi drivers steered clear of Brixton. I finally notice that Ty is smiling indulgently at me as I tell him about my experiences from the nineties, which makes me suddenly embarrassed. I stop talking to hear his version.

'I totally get everything you're saying about the energy and enthusiasm, but for me life in Brixton is about survival. Not some romantic idea, but survival: whether you have enough to pay the rent and look after your mental health; how you should look at somebody or not look at somebody, or whether or not the person coming down the street wants to hurt you. If the police who stop you are going to hurt you. That's how it is to live in Brixton. Of course, it's become less dangerous here, less stressful, but every time I step out of the front door I'm on the alert. These are things you don't have to live with,' Ty says.

He remembers the riots, and the conduct of the police. While I sat in safety, viewing the events with fascination from a distance, a war was playing out in his neighbourhood, among his family and friends. I risked nothing. As they walked around Brixton, Ty and his friends were constantly stopped by the police. For no reason.

'I remember I once took part in a workshop at Brixton prison, and I was shocked when I went in. Over half of the people I saw were people I used to know, who I thought had moved away. But they hadn't gone anywhere. They were in prison,' he says.[5]

Being a young Black man in London isn't easy. Ty is still stopped by the police. Completely at random.

'You know the feeling, when the police talk to you as if you're a child, even though you're physically towering over them,' he says with a sigh.

I can't imagine how it must feel. Ty says that the parties he and his friends held throughout the 1980s and 1990s were crucial for the London music scene.

It was during these years that Ty discovered rap music, just as his life took a tough turn. He prefers not to talk about that time. Today, he's an established artist and the father of small children. He tells me that Brixton has its own hierarchy, which made its mark on his childhood. Since the neighbourhood is the fort of the Caribbeans, people from West African backgrounds are often looked down upon. But the West Africans are no better – they look down on the Caribbeans. We decide to take a walk to Brixton Market. Ty would like to show me a shop he's collaborating with.

We walk down Brixton Road. Prosperity and poverty live side by side here, in an uneasy balance. Despite the enthusiastic media coverage given to Brixton, the neighbourhood is anything but polished. Older Caribbean women wearing hats limp past pulling shopping trolleys behind them, and I realise that there are plenty of staggering, dishevelled homeless people wandering around here, just as there always has been. The only ones who are really missing are the representatives from the Nation of Islam in their tight suits and bowties, who were a permanent sight here throughout the nineties. But they're only a stone's throw away. They hold meetings every Sunday morning for those who are interested, where they give passionate speeches about the racism of London's police force and the need to take care of the city's young people.[6]

We walk to Market Row in Brixton Village, where flags from all over the world hang from the roofs and everything is painted in happy shades of blue and yellow. Smart little eateries selling French cheeses, Spanish tapas, and wholemeal pancakes with sweet potato and goat's cheese served on wooden platters have been established here, with a clientele you would hardly have seen in the area five years ago. Most of the greasy spoons are gone. The cafés where the tea was scalding hot and the sliced bread white as snow, accompanied by an always generous helping of baked beans and served with an affectionate retort like, 'There you go, darling,' thrown into the bargain. As I look at all the well-dressed people, it occurs to me that Brixton is a place on which you could use endless volumes of antiseptic cleaning agents and still never get rid of the ingrained dirt. Perhaps this is what gives the neighbourhood its charm, and maybe it's good that the people who now use the market have money to spend. We arrive at the United80 store.

Ty introduces me to his friend Samantha-Jane Ofoegbu, the shop's manager, who is sitting at a sewing machine as we enter the little store with its bright yellow doorframe. United80 specialises in the cutting-edge of Black urban design. Here you can buy Afro Supa Star mugs designed by prize-winning illustrator Jon Daniel, backpacks in camouflage fabric I'm sure Don Letts would love, and college sweaters with 'Brixton' emblazoned across the chest. I smile at a T-shirt that bears the slogan 'Fook Twerkin. Try Workin''. All the clothes are created by local designers. The store was established in 2010, and is a collective run by local artists with West African and Caribbean roots.

Over the years, I've noticed that the shops selling African fabrics in Brixton are often owned by people from Pakistani backgrounds. Shouldn't they be owned by the Caribbeans or West Africans themselves?

'Yeah, it's a shame that we don't own these shops, but if we can't manage it ourselves, we just have to accept it. United80 is our way of giving something back to Brixton, and defining what Brixton Market should contain. We're not trying to exclude anyone. We have to contribute, not just sit around and complain.'

Samantha-Jane sounds like Ty. After buying one of the college sweaters with 'Brixton' on it, I leave Ty and Samantha-Jane. Everywhere I look, I see that Brixton is full of small stories of persistence and love for the neighbourhood. But without financial muscle, this trend may falter. Over the last decade, property prices have increased by over 70 per cent. And on the main roads, rents have also soared, from £5–6,000 to £20,000 a month.[7] United80 will hardly be able to survive such increases in the long-term.[8]

Happy Brixton Market feels like an entirely different universe when I visit Brixton again one week later.

Brixton's ugly duckling

'Get a life – bin that knife'. A tall, blue container with a discreet opening stands before St John the Evangelist Church in Angell Town. A sticker featuring a prohibited sign over a knife has been stuck on the front of the container, while two yellow arrows point towards the slit in it. I wonder how many knives are in there.

These kinds of containers can be found all across London, a service that makes it easy for people to dispose of these deadly weapons that have broken so many hearts here in Angell Town and in the rest of London. There are few people to be seen here on this estate, which has often been negatively portrayed in British newspapers; no gangs of boys in oversized hoodies and expensive trainers. The estate consists of squat, beige-brick buildings where damp threatens to devour the wooden window frames; net curtains keep out prying eyes. In some places the architects have attempted to brighten up the buildings by placing dark-blue stands outside them. What they're supposed to be used for, it's hard to say.

Angell Town is one of London's toughest council housing estates, just five minutes from busy Brixton town centre towards the slightly more upscale Stockwell – traditionally an area where the Portuguese have settled since the 1970s. Even more Portuguese arrived when Portugal joined the EU in 1986. Around 4,000 people live in Angell Town.[1] The crime rate here is twice as high as that in the rest of London, and the area is among the poorest 10 per cent in the UK. The chance of being robbed here is three times greater than anywhere else in London. The area was originally popular among the middle class, but during the 1970s concrete tower blocks were built here in a style that might be termed a kind of minimalistic brutalism, and those with a little less money in their wallets therefore moved in. During the 1970s and 1980s, the area fell into decline due to significant welfare cuts. Robberies and violence took over the streets.

Today, over 60 per cent of the area's inhabitants belong to Black and minority ethnic groups; the proportion of children who live with a single parent is the same. Abandoned shops line one of the squares. One store selling a slim selection of second-hand goods is open, and in one of the windows is a note from a professor at Goldsmiths University who is looking for test subjects for a project entitled 'Can education empower Black, Muslim and Migrant young women in British Schools?' Those who are interested are invited to meet up at Angell Delight Community Centre. When I see that the community centre has been named after one of Britain's most popular powdered deserts, I can't help but laugh. Angel Delight mousse – light and sweet, two adjectives that otherwise don't apply to Angell Estate.

CCTV cameras can be seen everywhere here – London has over half a million of them. Conservative Prime Minister John Major became a zealous advocate of the use of surveillance cameras after the IRA terrorist attacks on London in the 1990s. According to Major – who incidentally grew up in Brixton in the 1950s – people who were doing nothing wrong had no need to worry about the cameras: 'If you've got nothing to hide, you've got nothing to fear.' This increase in surveillance resulted in a sudden and marked increase in the number of boys wearing hoodies with their hoods up, and the term 'hoodie' became synonymous with suspicious, twitchy types.

I stand and stare, astonished, at one of the street signs: Angela Carter Close. The street is named after the author Angela Carter, who lived in Brixton in the 1960s. The mass-produced buildings with their pitifully meagre gardens have little in common with Carter's rich and surrealistic literary universe, I think, a little bleakly. But perhaps a resident or two will find their way to her books?

Luckily, there is a chink of light in Angell Town. A new outdoor gym was recently opened, paid for by the *Evening Standard* newspaper, which has founded the Dispossessed Fund.[2]

Darkness has truly fallen by the time I have walked down to Loughborough Junction, a five-minute bus ride from Angell Town. Imagine a TV crime series set in London, like *Luther*, with Idris Elba in the starring role and finding a corpse under a railway bridge, outside one of the warehouses that often exist in such places. I have rarely felt less safe in a poorly lit backstreet. It's probably my age. I would never have thought this way when I was twenty-five, or even thirty-five. I walk tentatively down the road, where wrecked cars and various tyres have been discarded. A young man walks past me, but he pays me no attention. I take a deep breath and stroll on, simultaneously starting to wonder whether I've actually told anyone where I'm going. What if something happens? I'm embarrassed by my own nervousness. At the end of the street I find number 282; as I open the heavy door a hint of sweat wafts towards me. Two young men are in a boxing ring, apparently in the middle of a fight. On the wall hangs a large photograph of a young Black man, Dwayne Simpson. The boxing club I've come to is called Dwaynamics, and was founded in Dwayne's memory. He was stabbed and killed on Angell Estate in 2014, just twenty-one years old.

It was Dwayne who originally started the club, and back then Dwaynamics was located in a small centre on the Angell Town estate itself. Dwayne wanted a way to keep himself and the other boys off the street. The street ultimately ended up taking his life. His mother,

Pastor Lorraine Jones, decided to continue her son's dream of rescuing the neighbourhood's children from the gang scene.

'I daren't even think about what would have happened to these boys if they hadn't started coming here,' general manager Richard Jones says to me.

He's a mature man, wearing a T-shirt and baggy jogging bottoms. Richard says that the boxing club has received a lot of support after London experienced what can only be described as an explosion in stabbings among young men – almost always committed by Black boys, who end up killing other Black boys in meaningless turf wars about postcodes and which areas they control. Young men killing each other, apparently over such trivial things. Dwayne's mother has previously told me that she had been warning politicians about the lack of recreational activities for years – and about the dangers that arise when boys don't have a place to go. They often have parents who work far too much to be able to keep track of them. This was precisely why her own son started the boxing club.

'The boys here come from homes where the parents are often suffering too, or not very good at taking care of their children because they never received love themselves. The parents of these boys are also often young, and some of them have significant problems of their own. They don't have the capacity to follow up, and when the boys end up in gangs, where money can be had quickly, they're unable to help them out of the destructive environment. Some of these boys have actually never even been hugged by their parents,' Richard says.

One of the boys comes over to us.

Brian is tall, and of indeterminable age. It turns out that he's fourteen – a year older than one of my own sons.

'Brian was stabbed last year, on the street,' Richard says.

Brian lifts up the vest he's wearing. A scar crosses his chest, just under his lungs. One ordinary afternoon he was on his way to visit some friends – there was nothing to suggest he needed to be extra careful. Without warning, a boy of around the same age as Brian came towards him. The boy walked right up to Brian – and stabbed him. The wound was deep. Brian collapsed. He doesn't remember much after that, he says. But it was OK. Because he's here now, talking to me. I have the urge to put my arms around him, the way I hold my sons.

Later, Brian found out that the boy who stabbed him mistook him for another boy he'd had a disagreement with. Richard says that Brian is one of the club's greatest talents, and that he'll soon be able to fight in a proper bout. Brian runs on to the mat to continue training.

Richard grew up in Brixton, and tells me that boxing is what saved him when he was young. He didn't have any adult role models, and when Lorraine contacted him to ask if he would join the team, he didn't hesitate.

'I think the parents have to get involved. They're far too relaxed. Teenagers need discipline. And the schools have to focus on physical exercise. There's far too little PE in schools nowadays. These boys have to be given the chance to express themselves in a sports hall. The chance to run. Fight. Interact. Their diet has to change, too. None of these boys have ever eaten anything healthy. None of them have fixed bedtime routines. All of this is connected,' Richard says.

To follow up with the young people at the boxing club, there are several police officers who are also boxing coaches. They try to teach the boys that the police can actually help them, and that they shouldn't view the police as the enemy. Richard supports the police's hard line. He goes across to one of the boys who is training on the mat.

The boy is small and quick, and Richard pushes him hard. I watch as the boy, who can't be very old, becomes more and more determined. Richard's punches are fast and strong. He sweats – a lot. But the boy holds his own. In the end, though, it looks like he's on the verge of tears. The mothering instinct in me kicks in, and I want to run on to the mat and stop them, but luckily the fight is over. Richard and the boy, whose name is John, come over to me.

'This one is an incredible talent, just you wait and see. I'm sure he's going to go far,' Richard says.

John looks down at the ground. He was brought to the boxing club by a social worker who understood he needed a way out of the gang scene. John had already been placed with several foster families, but none of them had managed to get him to stop dealing drugs. Who says no to earning thousands of pounds in a single weekend?

'I'd probably be dead if I hadn't started coming here. At first I was sceptical and thought it all seemed pretty stupid. But now I love it here,' John says. He tells me his father has started showing up to his fights, too.

'We're closer now, and he cheers me on. He was never interested in my life before.'

As John disappears into the small changing room, Richard moves closer to me. 'John is one of the boys I was telling you about, who had never been hugged by his parents,' he says in a low voice. 'After one match, he came up to me with tears in his eyes, and said: "Dad just gave me a hug." I'll never forget that moment.'

Back in my sister's apartment in Earl's Court, where I often stay when I visit London, I watch the news on London Live. Yet another young Black man has lost his life in a stabbing. The number of murders involving knives hasn't been so high for almost a decade. It isn't just young men being killed – older women and men who are simply in the wrong place at the wrong time are also becoming victims. Mayor of London Sadiq Khan is blamed for not doing enough, but the welfare cuts that have affected the city's young people were made during his predecessor's term. When Khan is interviewed about the knife-crime epidemic in the capital, he rages against drug use among the middle class in London. Cocaine use has never been more widespread. Nothing happens in a vacuum.

I have often felt annoyed at the fact that major American cities like Los Angeles, New York and Baltimore have a monopoly on pop-culture narratives about gangs thanks to TV series like *The Wire*. But London is just as bad, because London's streets hide hundreds of similar gangs and a vast illegal drug trade.

In 2011, *Top Boy* was released – a TV series that captures the melancholy and brutality of London's streets. The show follows Ra'Nell, a young man trying to avoid straying from the straight and narrow when his mother Lisa suffers a breakdown. He's torn between 'the right path' and local gangsters Dushane and Sully, who use all the young people on the council estate where they live. I know several people who haven't been able to watch the series because it's simply too realistic. In 2019 *Blue Story*, written and directed by Rapman, hit the movie screens, and was based on his own experiences of gang wars between Peckham and Deptford. Angell Town probably has more than its fair share of Ra'Nells, Dushanes and Sullys, because according to the Metropolitan Police this is a place where several of London's most dangerous gangs are based – such as GAS (Guns and Shanks), ABM (All Bout Money) and PDC (Poverty Driven Children).

There are many mothers here in Angell Town who have lost their sons, and as always there is a soundtrack to the madness. It is here, and in the adjacent areas of social housing like Tulse Hill and Stockwell, that one of the rawest musical genres in London began to take hold – drill. The style is too hard and too dark for it to have topped any charts, although a number of the genre's music videos have over a million views online.[3]

The videos show young Black men wearing characteristic hoodies, black sportswear from Adidas and Nike and huge parkas, hiding their faces as they smoke weed and drink, and pretend as if they're shooting people. The songs are also full of references to stabbings: splashing, dipping, touching and cheffing. The genre originated on the South Side of Chicago (known for its gangs), and made its way across the Atlantic to Brixton, where drill rapper M24 is notoriously popular. When it found its way into the bedrooms of boys in London, the style was quickly transformed, and given a new name and dedicated slang inspired by Caribbean patois. Unlike their American brothers who rap about violence and glamour, the London boys sing about their tough childhoods. One of the most well-known artists is Irving Adjei, better known as Headie One from Tottenham, who has served more than one prison sentence for dealing drugs. He was a promising footballer before he suffered an ankle injury. Drill music hasn't managed to evade the reach of the censors – the BBC refused to play it, believing it openly encouraged murder. But some have tried to approach drill in a more constructive manner. Youth worker and author Ciaran Thapar spoke to the BBC on 17 June 2020 about the organisation RoadWorks, and asked: 'How can we use this undeniably organically popular type of music, and our understanding of that music, as a way of connecting with young people who otherwise are being lost to the system right now at unprecedented rates?' But despite this more positive approach, there is no denying that the brutal gang violence and aesthetic of drill music haven't exactly helped to make Angell Town's poor reputation any better, but the tentacles of urban renewal have also started to make inroads into this area, with all the positive and negative consequences this entails.

'Where are the role models for young Black men?' the commentators in British newspapers often ask. They do exist – a few of them are professors – and at the time of writing, it's still quite the occurrence when they turn up at Oxford University.

One spring day in April I visit Wadham College, Oxford, where the Caribbean-British professor Paul Gilroy, who teaches English and American literature at King's College, London, and Linton Kwesi Johnson are going to meet to discuss Johnson's poetry.

I have previously spent time with Gilroy who became somewhat of a household name among anti-racist activists and scholars with the book *There Ain"t No Black in the Union Jack: The Cultural Politics of Race and Nation* (1987) in which he examines British racism, and later with *Black Atlantic*, published in 1993. He had a close relationship with the late Marxist and founder of British Cultural Studies, Stuart Hall. Gilroy and Hall are two of Britain's most renowned intellectuals with Caribbean roots.

When we met for coffee at King's Cross station before he headed off to a meeting out of town, Gilroy told me of his upbringing as a mixed race kid in east London in the 1960s: racism was part and parcel of his life, indeed also his academic life. Paradoxically enough, his work was recognised in the US long before it was recognised by British academia. I feel a sense of hopelessness rise in me when he shares his experiences. He was asked by Oxford University to remove his dreads when he was offered a position, a proposal he refused, and he has since felt uncomfortable whenever visiting the university. He has told me he will be leaving Oxford the minute the meeting is over. The two men will be taking part in a discussion led by Norwegian-Caribbean Louisa Olufsen Layne, who wrote her doctoral thesis on Kwesi Johnson, and is currently holding a post as a postdoctoral fellow at the University of Oslo.

This is a historic day. There are extremely few professors with a Caribbean background at British universities, and both Gilroy and Kwesi Johnson have achieved iconic status with their criticism of the British Empire.

In the auditorium, around a hundred people have gathered. A handful of them are students with African or Caribbean backgrounds.

Just before the event starts, a group of Caribbean women march in – mature women, wearing colourful outfits. They seem to know each other. Their presence is striking. When I ask a friend about them, she tells me that they probably work at a car factory near Oxford, and have come here today for the sole purpose of hearing Kwesi Johnson and Paul Gilroy.[4] When Kwesi Johnson reads from his poetry collection, the room is quiet enough to hear a pin drop. Even though the poems were written almost forty years ago, the texts are disquietingly relevant. Young Black men are still in trouble. They are still being stopped by the police. The road from the council estates of Brixton and Tottenham to Oxford is a long one – especially if you're a young man from the capital's tower blocks.

'He was just trying to find a way out, like everyone does. He just didn't manage it.' A young man in a black hoodie is sitting on a wooden fence beside a grave covered in flowers. Fuzzy images from CCTV cameras show angry young men running through the streets. 'He had no weapon in his hands. Still, he was shot down.' The lawyer's voice is clear. I see a city in flames. 'We're going to be here until we get justice for Mark!' shouts a mother.

The scenes that flicker past as I sit in the bar Upstairs at Ritzy, a small space in the Ritzy Picturehouse Cinema in Brixton, are heartbreaking. I think about Paul Gilroy and Linton Kwesi Johnson. These scenes must resonate strongly with them. They too were young men harassed by the police. I'm watching the documentary *The Hard Stop* (2016), which is about the murder of twenty-nine-year-old Mark Duggan, and his friends. One of them was convicted of having started the extensive riots that took place in London in August 2011, which began when Duggan was killed by police in Tottenham. The film's title refers to a tactic London police use when chasing down a suspect: three police cars drive towards the criminal's vehicle, from the front, from the back, and from the side. The criminal is therefore forced to stop – the aim is to paralyse and frighten him, preventing the suspect from pulling a weapon. The move doesn't always end well. Sometimes people die – like young father Mark Duggan. As to what really took place on that fateful summer night, Duggan's family and the prosecuting authorities do not agree. The police officers claimed Duggan was carrying a pistol and was about to shoot.

Two young men wearing large down jackets are in the auditorium with me: Marcus and Kurtis, Duggan's closest friends and the main figures in the documentary that examines both Duggan's murder and the violent riots that occurred in its wake. It was Kurtis who was charged with having started the commotion that led to shops and cars being destroyed and burned all across London. In grainy footage from a surveillance camera, we see him attacking a car in rage after the two friends have just been to the police station, and discovered that the policemen who shot Duggan will go free. His anger inspires the entire city, and the scenes we watch are suspiciously reminiscent of the images from Brixton in the 1980s. It's as if time has stood still. Kurtis ends up being sentenced to thirty-two months in prison for having started the riots. The film quietly documents the despair and chaos that followed Duggan's death, as well as the road out of crime.

Broadwater Farm Estate, where both Marcus and Kurtis grew up – as did Headie One – was built with the intention of improving people's standard of living. Instead, the twelve monstrous blocks ended up filled with darkness; when the situation was at its worst, 90 per cent of the estate's residents were out of work. Today, the area has been subjected to large-scale renovation, and the standard of living is better.

One of the boys converts to Islam in the hope that religion will help him get his life back on track, while the other gets a job – he spends hours commuting to it in order to feed his small family. After the film, I hurry to keep up with Marcus and Kurtis as we head out to Windrush Square. They're not tough guys – they're softly spoken. Almost shy.

'The documentary has given us a new life,' Marcus says. He towers over me in his big parka.

'We've been outside the council blocks in Tottenham. We've seen the world. We'd hardly been outside our neighbourhood before the documentary got made,' Kurtis says.

They tell me they were suspicious of the director when he told them he wanted to make the film – they thought he was an under-cover cop. Today, they're hopeful about the future.

'We've turned what happened into something positive, given young Black men a kind of voice. I've started a foundation to help young men in Tottenham who are involved in the gang scene, and hope it will do some good,' Marcus says.

It's easy to get hung up on all the problems Caribbean boys in London experience, but the figures speak for themselves: Caribbean families are more likely to struggle financially, and Caribbean boys are over-represented in prisons while being under-represented at universities. But at the same time, there is also another story – one of a growing middle class. British-Caribbeans are asserting themselves among the cultural elite, within finance, music and sport – and not least, politics. Sadiq Khan's Conservative Party challenger is Shaun Bailey. His parents are from Jamaica, and belong to the *Windrush* generation. He is not a privileged man – he grew up with his single mother in North Kensington.

It feels almost symbolic to stand here with Kurtis and Marcus this evening. Seventy years have passed since SS *Windrush* docked in Britain. The children and grandchildren of those who arrived full of hope and expectation have become true London citizens – shaped by a unique mix of cultural impulses from all across the world, here on the capital's streets.

It therefore came as a significant shock when the *Windrush* generation learned that the motherland had begun to expel them in secret. In 2013, rumours began to circulate that Caribbeans had been thrown out of the country; that there were Caribbeans who had lived their entire lives in Britain who had ended up being deported or placed in detention centres. In 2017, these rumours became all too real tears of despair when *Guardian* journalist Amelia Gentleman received a tip about an older Caribbean woman who was waiting to be deported from the country.[5] Paulette Wilson, who had lived in the UK for fifty years, working as a cook at the House of Commons and paying tax her entire life, suddenly received a letter declaring her an illegal immigrant and informing her that she would be returned to Jamaica – a country she left as a ten-year-old and had only visited once later in life. All the benefit payments Paulette was receiving were immediately stopped. She lost her home, and had to move in with a friend. She was told to report to the immigration authorities once a month. On one of those occasions, Paulette was ushered into a car and driven to a detention centre, where she was told she would soon be deported. She was then taken to Yarl's Wood Immigration Removal Centre, where illegal immigrants are held before deportation. There, she was able to call her daughter.

Paulette quickly received help from a lawyer, who was able to prevent the deportation, and in January 2018 was granted indefinite leave to remain. From that point onwards, Paulette dedicated all her strength to fighting for others who might suffer the same fate. She passed away in 2020.

Hundreds of stories bubbled up to the surface, and journalists from the *Guardian* travelled to Kingston, where they met several British-Caribbean citizens who had spent their entire lives in the UK, only to be deported to a country they hardly knew due to a lack of paperwork. When the *Windrush* generation arrived in London, they automatically had the right to indefinite leave. They began working and paid their taxes; they settled down. Nobody had ever asked for residence permits before – they were British!

These changes in documentation requirements were deliberate. Because in 2013, when future prime minister Theresa May was home secretary, she introduced the 'hostile environment' designed to force illegal immigrants from the UK. Lorries emblazoned with the message 'In the UK illegally? Go home or face arrest. Text HOME to 78070 . . .' were observed driving around specific areas of London – put there by the Home Office. The lorries quickly became the subject of extensive criticism, and were stopped. But public sector employees in both schools and the NHS were forced to ask employees and patients to identify themselves with valid documents. The *Windrush* generation suffered the brunt of this. They were treated as illegal immigrants, because so many of them lacked the paperwork they should have been given when they arrived in 1948 and over the subsequent years.

After my conversation with Marcus and Kurtis I stay sitting in one of the cold metal chairs on Windrush Square. The rage felt among members of the Caribbean community is entirely justified. The fates of those who were deported, or who were told they would be deported, created a deep feeling of unease among everyone I knew. Was this just a bureaucratic blunder, or a warning about the future to come? A compensation scheme was established, but has been harshly criticised both for being slow and because the compensation is too low.

I leave Windrush Square and walk towards Coldharbour Lane, past the faces of stars of African culture painted on the wall of the Ritzy Cinema, past the Satay Bar where the customers always look like extras from a Kendrick Lamar music video, over Electric Avenue where the market stallholders and shops have packed up and closed for the day, only rubbish and a few small rivulets of blood from the butchers remaining in the square, and on to Brixton Station Road. Brixton will continue to resist – always. And the Notting Hill Carnival will never die.

The music. The noise. The sheer joy.

A London without the Caribbeans would be a London empty of sound.

West African London
– Peckham

All mothers are queens

'Are you really going to Peckham?'

My mother looks at me. She's worried.

'Yes, it isn't dangerous any more,' I say.

'But somebody just got stabbed there,' she protests.

'Oh my God. They're not exactly going to go after a mature woman like me,' I say, putting on my new Nike trainers. They're gold, with a red logo. In London, trainers aren't just something you wear to go running. They also say something about how street-smart you are. I might be so-called mature, but my heart is still very much punk rock. I would not be caught dead in anything but the trendiest trainers.

'Be careful!' Mum shouts after me.

I close the door. Feel my mother's gnawing sense of unease all the way to the bus.

Gangster's paradise or hipster heaven? The jury is still out when it comes to Peckham. The area used to be compared to the Bronx, but now? A couple of years back *The Times* deemed the neighbourhood the best place to live in the city.[1]

The homeless person I glimpse under several colourful fleece blankets outside Peckham Rye station likely doesn't care about this debate, because the cool reality that lifestyle journalists like to call artsy can be a grim one for others. Despite the influx of mashed avocado, banana pancakes and pistachio brûlée, Peckham remains one of London's roughest neighbourhoods. I have often thought of Peckham as Brixton's little brother. The one who can't quite get his act together, no matter how hard he tries.

Peckham isn't quite as marked by political tensions as Brixton. A different atmosphere dominates the streets and shops: everyday West African life coupled with London's periodic merciless brutality. Look closely, and you'll discover that the grocery stores offer everything you need to make West African food: spices such as bese, mesewa and hwentia; millet, dawadawa, and vegetables like cassava, okra and yams. The reason for this is clear: over 50 per cent of the district's inhabitants are from Nigeria, and Nigerians have been in London for over 200 years. Peckham is London's 'Little Lagos'– and reflects a quite different reality than that presented in one of the most popular British comedy series of all time, *Only Fools and Horses*, which takes place in Peckham in the 1980s. The series is about two white English working-class brothers, Derek and Rodney Trotter, and their grandfather, who runs a market stall in Peckham. These days the series feels dated, and has been accused of racism.

The main thoroughfare of Rye Lane is always noisy and busy with people – no leisurely English village atmosphere here. You have to weave in and out between the well-dressed women in their traditional West African outfits, Somali women with small children in tow, a lonely hipster or two, and a strikingly large number of boys wearing expensive Adidas or Air Jordan trainers. The main streets of London's smaller well-off districts are always intense and insistent – and a dream for smart marketeers. This is probably why marketing executives at Nike used precisely these streets to create 'Nothing beats a Londoner', one of the sporting giant's most popular campaigns. Nike sent famous athletes out into a number of London's neighbourhoods, including Peckham's very own football star Rio Ferdinand, in an attempt to encourage more young people to participate in sports. In one of the advertisement's scenes, British sprinting superstar Dina Asher-Smith shouts: 'You think that's tough? I have to run through Peckham! At night!' as she runs through the neighbourhood's neon-lit streets in the evening dark. Well aware that they were balanced on a knife edge – quite literally – here, Nike was smart enough to get Giggs, a grime artist from the area, to comment on Asher-Smith's outburst with a twinkle in his eye: 'What's wrong with Peckham?'[2]

There's absolutely nothing wrong with Peckham. Not now. And nor was there way back in the olden days.

Were I able to scrape off our layer of contemporary history and look back in time, I would find a lush Peckham without a trace of asphalt or neon. Back then, the poet William Blake saw an oak tree on Peckham Common, 'filled with angels, bright angelic wings bespangling every bough like stars'.[3] This was in 1765, when Peckham was synonymous with clerical collars and fruit trees laden with peaches. Later, Peckham also became famous on a national level for a large-scale health experiment, begun by doctors George Scott Williamson and Innes Hope Pearse in 1926.[4] In the Peckham Experiment, families in Peckham were invited to a specially designed centre, where they received regular health checks and consultations with doctors who provided them with recommendations as to how to live a healthy lifestyle. Documentary *The Centre* (1947) provides an insight into the philosophy put forth by the doctors, which emphasised the importance of leisure activities for both children and adults. The centre also provided the families with meeting places, which were designed by enthusiastic interior architects with specific visions regarding how design could be used to promote social inter-action. Even the cots that infants were placed in were designed to stimulate communication. At the centre, families could go roller-skating, play tennis, and swim.[5] Through large glass windows, the centre's visitors were studied by doctors and biologists, who noted that the families were harmonious in their relationships, and worked well together. The experiment continued until 1950, but when it became clear that the institution's innovative attitudes were not shared by the British health service, the team lost its funding and was forced to close the centre. This socialist utopia stands in stark contrast to what Peckham would become known for over the years that followed.

In 1969, construction began on the North Peckham Estate – one of Britain's biggest council estates – to provide new properties for poor people who were living in dilapidated housing. But the seventy-two low blocks soon developed a reputation for being among the worst in all of Europe,[6] a so-called sink estate, which housed newly arrived Caribbeans and West Africans who didn't have a penny to their name. Like the Broadwater Estate in Tottenham, Peckham became known as a place best avoided. Throughout the 1980s and 1990s, journalists wrote fervent articles about the gangs of youths who terrorised the area. Robbery, vandalism, break-ins, graffiti, murder, poverty, alcoholism, prostitution and drugs have plagued Peckham for years, and are the reason for my mother's worry. But now it seems that little brother Peckham wants to get out from under his big brother's shadow – and this time, he wants to do it once and for all.

The inhabitants of Peckham probably thought they were dreaming the day they saw a Nigerian woman wearing traditional Yoruba dress riding on horseback down the main street. But it was no dream. What they were witnessing was a tribute to mothers and the area's Nigerian heritage, produced by multi-award-winning film director Adeyemi Michael.

'All mothers are queens, they lead the universe. Mothers give birth, they build families and they build the world. I felt it was my duty to celebrate the woman, the mother, the matriarch, the immigrant,' Adeyemi says of the idea behind his short film *Entitled* (2018),' which has attracted attention among Nigerians both in London and back in their native country.

The film touches something deep within me. Through dreamlike sequences, it depicts a mother's transformation from an ordinary woman into a conqueror as she is decorated by young Nigerian girls. As the horse trots around the council estate we hear Adeyemi's mother, Abosede, reflecting on her identity as an immigrant. Adeyemi's mum is a dazzling sight on Peckham's shabby main road.

'It's a fantasy documentary,' Adeyemi says. We're sitting in a minimalistic café in Elephant and Castle, where he now lives, a couple of kilometres from Peckham. This area was once full of Nigerians, but now the Latin Americans have taken over. The beloved shopping centre, which for fifty-five years used to wish everyone welcome with a pink elephant, is soon to be demolished to make way for a massive regeneration project. Hearts are broken.

'Your mother looks so proud, riding on the horse. Calm, and so proud,' I say.

'Yes, I know. She wasn't nervous, but determined. She had never ridden before, but nevertheless she got up on to the horse and stayed calm through the entire shoot, as if this was something she wanted, deep down inside. That's why I call the film both a fantasy and a documentary,' Adeyemi says.

'She could almost have been my mother – I recognise everything she said about the importance of remembering where you come from, your roots,' I say.

Adeyemi smiles.

'I've had that reaction from countless people – all of them with an immigrant mother. We know what our mothers have been through,' he says.

We sit there in silence, looking at each other. It's as if we're sharing a secret. I think about my mum, who worries every time I say I'm going to Peckham. I also think about Adeyemi's mum, who came from Lagos with her two small children to start a new life. They have much in common. Two women who left a life, each in their own region of Africa, to start again in a foreign land. Two mothers who had to find themselves again. Navigate unknown terrain, and forever carry the grief of never really belonging anywhere. I'm sure they would have lots to talk about.

Life didn't exactly turn out as expected when Adeyemi and his parents moved to Peckham in the early 1980s. Adeyemi was two years old. His father was a qualified pilot, and imagined he would have better career prospects in the UK than those available to him back home. Instead, despite his US education, he encountered a job market in which he wasn't wanted. He ended up at home, pacing restlessly around the house, while Adeyemi's mother went to work. Adeyemi was deeply affected by his father's continual struggle to cope in the new country.

He started school, where all the students were Nigerian or from other West African countries.

'My tribe,' Adeyemi explains. 'We were all West African, and we had our world. At home I was one hundred per cent Nigerian, but as soon as I walked out the front door I became someone else, somebody who navigated several identities. I think my childhood in Peckham made me wise, and gave me the tools to handle life,' he says thoughtfully.

Adeyemi tells me that through making the film, he wanted to give his mother her self-confidence back.

'I wanted to show that immigrants are conquerors too, and that we shouldn't edit ourselves. I feel that far too often, my parents' generation have edited themselves in order to survive. As my mother rides through Peckham, she's doing two things: she's conquering these streets, and as she does so it becomes absolutely clear that we're not here as slaves. At the same time, she's challenging the traditional image of the triumphant white man on a horse, but that isn't to say she's taken on the European heritage, no, she's continuing her Nigerian heritage. In the north of Nigeria, people have always ridden horses,' Adeyemi says.

The film secured Adeyemi the chance to participate in a prestigious talent programme at the BFI London Film Festival in 2018 – a big step for Adeyemi in his film career. The movie won Best Short Film at the Screen Nation Awards in 2019. The statistics are stacked against him. Coming from the working-class neighbourhood of Peckham opens no doors. And in the year 2000, the area's residents saw just how tough life really was for the neighbourhood's young boys. A murder in Peckham outraged all of Britain – and led to fundamental changes for the entire district.

On 27 November, ten-year-old Damilola Taylor was sauntering home from Peckham Library, the streets still a little unfamiliar to him. His mother Gloria had recently moved to London from Lagos, in the hope of getting her daughter who suffered from epilepsy better medical treatment than that available in Nigeria. Damilola accompanied his mother and sister to London, while his father Richard continued to work as a public servant back home in Lagos. Gloria and her children were allocated a council flat on the North Peckham Estate. Video footage shows Damilola at Peckham Library, where he was taking part in a computing course after school. It wasn't far from the library to his home on Blake Row – no more than a five-minute stroll. On his short walk, he was attacked by a gang of youths and sustained a deep, life-threatening cut to his leg. Damilola staggered home to the stairwell that led to his flat, where he was found bleeding by a random passer-by who had noticed the trail of blood. Damilola later died at the hospital. In the wake of his death, his parents had to convince the police that their son had been the victim of a crime. The police claimed the incident was an accident, and that Damilola might have fallen on to a broken milk bottle.[7]

Police officer Rav Wilding, who worked at the police station in Peckham at the time, talked of the significant challenges the police encountered when they began to investigate the murder.[8] People in the neighbourhood felt hostile towards the Metropolitan Police after the racially motivated killing of Stephen Lawrence in 1993, when it was revealed that the police had knowingly botched the murder investigation. The home secretary at the time, Jack Straw, ordered a report on racism within the police to be conducted in the wake of Lawrence's murder, and four years later the Met was found guilty of institutional racism. The report's conclusions sent shock waves throughout the UK. But not only were the residents of Peckham afraid of the police – they were also anxious about what would happen if they chose to provide information, because they risked reprisals from local gangs in the area. It was a challenging landscape for the police to navigate, but after a laborious investigation, brothers Danny and Ricky Preddie were identified as the perpetrators. The boys were just twelve and thirteen years old when they committed the murder, and already notorious in Peckham. But it would take three trials before the brothers were found guilty of manslaughter on 9 August 2006. They were sentenced to eight years in prison. The murder of Damilola Taylor and the subsequent trials stigmatised the area.

Two years after the murder, the blocks on the North Peckham Estate where Damilola was killed were razed to the ground as part of the extensive Peckham Partnership urban renewal project, which aimed to make Peckham a safer and more attractive area. Over £300 million was spent on improving people's living conditions. The blocks were replaced with rows of small, pale-brick terraced houses, in the hope of creating a better environment. Playgrounds were established and youth clubs started. Damilola Taylor's parents were crushed by grief, but decided to honour their son's memory by starting the Damilola Taylor Centre in 2002, where young people can go to get advice and participate in activities to stay out of crime. Damilola Taylor's murder changed Peckham, but not entirely.

Adeyemi is frustrated by the media's version of Peckham – a version that has grown roots and taken hold. He points out that life in London is inextricably linked to class and race, and is frustrated by those who ignore just how much these issues affect the lives of the city's population.

Adeyemi didn't realise just how deep these issues ran until he started at university.

'I met people there who talked to me as if I was from another planet. I was just being myself – I didn't know how to be any other way. But suddenly I understood that my life, my language, didn't work. I was sort of just in the way. But we Nigerians have a distinct style, we take up space in a way that the English aren't used to, and we dream big. We're also amazing entrepreneurs. I realised it wasn't possible to behave that way among the English middle class. But you know what? I really don't care,' Adeyemi says.

I have never met anyone from a Caribbean or African background who hasn't highlighted the role of discrimination when talking about their childhoods. London is a city where integration and segregation operate side by side. If you look at the stars of grime, like Skepta or Stormzy, and their music videos, white English youths are among those featured, and relationships that transcend ethnic groups are only increasing in scope. But at the same time, the artists talk about the racism that has been a constant presence in their lives, especially in school settings, where nobody ever thought they would amount to anything. What has changed is that young people like Adeyemi are now using their experiences from neighbourhoods like Peckham to redefine London's streets, and tell familiar stories from new perspectives. He points to John Boyega, Peckham's pride who has starred in several *Star Wars* movies and has not been shy in voicing his support for the Black Lives Matter movement or strong opinions about racism in Hollywood.

'I know so many young people from here who have gone on to get really great jobs. That's why I end *Entitled* with two little girls wearing my mother's shoes and headdress. They're the next generation. They'll never bow their heads,' says Adeyemi.

His words churn in the back of my mind for the rest of the day. Later that evening I attend a punk concert in Clapham: 'An evening of British Black Punk'. On stage, a young man dressed in a skirt and a nose ring screams the way only punks can. Screaming Toenail describe their sound as 'an anti-colonial militant queer punk band'. The trio Big Joanie, who are signed to Thurston Moore, founder of Sonic Youth, and Eva Prinz's label Ecstatic Peace Library, go on after them. They sound like a mix of the Slits and X-Ray Spex, once led by Marianne Elliott-Said, also known as Poly Styrene. The evening is celebrating Black British rebellion. I feel enthusiastic together with all the young punks around me who are in all colours, shapes and sizes. Together with the likes of John Boyega and Adeyemi, they represent a new future for London.

I can hear the old London creaking, about to be ripped apart at the seams, and a bold, new city emerging.

Idealism, fashionistas and afrobeats

'Isn't it just the same old story, all over again?!' says one of the sisters as she picks a fishbone from where it's got stuck between her teeth.

I look at the dresses hanging on a rack in the dressmaker's shop in Rye Lane Market, a small, slightly rundown shopping centre in Peckham, filled with treasures like the Caribbean Zionly Manna Vegan Rastarant. I've just asked Lewa and her sister what they think about the fact that West African fabrics have become so trendy. I'm sure designer Stella McCartney would like these outfits, because her recent collection bears clear signs of a fashionable love for all things West African. In no uncertain terms, the sisters let me know that they're fed up with European designers stealing their cultural heritage and earning tons of money, while they get nothing.

Lewa takes another piece of fish from the plastic box in front of her. West African food has also become trendy and a number of restaurants have opened, offering soups like *mpotompoto*, egg and okra stew, or plantain covered in chocolate and pistachio – they run the gamut from the highly stylish to those that are more like cultural projects, such as Zoe's Ghana Kitchen, run by British-Ghanaian Zoe Adjonyoh. An African food revolution is in the offing – there are apparently now over 300 Nigerian restaurants in London. But I struggle with the fish. When Lewa offers me a taste, I politely decline.

Lewa's sister is sitting at the very back of the cramped shop, sewing a dress. They have plenty of local customers, but the sisters also send clothes to Nigeria because they have a unique style, inspired by London. Forget Paris – it's on the streets of London that the latest trends within fashion have always been found.

In 2011, for the very first time, fashionistas were able to see West African models walk the catwalk in clothes designed exclusively by African designers when Africa Fashion Week was held.[1] Behind the curtain its founder, lawyer and fashion expert Ronke Ademiluyi, clapped with joy at its success. Africa Fashion Week has since showcased over 800 emerging designers and exhibitors from Africa, Europe and America, and welcomed almost 70,000 visitors.[2] Interest in the fashion week has increased in line with the ever-deepening pockets of the West African middle class. The Marvel film *Black Panther* has also led to a surge in interest in West African materials and African fashion. The prints, colours and fabrics all have their roots in various tribal traditions. The intricate, Arabic-inspired embroidery often reflects the heritage of the Islamic world, while the colours have specific meanings depending on which tribe you belong to. The Ashanti tribe use red for protection; yellow means fertility and vitality; while white is used to celebrate special occasions. The patterns allude to proverbs, animals or plants, but this doesn't stop the modern West African fashion world from being just as inspired by Valentino as ancient traditions, and the outfits on the catwalk during the fashion weeks are sophisticated, but never timid.

'We dream of being able to show our dresses on a proper catwalk,' Lewa says.

I fear the sisters' road there might be a long one.

I make my way to Peckham Levels, a former multistorey car park situated just over the road from the market. Trend bible *Wallpaper** has raved about the facility, because it now houses galleries, work-shops, a cocktail bar, a parkour centre and a playground for children.[3] I've arranged to meet Nicholas Okwulu, the driving force behind Pempeople (People Empowering People), an idealistic organ-isation that helps young people to help themselves. Nicholas turns out to be just as cool as Don Letts. Londoners have a certain style that's unmistakable: a combination of new and old, but with a twist. Street and glamour, all at once. The cut is different – indefinable. I somehow never manage to pull it off.

Nicholas grew up in Brixton, but he's now lived in Peckham for over thirty years. He's a good friend of Samantha-Jane and Ty from the United80 collective.

Nicholas isn't very interested in talking about himself – he's a man with a specific goal. He wants to show me the real Peckham, the version far from the sensationalised headlines about crime.

We pass the local independent cinema with its name, Peckhamplex, written in plump graffiti letters above the entrance. You can see the latest films here for just £5 – around a third of the price of an ordinary cinema ticket. When *Black Panther* premiered, 200 young people were permitted to watch it for free. The wall of the cinema is covered in images of idols with African backgrounds, and quotes. A narrow road decorated with murals leads to the entrance to Peckham Levels.

'I want you to meet the people who really need this place – young artists who were born and grew up here. Without it, I honestly don't know what they would have done, they would probably have ended up in criminal gangs,' Nicholas says, escorting me across a floor of the building that still bears the marks of its former life, but is now decorated with green plants.

Broad, yellow arrows once used to direct motorists now conduct us upwards. Where cars once parked, separate workrooms have been built. We stop at one of the doors, and can hear voices. Nicholas walks straight in. Two young men in their early twenties greet us enthusiastically. The walls are covered in paintings; cans of spray-paint lay discarded on the floor. One of the young men is a painter, the other a musician. All Inxsanixty's paintings feature motifs inspired by his Nigerian background. He tells me that he hasn't been to art school, and would never have had the opportunity to follow his dream of becoming an artist had it not been for these facilities.

His parents were not exactly happy when he told them he wanted to be an artist.

'But once I actually started to sell my paintings, then they calmed down,' he laughs.

In 1998, it would be an exhibition featuring elephant dung and glitter that would win the distinguished Turner Prize, worth £20,000. One of the paintings, depicting an African woman, was titled *Orgena*, and the artist who had impressed the jury was British-Nigerian Chris Ofili, who became the first Black artist in Britain to win such a renowned prize. Ofili's exhibition also included the painting *No Woman, No Cry*, which shows an African woman crying; each tear consists of a collage of murder victim Stephen Lawrence. The painting is a tribute to Doreen, Stephen's mother. Inspired by African and American pop culture, pornography and the Bible, Manchester-born Ofili creates art that affirms the well-worn myth that art should provoke and tear down boundaries. Two years before he painted *Orgena*, Ofili had created another work, *The Holy Virgin Mary* – an over two-metre-tall image of a Black Virgin Mary, adorned with elephant dung and collages of images cut from pornographic maga-zines. Rudy Giuliani, mayor of New York at the time, was furious when the work was exhibited in Brooklyn in 1999.

Artists with roots in Ghana and Nigeria have made their mark on the British art scene in recent years. Race, identity and postcolonial challenges have been central themes. Inxsanixty has many West African role models in London who inspire him, such as artist Yinka

Shonibare, whose roots are Nigerian, and film director John Akomfrah from Ghana. They have managed to assert themselves in a world dominated by white artists.

Inxsanixty's musician friend, Markland, suddenly pulls out his mobile.

'Look, I have to show you this!'

I stand beside him to take a look at what's on his phone's screen. It's an email exchange.

'A few days ago we tried to apply for exhibition space at a fancy gallery. We signed the application with our own names, but were rejected outright. But then we created a false profile with the most English name we could think of – Emily Huckabee. And we received this nice email, with an invitation to present what "Emily" had created.'

I stare at the name Emily Huckabee on the screen.

'What? Seriously?' I say.

They nod.

'But surely that's just not . . .' I hear myself say.

'That's how it is. The prejudices are there. And it doesn't exactly help that we're from Peckham,' Inxsanixty says flatly.

While the boys might be struggling to get exhibition space at snobby galleries, they're not simply sitting around waiting for somebody to discover them. At several places in the complex they have set up pop-up galleries, so they can exhibit the artworks they have created. Nicholas and other enthusiasts regularly hold workshops to help young people develop their skills within finance and marketing. Just yesterday, classes in tax, scholarships, crowdfunding, brand building and PR were part of the schedule, with an entire pack of lecturers with expertise in every field.

Entrepreneurship is regarded as a virtue in the Nigerian community, and the help Nicholas offers the neighbourhood is entirely in line with this culture. Other Nigerians in London have amassed fortunes.

To find them, you need look no further than across the river, in south-west London, where the rich Russians and Chinese live. Those Nigerians are on an entirely different level to most Nigerians in London – with a standard of living most can only dream of, and their wealth provokes ordinary Nigerians. There are a number of corrupt Nigerians here. Since 2016 the organisation Kleptocracy, led by Roman Borisovich, has run an extensive campaign to expose what it believes is the laundering of black money through property acquisitions in London. In October 2017, Borisovich conducted a guided tour of London's streets in order to document the dubious sources of Nigerian money. He pointed out the properties of very high-ranking Nigerian politicians, who both own properties worth over £11 million.[4] In recent years, British publications have contained several reports about rich Africans.[5] In 2014, *Tatler* – the magazine read by everybody with money – published a lengthy article about Nigerians in London with the title: 'The Nigerians have arrived . . . and London is paying attention', in which the interviewees, all from the upper class – whether through old money or as nouveau riche entrepreneurs and businesspeople – describe their extravagant lifestyles. They shop only at Harrods or Selfridges, and send their children to the best British schools like Eton and King Edward's in Surrey.[6]

We continue up the stairs, which are lit by a blue neon strip light. The floor we reach has been transformed into a playground, where children romp around on brightly coloured wooden blocks, and several eating areas and bars have been set up. Wallpaper featuring palm trees and sober colours covers the walls. There are lots of plants and large tables, along with many people in their thirties and forties.

'This is for the people with a big disposable income,' Nicholas says laconically.

The vast majority of the people here are white. There's a view of London in every direction – I can make out the Shard and the Gherkin, along with a large number of cranes.

Nicholas has been running Pempeople for several years, after giving up his career in the pharmaceutical industry where he never really felt he belonged. He's now acquired several buildings in Peckham that he uses to help young people, and runs the organisation himself full-time. He spent his formative years in Nigeria, where his father was a farming entrepreneur.

'I learned a lot from him, including about how important it is to obtain knowledge and the right tools in order to succeed. That's what I always try to tell the young people I work with. Don't wait for other people. But I understand how they can become disillusioned, because Peckham struggles with major social problems, and even if they're suddenly reading headlines about how cool it's become here, they're not affected by the success stories. They don't have the money to go to the new bars, and if they turn up here in the bar in Peckham Levels, people look at them strangely. They don't understand the social codes of the middle class,' Nicholas says.

Nicholas believes that one of the problems is the language used by those who have the power to initiate change, and that the measures implemented often feel unfamiliar to those who have long lived in a neighbourhood with entirely different economic conditions.

'I don't want to complain – I try to contribute and instead inspire the locals, so they can use the available funding in ways that will best benefit them. The problem is that those who make the decisions don't listen.'

We leave Peckham Levels and continue towards Peckham Library, which has won several awards for its architecture. The library contains one of London's largest collections of Caribbean and African literature.

New research has been conducted into the history of Africans in the UK in recent years, through documentary series produced by British-Nigerian historian David Olusoga, and his comprehensive book *Black and British: A Forgotten History*, which was published in

2016. He grew up in Newcastle in the 1980s, the son of a Nigerian father and a British mother who met at university. Just like Adeyemi, Olusoga also insists on rewriting stories and depicting the course of history through other sources and gazes than those of the established white English historians. There is a clear connection from Olusoga to Peckham and Brixton. Here in the heart of south London, a revolution is underway that cannot be ignored. Nicholas is one of its footsoldiers, along with Ofili and Adeyemi.

The British colonial period and transatlantic slave trade remain an unshakable part of the Nigerians' history in London. Among the British, some sympathetic souls managed to abolish the slave trade in 1807, before it was abolished in the US, following pressure from figures like the formerly enslaved Nigerian Olaudah Equiano. He was a member of the London-based group Sons of Africa, who fought hard to convince the British of the horrors of the slave trade. But even though the slave trade was abolished, Lagos was annexed as a British colony in 1862, and by 1903 all of Nigeria had been colonised. But the Nigerians didn't travel to London as migrant workers. Both before and after the country gained independence in 1960, many Nigerians came to the UK to study. Among them were Nicholas's parents, who after a few years realised they could have a better life in Nigeria than in England. The next wave came in the 1980s, when Nigeria experienced an economic downturn, and later when dictator Sani Abacha was in power between 1993 and 1998. While Peckham has long been a neglected neighbourhood, the children of Nigerians in the UK have in recent years belonged to the proportion of students who do best at school on a national basis, and along with the Russians it is now the Nigerians who take many of the places at private schools. Nigerian authors are also making their mark, and in 2019 the British-Nigerian author Bernardine Evaristo won the Booker Prize, together with Margaret Atwood, for her novel *Girl, Woman, Other*.

Nicholas leads me to a small centre where a group of young people seem to be having a party; they greet Nicholas warmly. Peckham has always been known for its music. Secret clubs have always existed, where a mix of Caribbean and West African music with close ties to the area's gangsters developed. This music laid the foundations for the genre of grime, which for a time only ever attracted media attention when something went wrong (read: shootings).

Nicholas wants to show me what's going on in the cellar. We go through a narrow doorway, down some poorly lit stairs and straight into a music studio. In it sit five young Black men, all wearing sportswear. I've hardly ever seen young Black men wearing anything else, it occurs to me. My sons, too, come to think of it. It seems as if every young man wants to look like a football player.

'Oh my God, superstars in the house!' shouts Nicholas.

The boys laugh. Two of them, Kwamz and Flava, are actually celebrities if you listen to the genre of afrobeat, which in 2020 got its own first official UK chart due to the enormous popularity of artists such as Nigerian-born Burna Boy, J Hus and NSG. The video for Kwamz and Flava's song 'Takeover' has had over 2 million views on YouTube and Kwamz has just released his first solo single, 'Wake Up'. I suddenly feel very old, standing there in my smart wool coat. In an attempt to excite the young men I hear myself say: 'You know, I've actually interviewed Snoop Dogg.' The boys holler, impressed. Several British-Nigerian artists have focused on making a career for themselves in Nigeria and other West African countries rather than Britain, because afrobeat is more widespread there. Even though the boys have achieved a certain level of stardom, they tell me they're completely dependent on being able to borrow this studio from Nicholas.

'I dream of getting proper rich. I've promised to buy a house for my mum,' says Kwamz.

The other boys laugh at him. I have to ask them about the wave of stabbings. They turn serious.

Kwamz looks dejected as he tells me about all the times he's seen far too young boys with knives.

'They don't have anywhere to go,' says Flava. 'No after-school clubs. We actually used to have a few different places where we could hang out after school. The politicians keep saying they're going to do something, but it never happens. It's easy for boys to get involved in gangs when they just spend their time walking around, hanging out.'

In Olusoga's documentary series *Black and British: A Forgotten History*, which was related to his book and aired on the BBC in 2016, one of the episodes was about how hard it is for Black boys to achieve good grades at British schools. The programme showed how it's almost impossible for them to become prime minister because of the class divide in the school system. It is twelve times less likely that a Black boy will attain that position than a white boy.[8] As adolescents, they also struggle to get attention from their parents.

Kwamz and Flava have been lucky – they have parents who have been able to take good care of them. They haven't had to turn to gangs in the search for a place to belong.

The boys insist that I have to watch their music videos. They tell me that they always purposely film in south London, and that the sound of London here is full of warmer, more affectionate beats than grime.[9]

'We want to spread happiness and positive vibes,' says Flava.

I think this is probably a smart tactic. Nicholas escorts me onwards through Peckham's streets.

Nicholas rarely speaks about racism explicitly when we discuss life's challenges in Peckham. For him, life here is about people being deprived of opportunities. He wants to give people in Peckham faith that they can make a difference.

We walk on towards Queens Road Peckham station, where I'll take the train back to Croydon. We walk past the closed-down police station; small, simple West African restaurants; a newly built hotel. Nicholas continues to tell me about everything that can be found in the neighbourhood: about how nice the council estates have become, now that the tower blocks have been replaced by houses with small, well-kept gardens outside them. About the Persian restaurant, Persepolis, which is chaotic and cosy at the same time, and the Prince of Peckham pub, where ambitious MCs can perform their texts to select beats. Or about Peckham BMX Club – a sanctuary for young people who don't want to get involved in the gang scene. There are so many passionate souls in London. I almost daren't think about what life would be like for the most vulnerable in Peckham without people like Nicholas.

A tree without roots will fall

If you find yourself on one of London's many buses, making your way south on a Sunday morning, you'll quickly realise that many of the female passengers are astonishingly well dressed in beautiful West African outfits. The men are dressed no less finely, in attractive suits, often with a well-thumbed Bible in their hands. The girls wear party dresses and bows in their hair; the boys dazzling suits and polished shoes. All of them are on their way to the churches that can be found in and around Peckham.

The Borough of Southwark, of which Peckham is a part, contains several hundred African Christian churches. A dozen or so can be found on the Copeland Industrial Estate, just five minutes from Peckham Rye station. A sign at the entrance to the area clearly indicates what can be found here: Christ's Gospel Church, Church of Kings, Shalom International Ministry, Salvation Parish Church. While the Church of England is struggling to get people through its doors on a Sunday morning, the number of West African church-goers is growing, and nowhere else in the world are there so many African churches outside Africa than here in Peckham in Southwark.

Two little girls in white dresses are about to run straight into me, hurtling towards me at full speed as they run out from a path behind a Jamaican snack bar. When they realise that I'm standing there, they giggle shyly. They appear to be of West African descent, and are laughing and jumping around, when a third girl appears. Curious, I walk over to the footpath from which they emerged, and discover that behind the snack bar, an extension has been built. More girls in white are standing there outside it – the outfits they're wearing are not dresses, I now realise, but tunics. Their angel-like radiance looks peculiar against the backdrop of the simple building painted in white and blue they are playing in front of. An older West African woman glowers at me – I must look quite stunned, just standing there.

'You can come in, but you have to take off your shoes!' she commands.

I do as I'm asked, and enter the premises. To the right of the entrance is a small room, the walls of which are painted brown. Rows of chairs have been set out facing a small altar. The concrete floor is cold beneath my feet. The woman shows me down a steep staircase, and I enter a room painted in shades of turquoise. One wall is covered by something that looks like white rose petals, and at the top of the wall are the words 'Holy, holy, holy'. Something that looks like an altar is covered by a blanket, which features the same words in gold. In this basement room, men, women and children have gathered. An older man, who is obviously the priest, comes across to me and bids me welcome. I have entered one of the branches of the Celestial Church of Christ (or CCC for short) – one of the many African parishes in London. They are Pentecostalists, and therefore belong to a charismatic church in which speaking in tongues is not uncommon.

'We meet here to pray to God and find peace of mind,' the pastor tells me.

The service has just finished, and now the members of the congregation will stay for a while, to socialise with the rest of the community. The church was originally founded in Benin in 1947 and has over a million members, most of them from Nigeria and Benin. They are visible on London's shopping streets, where they undertake extensive missionary work, often carrying placards paying homage to Jesus, singing together and handing out leaflets to passers-by. Their dogma is a mixture of tribal religions and Christianity – a hybrid adapted to the West African heritage. The congregation seems reserved, and when I ask its members whether I might have a chat with them, they shake their heads. I have a few vague suspicions about why they might want to keep me at a distance.

The expansion of African Christianity in London has attracted significant attention – not just because the number of churches has risen exponentially in just a few years, but also because of reports of dubious pastors promising help with financial problems, infertility, weight gain and bad luck in exchange for fistfuls of money. At the same time, the UN Committee on the Rights of the Child has established that London is the world's major hub for the trafficking of children – and a large proportion of these children come from Africa. Upon hearing these details, it is easy to stumble into all the worst possible assumptions a European can make when encountering the unknown – especially when it comes to Africa, a continent so permeated with myths and shrouded in stereotypes.[1] My own perspective can easily fall prey to exoticism when I hear about healing through dreams, about visions and spontaneous prayer – despite the fact that this is all completely ordinary within the Pentecostal movement. However, there are also terrible stories that confirm London holds the darkest of secrets, which cannot be simply brushed under the rug.

One of these stories starts with a stroll across Tower Bridge.[2] One afternoon in September 2001, a pedestrian noticed something strange floating in the Thames. He thought it was a barrel at first, but slowly realised that it was the torso of what appeared to be a child. The police were called, and divers fished the body from the river. The head, arms and legs had been dismembered; the only thing the boy was wearing was a pair of orange training shorts.

Investigators decided to call the unknown boy Adam. After several years of meticulous investigation, in which the contents of the boy's intestines were analysed with the assistance of botanists at Kew Gardens, experts were finally able to say that based on the presence of a unique bean in his system, the boy was likely from Benin. Then, based on analyses undertaken by Professor of Theology Robert Hoskins, came the awful conclusion: in all probability, Adam had been sacrificed as part of a ritual killing.

The hunt for the killers has led investigators to such disparate countries as the Netherlands, Scotland, the USA, Ireland, Nigeria, South Africa and Benin, but the murder remains unsolved – and Adam's story is just one of several extremely disturbing incidents involving West African children. The year before, eight-year-old Victoria Adjo Climbié was murdered by her aunt and uncle because they believed she was possessed by the devil. Her guardians were members of the controversial Universal Church of the Kingdom of God. At the time of her death, Victoria had 128 marks resulting from abuse on her body.[3]

Attempts were also made to link the discovery of Adam's body to two other murder cases, in which two girls were grossly abused and murdered by their guardians because they were supposedly 'possessed by the devil'. In one of these cases, the girl who was murdered had been taken to various churches and subjected to exorcisms. Several documentaries have been made about this kind of child abuse undertaken in Jesus' name, and they contain shocking scenes – small children being shaken and slapped in order to force the devil from them. The British authorities have exhibited firm resolve in hunting down pastors who perform such exorcisms; the problem has been so widespread that the Metropolitan Police established a dedicated working group, named Project Violet, to handle such cases. The group collaborates with AFRUCA – Africans Unite Against Child Abuse – an organisation founded in 2001 in the wake of the murders of Victoria Climbié and Adam.

In early 2014, a pastor and self-proclaimed witch-hunter came to London. She handed out brochures which stated that 'if a child under the age of two screams in the night, cries and is always feverish with deteriorating health, he or she is a servant of Satan'. She also made a shocking film in which children are presented as demons and subjected to grotesque rituals. She was subsequently identified as a threat to British children and was deported.

After my encounter with the Pentecostal church I walk along Rye Lane towards the station, where I've agreed to meet Abosede, film-maker Adeyemi Michael's mother. On one of the small stalls selling mobile SIM cards, I see that they also have West African DVDs for sale – films in which demons and witchcraft form an integrated part of the narrative. The DVDs are packaged in garish covers featuring blood and people screaming: they look like horror films. Abosede is waiting for me beside the train station. It starts to rain, so we seek refuge in a Costa Coffee. We talk about the films I've seen, and about the tragic stories of child abuse.

'You'll find evil in all cultures – the good and the ugly. What you choose to follow is up to you. But I think it's so sad to witness how these forces are ruining our reputation. The solidarity offered by the churches is beneficial to most people. We find safety there. Many people feel so isolated. The churches become their second home,' says Abosede.

Abosede believes the churches meet the fundamental needs of African immigrants used to living in close-knit communities that are not always so easy to find in a city like London, where life can often seem like a battle to survive. For the most vulnerable, this battle can seem completely insurmountable without faith in Jesus.

'Life isn't easy for immigrants. Even if you have family, you might feel lonely because your relatives are back in Nigeria. If something happens to you, it's easy to end up destitute. The pastors can provide advice about difficult financial situations, and ease people's loneliness. They can listen, provide care. We have solidarity. My experience is that ordinary Englishmen don't understand this – they never enter our churches, and only ever see us wearing nice clothes and dancing,' Abosede says.

I think back to the Italians at Casa Pallotti in Clerkenwell. I think of the Irish, the Caribbeans, the Muslims and Sikhs. All of them point to this solidarity. The imams, the pastors and the priests are all social workers – and whenever the flock gathers, it's often just as much a celebration as a prayer meeting.

We come around to the topic of Adeyemi's film, and I tell her how amazing it was to see her in the purple outfit with gold embroidery.

'I like the way that it fused the Nigerian with the British. The colours I was wearing – they had associations with wealth, and I like that. Nigeria is a rich country. The image of me in those clothes shows that I'm proud of my country and my traditions. Even if Peckham and Britain are my home now, I'd really like to preserve my Nigerian heritage. When I go to wedding parties, everything is about putting on the finest clothes I own, and throwing money around the couple to wish them good luck. This is a tradition I've grown up with. And if a Nigerian boy marries a Nigerian girl, the families have to be introduced to each other. That's just how it is – there's nothing wrong in that. Everything is about roots. You can't forget them or pretend that they don't exist. It's like a tree – it would fall down if it didn't have roots – it wouldn't survive. You understand?'

I think I do, even though the term 'roots' is a complicated one for me. Abosede tells me that Nigerians in the neighbourhood have asked her many questions about Adeyemi's choice of career. The West African churches, and especially the Pentecostal movement, are proponents of a conservative lifestyle in which the parents are to be honoured, and a traditional family life in which the mother is the caregiver and the father, as the head of the family, is at the centre of things. Abosede says she realised that Adeyemi had a talent early on, and that she wanted to give him freedom because she wanted him to be happy. Something that isn't always a given within immigrant families.

We go back out on to the street; the rain has stopped. We walk past the many Korean and Vietnamese nail salons where the young women might be victims of human trafficking. I can also see the famous Khan's Bargains Ltd which was founded by an Akbar Khan, an Afghani, in 2000, and quickly became a favourite among the locals. A beautiful art deco ceiling consisting of a thousand glass bricks was found in 2017 while restoration work was being carried out. Peckham is Abosede's village now. She remembers a time when street violence was an everyday occurrence, and she's glad that North Peckham Estate has been razed to the ground.

'I decided to keep my kids indoors after school and fill their weekends with outdoor activities. The playground is where everything happens – what happens there can either destroy you or make you stronger,' she says, explaining how the young Adeyemi used to sit and stare longingly out of the window while his friends played outdoors.

'Did he protest?'

'Oh, yes. I know I was strict, but I'm sure that's why he's a film director now, and why he wasn't stabbed to death or sent to prison. Here in Peckham, young boys have to be kept a close eye on at all times to make sure they don't end up in trouble,' Abosede says.

Abosede tells me that despite its problems, Peckham is a neighbourhood where people care about each other, no matter their background.

'The Pakistanis who own many of the shops around here understand us Nigerians, they understand respect – unlike the English. The Asian shop owners always say "auntie" and "uncle" to anyone older than themselves, just as we do in our culture. It takes so little to acknowledge each other's traditions, and the greatest thing of all is that we have so much in common, no matter where we come from,' Abosede says.

I can hear the protests of the immigration critics at this – of course, not everything is unproblematic. But regardless, I feel great joy at Abosede's attitude to life. Like many other women in her situation, she's done well for herself here in London and raised her children to dare to blaze a trail for others, even though it would have been so much easier to simply go along with the status quo. She reminds me of my mother.

Indian London – Southall, Brick Lane, Tooting

Lost sailors, nannies and hipsters

My preferred entry point to Brick Lane has always been Aldgate East Underground station: dark and inhospitable. Flaking paint in safety yellow and blue. Down a narrow backstreet right next to the station is Freedom Press Bookshop and Publishers, which I've frequented since the mid-1980s when I saw myself as an inquisitive anarchist. Since 1886, those with unruly hearts have wandered purposefully into this side street with a desire to change the world.

When I was young, the bookshop was on the first floor at the end of a crooked staircase. Unshaven men in corduroy jackets, all with revolution on their minds, sat there surrounded by wonky old bookcases containing books by Russian revolutionary Peter Kropotkin and Stuart Christie, along with pamphlets created by city guerrillas the Angry Brigade and the latest issue of the uncompromising newspaper *Class War*. I was in heaven. The small enterprise is active even today. Now, it's young anarchist hipsters who have taken over. They've moved the bookshop down to the ground floor, and the entrance has been renovated beyond all recognition. Gone are the huge piles of old books and periodicals that used to be stacked up everywhere, as is the old bookshop's distinctive musty smell.

Almost right next door is Whitechapel Gallery, and directly across the street, where Adler Street, White Church Lane and Whitechapel Lane meet, is Altab Ali Park, a green breath of fresh air away from the thundering traffic – once a cemetery, and today a memorial to a twenty-five-year-old textile worker from Bangladesh who was murdered by racists in May 1978.[1] That was also the year the influential ad hoc organisation Rock Against Racism (RAR) began arranging concerts in east London, where both reggae and punk artists united in taking a stand against the increasing number of racist attacks that were taking place in London.

Technocrats, anarchists, hairdressers, bakers, poets, Orthodox Jews, Muslims, street sellers, artists, accountants, gangsters, urban elitists, tailors, fashion designers . . . Brick Lane has everything and more besides. This wondrous street, which winds its way through the east of the city, from Bethnal Green in the north on to Shoreditch and Spitalfields, and all the way south to Whitechapel, is a microcosm of London. To take a walk here is to embark on an incredible journey along worn-out pavements and chequered asphalt, beside graffiti in all conceivable and unimaginable nuances of style and colour, through meaningless and meaningful chaos and spectacular architectural visions that stand shoulder to shoulder with Victorian houses with flaking paint and crumbling brick. Brick Lane contains many stories – about Huguenots, Irish, Jews and Bangladeshis in a kind of chronological order – with the bearded, tattooed hipsters in their lumberjack shirts the representatives from the current century.

An arch with red lights shaped like small minarets signals the entrance to Brick Lane. It must have shone once but is shabby now, bearing witness to the pervasive weariness that marks the streets here, too. In 1997, Brick Lane was officially dubbed Banglatown. The street is thick with restaurants, interspersed with small bakeries offering tempting Indian baked goods in vibrant colours, and threadbare grocery stores where older men in tunics and beards dyed with henna sit on chairs, watching the street life that flows past. On Friday evenings, smiling young men in shirts and waistcoats tempt hungry passers-by into Bengal Village, Café Naz, Meraz Café, or

Brick Lane Brasserie – all of which offer pungent-smelling garlic chicken with naan bread that will ensure the cocktails and wine won't cause any unnecessary staggering on the cobbled streets later in the night. At some of the restaurants the chefs have been deemed worthy of a Michelin star; at others the rice is old and the curry sauce thin as tea, obviously reheated from the day before. Between the restaurants, with their large banners proclaiming that they have won various titles for the best meal, are small vegan alternatives or minimalistic doughnut shops.

The contrasts are never far away as you wander around here – all you have to do is walk a few hundred metres from Brick Lane for the blocks of council housing to appear. Here there are young bearded men in tunics, and young women wearing hijabs. The mosques stand side by side with ever more luxurious apartment buildings, tailor-made for the bankers who crack mathematical formulae in the City, just a Porsche ride away. In Hackney, property prices increased by 702 per cent between 1996 and 2016.[2] Once a neighbourhood known exclusively for its slums and notorious for its high crime rate, today the streets around Brick Lane are full of new money, and have almost become a theme park. London's brutal social divides are perhaps more visible here on Brick Lane than on any other street in the city. The flashing neon lights might fool us into believing that there is glamour to behold here, but behind the facades the apartments are cramped and infested with mould.

A clear illustration of the divide between rich and poor in east London is a residential complex at One Commercial Street. The building used to have two entrances: one for those who could afford to buy one of the complex's attractive apartments, and another, hidden away in an alley, for the people who lived there with social support. The solution was much protested and eventually removed, but this is not an uncommon practice. Contractors have chosen to use such solutions in several places where they have promised 'mixed' housing in order to obtain permission to build in areas where poorer people also live; but the poor are allocated their own floors, their own lifts – yes, even their own areas for waste disposal – so the rich never have to mix with those who are less well-off.

The relationship between the British and the population from the Indian subcontinent has always been marked by a curious mix of hate and love, arrogance and humility. This strange relationship has also coloured my own relationship to Britain and the Empire. These connections go all the way back to 1600, when a group of merchants and aristocrats founded the East India Company, and were granted the right to a monopoly on all trade beyond the Cape of Good Hope and the Magellan Strait by Queen Elizabeth I. The trading of tea, spices, silk and other luxury goods brought the Indians and British together in a way that would have social, political and economic consequences for the entire subcontinent for hundreds of years. It would forever characterise the political landscape of the UK and London – and continues to characterise Brick Lane today.[3]

When the East India Company began its operations, India was ruled by the Muslim Moguls. In their heyday, they ruled almost the entire Indian peninsula. But in time the Moguls were starting to lose their foothold, and in several regions this led to riots breaking out against the Great Mogul. This unrest made it easy for the East India Company to secure land and trading rights across the vast continent with its intricate system of religions, castes, languages and traditions. Thousands of Indians started working for the company. Some of them found their way to London on the ships that regularly sailed between England and India. The first Indians arrived in England as early as the 1600s, and the first Christianisation of an Indian is said to have taken place in a church in the City of London.

The Indians who came to Britain were mostly sailors who stayed in the port towns from where the large ships would cast off. A number of these seamen came from the Sylhet region, in what is now Bangladesh. They were known as Lascars, and made up a significant proportion of the crews on European ships. A number of them remained in London as cooks when they were unable to find other work. Hundreds of Indian women were also employed as nannies – ayahs – for prosperous British families. When these families had seen enough of India and returned home to London, they took the nannies with them. The streets of London gradually filled with Indian family stories.

In 1947 it was decided that India would be divided in two through the partition, to form Hindu-dominated India and Muslim Pakistan – the land of the pure. Mahatma Gandhi strongly opposed partition based on religious affiliation, while Muslim politician and nationalist Muhammad Ali Jinnah saw it as a victory. The partition of India was a tragic and traumatic event. Over 14 million people were affected when the border was drawn. Roots were brutally ripped up. Hindu families who for generations had lived in what became Pakistan were forced to flee, as were Muslim families on the other side. People were murdered in horrifying numbers.

The partition of India continues to affect families from the continent, and it has also left deep traces among London's South Asian population. Some of my own relatives who hadn't emigrated to Kenya were forced to flee to Lahore, losing so much in the process, and I've heard terrible stories of violence and despair. The Sikhs were hit especially hard, which meant that thousands of them decided to travel to Britain. They had little to lose.

When the immigrants from the subcontinent arrived in London, whether as sailors, students, lawyers, politicians, nannies or doctors, they were like a river that flooded its banks. They created small distinctive brooks in the south in Tooting, then moved north-east to

Tower Hamlets and north-west to Wembley's Ealing Road and Neasden, where BAPS Shri Swaminarayan Mandir is located – the biggest Hindu temple outside India, constructed from limestone and Italian marble – and west to Southall and Ealing, not far from Heathrow airport, where the Sikhs in particular found a home. Immigrants also arrived from Sri Lanka, once known as Ceylon – they too consisted of several distinct groups, including the Sinhalese, Tamils and Moors. All with their unique heritage and culture, but inextricably linked through a constructed British fellowship that is still filled with tensions, but also love.

It's impossible not to feel somewhat overwhelmed and moved by this historical backdrop as I wander down Brick Lane. I have no connection to Bangladesh or the people who live around Brick Lane, but we are nevertheless inextricably linked through a shared history. And we all came here because the British wanted us to.

Friday prayers have just finished at the local mosque, Brick Lane Jamme Masjid, as I walk past. Well-dressed men, the older ones in traditional Bangladeshi clothing, the younger in more modern outfits, are coming out of the door, greeting each other warmly. The building is old. Were it not for the modern minaret, you would never guess that this was a mosque, because there is no South Asian aesthetic to be seen here, no cupolas. I don't see a single woman.

I notice a small group of tourists, who are watching the men leave. They point at the mosque, exclaiming in their American accents: 'There used to be a synagogue here!' They're right. The mosque occupies a building from 1743, L'Eglise de l'Hôpital, which was originally a place of worship for persecuted French Huguenots who sought refuge in London. In 1809, the organisation London Society for Promoting Christianity Amongst the Jews took over the building in an attempt to convert the Jews who had arrived in the area after facing persecution throughout Eastern Europe. Ten years later, the building became a Methodist Church, before it became clear that the conversion efforts hadn't quite gone as planned and the church was transformed into a synagogue. Jews made up 95 per cent of Spitalfield's population in 1900, so there was an obvious need for a Jewish place of worship here.

The largest migration of people from Bangladesh happened in connection with the partition of India. After the creation of Pakistan, which also included five provinces known collectively as East Pakistan, the Bangladeshis became agitated, believing they had been cheated out of self-rule. Culturally and linguistically, East Pakistan and Pakistan were extremely different, and there was an uproar when Urdu was adopted as the official language for the entire area. In 1971 a bloody civil war broke out, in which millions fled East Pakistan for India, which allied itself with those of Bangladeshi descent. India actively participated on the side of East Pakistan, which led to Pakistan losing the war and being forced to relinquish the provinces. Bangladesh was thereby established as a separate nation.

The civil war caused many people from Bangladesh to leave their homes for Britain. In the 1970s it was almost exclusively men who made the journey, but throughout the 1980s women and children came too. Like the first Bangladeshi sailors and ayahs, they settled in Tower Hamlets. Today, over 600,000 Bangladeshis live in Britain, 70 per cent of them in London.

On Brick Lane, the events of history are insistent, pressing. The mosque, which opened in 1976, is situated on the corner of Princelet Street and Fournier Street, and I don't know how many times I've come to a stop in front of one of the old, narrow houses on these streets, wanting to scrape off the paint, as if that could transport me back in time. I've stood still here for a long time. Over and over again. Closed my eyes, taking a deep breath, to feel the closeness of all the stories here. Fournier Street, named after a French Huguenot refugee, runs between Brick Lane and Commercial Street.

The narrow, terraced houses span three floors, and were built in the 1720s. Back then the Huguenots dominated the silk trade in London, and it was in these houses that they wove the silk garments high society loved to wear. Some of the doors are painted in cobalt blue or green, and if you take a peek through the windows it is clear that it's London's well-off who have now taken over here. I've always dreamed of being able to step inside one of these houses – not to mention the gardens. I've seen photographs of the back of the properties, where the gardens are like small botanical treasure troves. Many of the doors are maintained in their original condition, and some of them feature the word 'Tradesmen' as a reminder of the street's original function; on others the paint is flaking off, revealing the colours going back in time. Above one cobalt-blue door hangs a plaque: Bangladesh Welfare Association – the office where Bangladeshis have been able to obtain advice from within their community since 1964.

Princelet Street seems even narrower, and at the bottom of it is Huguenot Court, where the once so dilapidated buildings have now been transformed into new apartments. At 19 Princelet Street is a museum: Europe's first museum of immigration and diversity. The building, from 1719, was the home of the French Huguenot Ogier family, who quickly became affluent through the silk trade. They had fled persecution from the Catholics in France. Later, the building was taken over by Irish who had fled the Great Famine of the 1840s, and then came the Jews, who were fleeing the pogroms in Russia and Eastern Europe. They used the small back garden as a synagogue.

In the 1930s, the house functioned as a base for the Jewish East-Enders, who fought against the Blackshirts – the troops of fascist leader Oswald Mosley – who marched here. The museum is rarely open because the building is unable to tolerate the frequent, enthusiastic steps of visitors. On the few occasions that the doors are opened, the queues are long. The building's loft also contains a mystery. In 1980, the door to the attic space was opened for the first time in eleven years. This was where the self-taught rabbi David Rodinsky had resided, but he disappeared without a trace in 1969. To this day, nobody knows what happened to him. The people who discovered the room were overwhelmed by all the documents, notes and books they found there, which were mainly about Kabbalism, and in the east of the city the attic has become just as legendary as gangster twins Ronald and Reginald Kray. In the 1990s, Jewish artist Rachel Lichtenstein began the arduous task of trying to find out who Rodinsky was, and the result is the curious book *Rodinsky's Room* (1999), co-written with author Iain Sinclair.

The Jewish presence in Brick Lane likely provides much of the explanation as to why east London is known for its uncompromising attitude to far-right forces.[4] In the 1930s, the British Union of Fascists (BUF) was a rapidly growing movement with influential supporters. The organisation's members proudly walked around wearing black shirts and boots. In Chelsea, the group at one point recruited 200 unemployed youths to live in a disused barracks in exchange for a few shillings and three square meals a day. They formed their own army, and were active on the streets. In 1936, the BUF added the designation 'National Socialists' to their name, making their anti-Semitic stance even clearer. They described Jews as 'rats and vermin' and 'hook-nosed, yellow-skinned, dirty Jewish swine'. But the fascists encountered resistance from several sides. Their most ardent opponents were the Communist Party (CP), the Independent Labour Party (ILP) and the Jewish People's Council Against Fascism and Antisemitism (JPC).

On 4 October 1936, Oswald Mosley and his party decided to march through east London, but the left mobilised quickly. Walls all across the neighbourhood were covered with the slogan 'No Pasaran' – taken from the Spanish Republicans who fought against Franco in

Spain – written in chalk and sung loudly by marching anti-fascists. Huge barricades were set up, lorries were overturned, streets were covered in mattresses and furniture, shops closed in solidarity, and from windows rotten fruit and urine poured down over the many hundreds of fascists who attempted to march through the streets.

A wild brawl broke out in Cable Street, where the police attempted to protect the fascists. But in the end the police were forced to give in, and asked Mosley and his crew to withdraw. The anti-fascists had won. Oswald Mosley continued tirelessly in his endeavours regardless, but in 1940 the BUF was banned and Mosley imprisoned. In the years between 1979 and 1983, a mural inspired by Mexican communist Diego Rivera could be seen in Cable Street, in honour of those who had fought during the march of 1936. Every year, the victory is marked with a celebration, and speeches are given by participants who are still alive, to remind everyone of the ghastly attitudes promoted in the name of the fascist cause.

Lacking other opportunities, enterprising Bangladeshis understood early on that they could start small restaurants to satisfy an ever-growing group of customers who were curious about Indian culinary culture. In the 1950s and 1960s, Indian restaurants were popular among those who had served on the subcontinent, and curry became a popular dish among students because it was cheap. Today, almost 90 per cent of all Indian restaurants in London are owned by people with a Bangladeshi background, not Indians or Pakistanis, even though the food contains ingredients from across the entire Indian subcontinent. You have to be well versed in Indian culinary culture in order to be able to identify where the various combinations of spices originally come from, and in which regions it is common to use mustard oil, pickled lime and mango or coconut in the various sauces.

'The English are completely fooled by meaningless labels,' my aunt in London always chuckles whenever we eat lamb curry and steaming hot chapatis at her house, and my mother wrinkles her nose if she catches even a hint of sugar or coconut in the curry sauce when we visit a new Indian restaurant. Every family has its own distinct mix of spices, and everybody believes that their region's spice mix is better than everyone else's.

The first Indian greengrocer in London was established as early as 1931: the Bombay Emporium (BE) in Grafton Street near Tottenham Court Road. Today, the company is called Bombay International, and is run by the sons of its Indian founder. The brands it imports – Rajah, Lotus and Amoy – are now permanent fixtures in super-markets all across the UK. The British fascination with Indian food would turn out to be the key to success for a number of families.

Shanta Gaury Pathak Pandit was born in Zanzibar in 1927.[5] When she was eighteen years old, she married Laxmishanker Pathak, who was living in Mombasa, where his older brother had started a bakery to satisfy an ever-growing and sugar-hungry Indian population. In 1956, Shanta and Laxmishanker moved to London, reportedly with just £5 between them. In London, Mr Pathak found a job cleaning the drains for the local authorities – a job his wife didn't like in the slightest. She instead convinced her husband to start a food company from the small flat in Kentish Town where they lived. After a few hard years, they had managed to save up enough money to open a small shop in Euston. Later, they had the funds to start yet another branch in Bayswater, but soon received complaints from the neighbours, who were none too keen on all the exotic smells. They ended up having to leave, and decided to move to Northamptonshire in the Midlands, where from a disused mill they started a hugely successful company, almost completely by chance. Because in 1972, 50,000 Indian refugees arrived in the UK from Uganda, after having been expelled by Idi Amin. The British authorities needed someone who could provide them with food and organise the camps they were lodged in, and put the project out to tender. Shanta saw a unique opportunity, and won the job. The Pathaks completed their assignment faultlessly, and rumours of the proficient family business began to spread. By the end of the 1970s, Patak's had over 500 employees and was producing sauces and spices for over 7,000 restaurants, as well as exporting products to forty countries. In 2017, the descendants of Shanta Gaury Pathak Pandit sold the firm to Associated British Foods for £105 million.

But over the years the British have become more sophisticated in their tastes, and many now turn up their noses at the Bangladeshi version of Indian food. Yawar Khan, head of the Asian Catering Federation, says the traditional curry houses are struggling to compete with the new Indian restaurants that are now starting to open. Chicken floating in cream, butter and rice is now up against beansprouts, kale, seeds and salad.

If Brick Lane, with its older Bangladeshi immigrants, is a testament to a bygone past, just next-door Shoreditch is a vision of an entirely different era. A new age in which successful Indians wish to promote a different experience of what being Indian can bring to London – aesthetically, politically and philosophically, as well as culinarily.

Hidden away just off Boundary Street, in a discreet passage a couple of minutes from the ultra-trendy Ace Hotel, is a manifestation of the modern Indian London, completely in line with the stories we hear from the ambitious middle class in Mumbai and New Delhi. Glass walls and green plants. Plush chairs and the unmistakable fragrance of coriander. Dishoom is an assured, stylish restaurant with soft carpets and dark wood.

'We wanted to show that Indians are stylish and challenge the restaurants in Brick Lane that don't really serve Indian food, but more like a British version of Indian food from the time of Henry

VIII,' says Shamil Thakrar. I meet him at his office, an equally sophisticated place, on Shoreditch High Street.

He's just as elegant as the restaurant, wearing jeans and a waistcoat over his shirt, which is clearly influenced by the kurta, an Indian garment. Dishoom is inspired by the old Iranian cafés that arose in Bombay when a group of Iranians fled to India in the early 1900s due to their links with Zoroastrianism, a religious movement founded by the prophet Zarathustra. The cafés became popular institutions among Bombay's population, unpretentious and homely, almost like American diners. Their interiors were inspired by the brasseries of Paris and the cafés in Vienna and Prague. In 1950, there were more than several hundred of these kinds of cafés in Bombay, while in today's Mumbai only a handful remain. Dishoom has copied their style with marble tabletops, lots of mirrors, and wooden bistro chairs. Nothing has been left to chance – everything from the tea glasses to the plates the food is served on has been planned down to the tiniest detail. Everything has a history.

'The cafés were unique gathering places for all kinds of people, regardless of religious background. In a society like India, where people were carefully divided by class, caste and religion, the cafés were neutral and unifying. They promoted a tolerant view of life, which I believe India actually represents. Tolerance is a value I hold in extremely high regard. We celebrate Christmas, Eid and Diwali here,' says Shamil.

Shamil grew up in north London, the son of Indian parents who sent him off to boarding school as a ten-year-old.

'I was terrified. There were just two of us from Indian families there. Me and an Indian prince,' he laughs.

His privileged upbringing led him to a solid job in an international investment bank, where he and his Eton-educated cousin Kavi earned enough money to realise their dream of starting their own restaurant. They now own five restaurants in London as well as ones in Edinburgh, Manchester and Birmingham. They currently employ 900 people. Another part of the story is that the family is also behind rice giant Tilda Rice – yet another fantastic success story of Indian immigrants with a good nose for business.

Dishoom in Carnaby Street has been decorated with a predilection for the time when the Beatles fell in love with yoga and Indian mysticism, and when the Indian music industry was also influenced by 1960s counterculture. All the doors in the restaurant feature the titles of Beatles songs written in Hindi. Books and vinyl are set on shelves around the premises.

'I love this period in Indian history – everybody looked so cool, and the world was genuinely interested in Indian culture,' says Shamil. 'Most people don't believe me when I tell them, but there was a proper rock 'n' roll scene in Bombay in the 1960s. The author Sidharth Bhatia has written a fantastic book called *India Psychedelic*. That's how I discovered that there was a band called the Combustibles that existed in India. We incorporated this heritage into the design work for our Carnaby Street restaurant.'

Shamil is passionate about showing another India than the one usually depicted through clichés about cricket, the British Raj, Bollywood and the traditional curry restaurants. I so understand what he means. There was something un-chic about India throughout the 1970s and 1980s. Young people from the Indian subcontinent were rarely at the cutting edge of fashion, music or design in the 1980s. Most of them were totally off – it was the Irish and Caribbeans who always seemed to represent the cultural vanguard. I was slightly offended when in 1988 Morrissey released the album *Viva Hate*, and on it I found the track 'Bengali in Platforms', about a young boy who so wants to impress the English with his style but completely misses the mark – but he was right. This lack of aesthetic sense, however, changed dramatically in the 1990s. Boys and girls from Indian backgrounds, born and raised in

London, decided to take action: off with the Terylene bell bottoms and on with the Levi's and cool trainers.

Brothers Avtar and Tjinder Singh burst on to the music scene in 1991 with their pop-punk band Cornershop, and immediately made the headlines. The band burned an image of Morrissey in front of the entrance to EMI records, in protest at Morrissey's alleged racism. At around the same time that Cornershop appeared, record label Nation Records was established in Notting Hill. They released albums by Fun-Da-Mental and Transglobal Underground, bands that created a unique mix of so-called 'world music', and rap and punk. I had a new hero: Aki Nawaz, frontman of Fun-Da-Mental – an uncompromising and fiery soul with the rare background of being a Pakistani punk. The record company was also home to younger forces, because in east London, at a youth club in Brick Lane, several young boys were ready to conquer the world. Inspired by ragga, rap, punk and rock, they called themselves Asian Dub Foundation. In 1995, their album *Facts and Fictions* was released on Nation Records. In the music video to Asian Dub Foundation's 'New Way, New Life', vocalist Deeder Zaman sits on the floor surrounded by family and friends as he raps a unique mix of patois and unmistakable east London dialect, speaking about the new life that generations before them had created in London, and about the legacy now entrusted to their descendants. I force my sons to watch this video at regular intervals, to remind them of their roots.

In 1995, a tabla-playing young man by the name of Talvin Singh also attracted a certain amount of attention. Not only because of his dishevelled blue and black hair, which was unusual among young Asian men at the time, but also because he combined traditional Indian music with the genre of drum 'n' bass. That same year, he and event organiser Sweety Kapoor started the club night Anokha in Hoxton, north-east London, at London's hippest venue the Blue

Note. Three years later, Singh released his album *OK* to critical acclaim.

I'll never forget my first encounter with the club: I was surrounded by people dancing, all clearly from Indian or Pakistani backgrounds, while DJ Sam Zaman played a hybrid of electronica and old Bollywood music. I was used to being the only person of Asian descent when I went out to concerts or clubs. The night was an immediate success among an entire generation who had felt out of place on the London club scene. Of course, the British press had to find a label to slap on this movement taking shape on London's streets, and dubbed the scene Asian Cool and Asian Underground.

After my meeting with Shamil, I have the urge to go to Hoxton Square – or 'Oxton, as the true locals say. The small square, five minutes from Shoreditch, is one of the city's oldest. In the 1990s, the little patch of grass and buildings around it was a magnet for music lovers and artists. Here, vintage Levi's 501s and irony ruled. Cool Britannia. The area has since become thick with hotels, bars, second-hand shops and cafés, and it isn't so easy to see the entrance to internationally renowned nightclub the Blue Note today.

Talvin Singh and his peers have long since grown up, as have I. Today, young people whose roots go back to the Indian subcontinent listen to the BBC Asian Network, where new music artists can be heard in a mix of rap, grime, R&B and electro. Many of them have probably never even heard of Anokha. They live in a new reality, where access to both Bollywood music and American rap are taken as a given.

London is also full of young Indians who commute between Mumbai and London. Rich Indians plough money into the property market in order to secure accommodation for their sons and daughters, who study at the city's best universities. The *Daily Mail* has long since dubbed London 'Richistan'.

As I walk past the shop windows in Hoxton, I suddenly catch sight of a younger version of myself, with a quicker step and more make-up – wearing trainers, of course – and I glimpse tiny snatches of a life lived from young rebel to grown woman. The stretch from Brick Lane to Shoreditch and Hoxton consists of several layers of memories, all the way from back when I took the Underground to Aldgate East for the first time as a teenager, to when I first brought my sons here, wanting to inaugurate them into Hackney's countless secrets. It is now my sons' curious footsteps that pound the asphalt of east London. Just like me, they have London in their blood.

The cultural revolution

One evening, as I'm looking through an old photo album at home in London, I come across photographs of my father from when he was a student at King Edward Medical College. He's lanky and has thick, black hair, combed back in an Elvis-style quiff. After finishing high school in Mombasa, my father was sent to Pakistan to study medicine. The university is one of the oldest in the Muslim world, and was founded by the British Raj. My father was no Nobel Prize winner, but he was well known at the university for his sporting achievements – M. M. Khan was a household name. Along with his brother, he had won several table-tennis championships in Kenya, and ranked number sixteen in the Asian league. At King Edward, it was tennis that would come to take up much of his time, but the other med students were more concerned with politics. One of them – who my father also studied with back then – was the charismatic activist Tariq Ali.

When my father set aside his tennis racket and dived into his medical textbooks, Ali went to Oxford to continue his studies, attracting attention from the very first moment he stepped on to campus. Since he was born into an affluent family, with a father who was a famous journalist and communist, Tariq Ali was schooled in socialism from an early age – a background that has influenced his entire life.[1] In 1965, as the leader of the Oxford Union, he met civil rights activists Malcolm X and Stokely Carmichael; during the demonstrations against the Vietnam War, he appeared in the media alongside actress Vanessa Redgrave. Glamorous rebels. Later, he became friends with John Lennon and Yoko Ono. How could anyone fail to be captivated by him? My father has always been fascinated by Ali, and I think this is because their lives have been so different. Ali broke with all conventions; my father, on the other hand, followed them. Ali entered into a relationship with a wealthy Englishwoman, and for a long time lived in the exclusive area of Highgate. And he hasn't mellowed with age. He continues to write books raging against American imperialism, but strangely enough found himself on the same side as Boris Johnson and the xenophobic UK Independence Party (UKIP) during the referendum on Brexit. 'The EU is an undemocratic and bureaucratic organisation which is not account-able to the people of any country,' was one of the explanations Ali gave when he was interviewed about his standpoint.[2]

Ali was far from the only person from British India to influence London's cultural scene throughout the 1960s. The city was seething with energy and rebellion from the former sons and daughters of empire. But some of them helped to bring about change in quieter ways – and their contributions were no less important.

Rays of sunlight enter through the windows of the three-storey house in the neighbourhood of Parsons Green in Fulham, west London. An older man with a cast on his foot is sitting in front of me. The house is full of art and books. Indian Amal Ghosh was actu-ally supposed to become a doctor, but after he convinced his father that he wanted to become an artist, he travelled to London to study at prestigious art school Central Saint Martins in 1958. Little did the young Ghosh know that in doing so, he would make history.

'I was terrified when I first came to London. I was staying at the YMCA in Tottenham Court Road – mostly it was Indian doctors and engineering students who were staying there. But I quickly found myself a room in a house in Acton. I got a true culture shock during those early days at St Martins, let me tell you. I was used to Indian discipline, but here I met the most rambling Englishmen,' says Amal Ghosh.

Ghosh remembers how he was shocked at the university's liberal attitudes, and the tutors' lack of authority.

'It wasn't that the tutors weren't engaged or strict, but they didn't force us to perform in the way that I was used to from my studies in India. Instead, they chose to inspire us. When I showed one of the tutors some of my work he was ruthless, and told me that it was a pastiche of something that was sort of supposed to be Indian. He commanded that I go straight to the British Museum,' Ghosh recollects.

At the British Museum, Ghosh's eyes were opened to what Indian art had been and could be. He also experienced a London in flux, where British artists were popular and a natural part of society. They found Ghosh peculiar, and treated him with a combination of aloof fascination and genuine interest.

'You have to remember that there was almost nobody from India who was studying art at the time, everybody was studying medicine, so I stood out,' he points out.

But things haven't really improved all that much over the years, I think to myself. Parents with backgrounds from the Indian subcontinent will always want their children to become doctors. Always. Ghosh also found that many landlords in London didn't want to rent to foreigners. After an endless string of rejections, he obtained a reasonable loan through the local council, and with it access to London's property market. He used the loan to purchase the house we're currently sitting in. It has turned out to be a solid investment.

In 1966, Ghosh began teaching at Central Saint Martins – an appointment not everybody was equally enthused about. Ghosh tells me that several of his English colleagues attempted to undermine his authority, an experience he could have done without. He became the first person of Indian descent to be employed as an art tutor in Britain. He worked at Central Saint Martins for over twenty-five years, and maintained an active career as an artist alongside this.

Ali and Ghosh belonged to a circle of intellectuals who challenged the British cultural scene. A significant number of those who would change the cultural landscape of Britain came to London with the help of scholarships, one of them being Indian-Caribbean author V. S. Naipaul, who came to the city from Trinidad in 1954. Before he settled in London he had won a scholarship to study at Oxford, but after completing his education struggled to find his place. He lived with a cousin in West Kilburn, and worked cleaning public baths. He then got a job at the BBC, where he read short stories aloud on the programme *Caribbean Voices*. He began writing himself, and was discovered by influential British publishers. He climbed the literary ladder and was welcomed into the upper echelons of British society, who loved his acerbic texts.

'He was terribly arrogant!' Ghosh says with a grimace.

I know what he means. And over the years, it only got worse. Naipaul was unfriendly. Downright caustic, even. He indulged in a fair amount of self-flagellation and spoke of Muslims with disdain. But maybe it's too easy to simply dismiss him as pompous and narcissistic? Perhaps he was just trying to beat the English at their own game, giving them a taste of their own medicine now that he was deemed so brilliant.

Class differences have always been an important ingredient in the relationship between the British and their subjects. It was easy to control the weak, those without an education. But when the subjects demonstrated their intellectual ability, the rules of the game changed.

I can just imagine Naipaul, standing before a window with a whisky glass in hand, furious at the inescapable sarcasm the British upper class so casually throw around and plotting his revenge. I'm sure he was thinking: *Now I'll show them. We can be just as scheming and arrogant as they are.*

Ali, Naipaul and Ghosh paved the way for other intellectuals from the colonies, and several other authors wrote their way into the British literary scene. One of the most important was Muslim-born Salman Rushdie. In 1981, he attracted attention with his novel *Midnight's Children*, which examined India's journey from British colony to independence. In 1988, he published a work that would change the world – *The Satanic Verses*. The novel is partly inspired by the Prophet Muhammad's life, and the alleged Satanic Verses of the Koran. The book was banned in India, where the authorities believed it incited hate. At the same time, it received significant acclaim among literary circles in the UK, but here too the book's publication gave rise to outrage. In Bolton, a town in Greater Manchester, the book was burned and thousands of Muslims marched to protest it. On 14 February 1989, Ayatollah Khomeini issued a fatwa calling for Rushdie's murder, which meant that Rushdie had a death warrant on his head. But was the book really about Islam, or was it about migration, rootlessness and alienation? The debate around freedom of speech was put on the agenda, with far-reaching consequences for the Muslim communities in Britain – and the rest of the world.[3]

Inspired by Naipaul and Rushdie, other authors also appeared. Not all of them incited riots. But they certainly made waves.

When I was seventeen years old, my life changed. One night in London, I sat and watched the film *My Beautiful Launderette* (1985). Infidelity? Homosexuality? Punk? Pakistanis? All in one and the same film? I could hardly believe my eyes – a Pakistani boy who falls in love with a young punk with nationalist sympathies? I ran to my mother and told her about what I had just seen. She stared at me in shock. I found out that the screenplay had been written by a young Pakistani-British man named Hanif Kureishi, and all at once I felt that there was somebody else like me. That I wasn't alone in dreaming about squats, punks and anarchy, and that my complex cultural heritage had been acknowledged. From that moment on, I idolised Hanif Kureishi. I knew a number of people who felt trapped by traditions, plans for arranged marriages and endless nights spent watching Bollywood films. I had infinite freedom myself – it would never have occurred to my parents to arrange a marriage for me – but I lacked role models. Kureishi showed me that it was possible to forge your own path – even for those of us with a Muslim background. I felt wonderfully assured.

Two years later, I saw the film *Sammy and Rosie Get Laid*. Again, Kureishi had written the screenplay, and the film was a riotous critique of Thatcher's Britain and the strict norms within the Asian diaspora. The film featured a lesbian couple – not just any old lesbian couple, but one in which one partner was Asian and the other Afro-Caribbean. Unheard of! Again, I was speechless with admiration. And I felt even more assured.

In 1990, Kureishi published a work that would secure his position as a literary star: *The Buddha of Suburbia*. I'm sure his agent must have realised that the manuscript was gold from the very first page. Never before had literature been the medium for such a burlesque depiction of the identity challenges faced by a young Pakistani-British boy. Once again, Kureishi would show that he could change lives, and that there wasn't just one way of being Indian or Pakistani. The book was later adapted into a television series, and the explicit sex scenes meant I had absolutely no desire to watch it with my parents, who would have sat there, eyebrows raised, exclaiming: 'How vulgar!' at regular intervals. A cultural revolution was underway – Kureishi inspired a new generation of authors who would write about what it was like to belong to several cultures. When I finally met him in the 2000s, Kureishi was like an old lion; proud and satisfied. And although his books no longer engage readers quite as intensely as they used to, he remains a literary legend. A knight for the hybrids among us.

Rushdie, Naipaul and Kureishi are chroniclers of stories and narratives from London's streets. Now new talents have taken over, including the award-winning Hari Kunzru, Kamila Shamsie and Nikesh Shukla, but few seem to have been as influential as these three men. Rushdie and Kureishi continue to be held up as unrivalled role models. Perhaps it isn't so strange that this sense of homelessness and confused identity seems so strong among authors with roots in the Indian subcontinent.

London is a city where you can redefine yourself, and simultaneously disappear back in time should you wish to. In the west of London, not far from where the planes, filled with new and hopeful visitors, touch down, there is a world where some believe time has stood still since the 1960s. Where cultural conservatism breathes heavily, lying like a clammy hand over individuality and freedom.

Southall – a bell jar

A mixture of excitement and wistfulness fills me as I step aboard a local train from Paddington station one morning in August. I'm going to Southall, for the first time in several years. At some point my parents stopped making their trips to Southall in the car. Perhaps the drive became too tiring as London's traffic increased.

The station is under construction – like everything else in London. The Southall sign is written in both the Latin alphabet in blue, and in Gurmukhi in green – the script used by the Sikhs. The kebab shop on the railway bridge that we frequented when I was small is now gone, and I feel a brief tug at my heart. I stroll to the shopping streets I've visited so many times before with my mother. This was where she was always on the lookout for a bargain from the people selling 20-carat gold jewellery or silk fabric for a dress. A large, yellow sign glows on a warehouse-like building at the end of the bridge: Gurdwara Sri Guru Singh Sabha – one of the many Sikh temples in Southall. The first of them was founded in 1958, in a converted Methodist Church, while a youth club was simultaneously transformed into a Hindu temple to house the ever-growing group of Hindus that also settled here. It's not for nothing that Southall has been dubbed 'Little Punjab'. When India was partitioned, the state of Punjab was also divided in two: one part for the Muslims, and another for the Sikhs and Hindus. A large number of those who came to London after the Second World War came from Punjab.

Almost half a million Sikhs have settled in Britain. They are the largest group of Indians here, and there are over 300 gurdwaras. The Sikhs regarded the British Isles as the land of opportunity. They had remained loyal to the British Queen after the Indian Rebellion of 1857 against the East India Company, an extension of the British Crown. They had also served as soldiers in the British Army during the First and Second World Wars, and therefore felt a deep affinity with the United Kingdom.

India's prime minister, Jawaharlal Nehru, was not especially keen on this emigration. After several years at the University of Cambridge he had grown fond of British culture, and was worried about what would happen to India's image in England when so many uneducated Indians moved to the motherland. But it was not only those from the villages and army who set out to seek their fortunes in England – the Indian elite, who had been educated at British institutions, also wished to try their luck. They would soon discover, however, that there was a huge difference between them and 'the British'.

When I mention Southall, a special expression crosses the face of almost everyone in London I speak to who has roots in the Indian subcontinent. This district, where the shops so clearly reflect all that is Indian in both their names and what they offer, isn't a place you visit because it's so irresistible or exciting. Nor is the neighbourhood a magnificent area with broad green avenues or well-tended, elegant buildings, like Chiswick or Gunnersby, which are not very far away. It isn't especially nice or posh here. The pavements are narrow and dirty; the houses shabby. The gardens are often full of junk. The busy shopping streets are few, and any tourists who happen to stop by can see all there is to see within half an hour. Southall is an imaginary place, the stage set for dreams and clichés about what it means to have roots in the Indian subcontinent.

Every step taken along these streets in Southall is a reminder of a greater journey. Every woman I see wearing a sari or shalwar kameez, every man in a turban and with a distinctive thick silver bracelet around his wrist, seems in the grip of the confusion Salman Rushdie writes about in his novel *Shame* (1983) – the questions around what they should preserve, what they should scrap – as they carry thin plastic bags full of coriander and onions home to the houses in which they live. As if balancing fragile identities.

Familiarity breeds contempt, or so the saying goes. Perhaps it was this intricate intimacy between master and servant that was revealed when the Indian elite moved to London and discovered that despite their mastery of the British lifestyle, they were not regarded as equals. Although the Indians could look back on thousands of years rich with history within their own multicultural and multi-religious region, intellectual Indians with a British education felt that the British civilisation was somehow superior. The growing Indian middle class wanted to show that they too could be British, with all that entailed in terms of language, education and manners. Some Indian traditions were continued to preserve a certain sense of dignity, but mostly people learned to follow British customs.

A mild contempt gradually formed towards the ordinary Indians who had no education. The Indian elite generally dressed like the British, and were educated at Britain's best universities, like Gandhi, who had graduated with a law degree from Oxford. But whereas Gandhi denounced the British style of dress when he became politically active, his political friends like Muhammad Ali Jinnah, leader of the All-India Muslim League, wore a suit and tie. Regardless, it was believed that the Indians shouldn't have too much to do with the British colonial powers, and marrying English women was looked down upon.

I go into one of the shops to bring myself up to date, and look longingly at the rolls of fabric. Silk, brocade and cotton, side by side on specially made shelves. Gold embroidery. Silver embroidery. All ready to be sewn into saris or shalwar kameez. It is of silk that dreams are made. I pass my hands along the rolls of fabrics, close my eyes, and try to remember the few Pakistani weddings I've attended. I'm bombarded with sensory impressions, with smells and sounds. Muslims, Hindus and Sikhs from the subcontinent share many of the same wedding traditions: hundreds of guests, a bashful bride, and wild dancing late into the night.

I'm struck by how little I actually know about Hindus and Sikhs. I've visited Hindu temples, but never those of the Sikhs. The religious and cultural differences are real, and run especially deep in my parents' generation, where the partition of India is still in the blood, so to speak. On my way out of the shop I decide to visit the biggest Sikh temple in Britain, Gurdwara Sri Guru Singh Sabha Southall (SGSS) in Havelock Road. It cost £17.5 million to build, and was financed through contributions from affluent Sikhs over several years. I'm curious to see what it looks like.

The shops are smaller and the streets even narrower in the part of Southall where the temple is located. There are also many Somalis in this area, the last group of immigrants to have found their way here. The 6,000-square-metre building, with space for 3,000 visitors, is easily recognised. Muslims and Sikhs have traditionally always had a somewhat strained relationship to each other, since the Sikhs opposed the Muslim Mughal Empire in India and founded a separate kingdom in Lahore, in today's Pakistan.

Contemplating these tensions, I walk up the wide steps and into the changing rooms. Here, there are separate booths for men and women. Just in front of the entrance for women I see a box of shawls – I'm clearly not the first to forget to bring something to cover my hair. Everyone smiles warmly at me as I enter, but I'm uncertain as to how they would feel if they knew I was Muslim, not Sikh. They would probably have wished me welcome just the same. Up in the enormous hall there is dark blue wall-to-wall carpeting with geometric patterns, covered in white mats. Older women sit on benches along the walls, while the spaces for those who pray on the floor are divided by gender: the women sit to the left, the men to the right. It's almost like being in a mosque, but the segregation of the men and women is considerably more relaxed.

Sikhs seem to be less strict than Muslims when it comes to gender roles, but common to all ethnic groups with roots in the Indian subcontinent is that there are certain rules that apply to girls, and other rules for boys. Education is encouraged regardless of background, but young people are expected to marry. Preferably before they turn thirty. Divorce is often taboo, and thought to bring shame on the entire family. And interfaith marriages are often frowned upon.

I soon begin to feel restless in the Sikh temple. On my way out of the hall three elderly women give me a handful of warm halwa, a soft, unbaked dough made of semolina, flour and sugar, which has a slight hint of almond. The women have warm hands, and with their kind eyes and white dupattas covering their hair they remind me of my grandmothers, who have passed away. I walk down the wide marble staircase to the canteen. Rows of Sikh men are standing behind the enormous pots, handing out food that is served on a thali, a steel plate with five depressions in it. They chatter and laugh. High brushed steel tables have been set around the outer edge of the room, where some people are standing and eating, while others sit on the floor, completely at ease. Community is a core value among the Sikhs, and is often given as the explanation for why the Sikhs have had such great success within business and culture in Britain. All gurdwaras hand out free vegetarian meals consisting of rice, pickled vegetables, a little cucumber and tomato, chapatis and lentil curry. The meals are served every day, and it isn't just the Sikhs who come here to eat. An increasing number of people who do not practise Sikhism have found their way to the gurdwaras: the homeless and the poor. They are welcome as long as they cover their hair, and as long as they are not intoxicated.

I'm glad that I've visited a gurdwara, because the next day I travel to Ealing to meet an older Sikh woman. Harbinder Sodi welcomes me into her apartment in a well-kept street. She moved to London in 1960, along with her mother and two sisters. She roars with laughter when she tells me about the wine the Indian women drank every time a meal was served on the Italian-owned ship on which they came to England.

'I remember they got more and more funny the more they drank, they had no idea that it was alcohol they were drinking – they thought it was squash,' she laughs.

But life in Southall would turn out to be more challenging than Harbinder could have imagined. The seriousness of the situation became clear when she was met by her father at Victoria station. She hadn't seen him for three years. For the first time, she saw her father without a turban. His hair had been cut short. This wasn't a sight she had ever expected to see – Sikhs were not supposed to cut their hair. The prohibition was only relaxed in 1969 after significant debate.

Finding work was no easy task for the Indian immigrants who arrived in the British Isles, regardless of whether or not they shaved or removed their turban. Like the Caribbean immigrants, they were subjected to discrimination in both the property and labour markets. They were completely dependent on help from those who had arrived before them, and it was often the men who first tried their luck alone, before later reuniting with their families. The financial pressure on the men who came first was intense. The families who had stayed behind in their villages in Pakistan, India and Bangladesh expected money to be sent home. The men often saved as much as half of their income; by comparison, Englishmen saved hardly 5 per cent.

Workplace discrimination also affected those with a solid education. Endless stories of hundreds of applications being sent without receiving a single job interview circulated among frustrated academics, who had to make do with manual labour in order to provide for their families. Before leaving home, they had been issued an official certificate that documented their education, which was supposed to help them in their encounters with English employers, but the certificates turned out to be of little use. Nor did it help if they had studied at a British university.

Harbinder's father took the family to Southall. They lived in two rooms, which they rented from another Asian family. The home was of an entirely different standard than that Harbinder was used to in India, where the family belonged to the middle class. Older children who arrived were put in special classes for at least six months, to learn English. The school dinners also came as a shock. They weren't used to eating meat, boiled potatoes and peas – all without flavour. Harbinder took a packet of biscuits to school instead. But in Southall, Harbinder and her sisters quickly settled in, even though their parents often talked about going back to India. They sent money home, and also bought land in case the family should want to return, but Harbinder says that as the years went by it became clear that returning to India wasn't an option. The India they had left no longer existed.

She looks at me for a while, as if thinking about what she wants to say.

Then she leans forward.

'They didn't like us, I remember that to this day. After all these years, I still don't feel British. I've thought a lot about our clothing style, and wondered about why we were teased so much. I thought there was a whole world out there that the English ought to know more about, why did we have to adapt to everything that was English? I was even mocked when I took the table and chairs out of the house in the summer, so we could eat outside. The English people I knew said this was a very strange thing to do, but in India it's normal to follow the seasons and eat your meals outside when it's warm enough. The English did whatever they liked in India, so why shouldn't we do the same when we came to London? India was always depicted as being poor and awful in the newspapers. The ignorance was immense, and we were expected to adopt all the English customs. I'll never stop thinking that it's the hard work of immigrants in this country that has enabled Britain to become the nation it is today. We suffered under racism, accepted long working hours and changed ourselves to satisfy the requirements of the English, but even today we're regarded as foreigners. The Caribbean immigrants experienced exactly the same thing. But maybe it's our fault too, maybe we shouldn't have changed, and accepted all the demands that were made of us. Everything that made up our identity was erased.'

Her kind eyes are now full of anger.

Southall was gradually marked by white flight. The English disappeared from the neighbourhood, while an increasing number of people from the Indian subcontinent moved in. Southall became 'Little India'. These changes irritated the National Front, which had large groups of sympathisers in the 1970s. A number of them lived in Southall.

In 1976, eighteen-year-old student Gurdip Singh Chaggar was murdered in a racist attack. Hundreds of Asian youths took to the streets to demonstrate against the killing. And things would get worse. On 23 April 1979, the Anti-Nazi League arranged an anti-racist mustering in connection with a speech that was due to be given by the National Front.[1] Over 3,000 demonstrators turned out to protest; 2,000 police officers were ordered out on to the streets. The atmosphere was aggressive. In the clashes that followed, thirty-three-year-old anti-racist teacher Blair Peach died after receiving a blow to the head. The next day, 10,000 demonstrators took to the streets to protest the violence and racist attitudes of the police. The unrest united an entire neighbourhood.

While Southall's inhabitants struggled with riots and racism, life became difficult for Harbinder. Her father was suffering from depression, and her mother died. Harbinder and her sisters were left to themselves. During a summer holiday in India, Harbinder met a policeman and fell in love. They got married, and had two children, a boy and a girl. Harbinder's daughter Remy graduated with a law degree from Queen Mary University in London, and now lives in New York where she works as both an activist and documentarian.

'Southall is a place where time stands still. When I come here to go shopping, I'm shocked at how the people don't seem to have realised that the world has moved on,' she says, a sad expression on her face.

I've heard others say the same thing. They're right – these kinds of neighbourhoods recall memories of a bygone era, and are places that provide refuge to those who cannot or do not wish to accept the changes society insists upon. The problem is that at some point or other, these kinds of bell jars also start to suffocate those they protect.

*   *   *

Despite the apparent standstill in Southall, in the 1980s the neighbourhood was the birthplace of one of London's many cultural revolutions. Towards the end of the 1980s, while I was listening to punk and trying to be cool, my peers in Southall were starting to dance to some new pounding rhythms, their arms in the air. I quickly understood that something was afoot. The genre was bhangra, and it had originated among the Sikhs in the agricultural regions of Punjab. The music united everyone from the Indian subcontinent, and one person who especially loved to jump around to these beats was Bobby Friction from Southall. His enthusiasm for the music led him to the BBC, where he is currently one of the most popular DJs on the Asian Network, a flagship channel for British-Asian pop culture.

In the documentary *Pump Up the Bhangra* (2019), we follow Bobby as he traces the roots of this Indian music, showing how a generation of young Asians suddenly discovered dance music from a culture to which they belonged. Not Black, not white, but *brown*. 'This was our music. Finally!' Bobby says. The video clip from the 1980s shows a slender young man dancing to the heavy beats bhangra is known for. Today Bobby is almost fifty, but he still wears a leather jacket and an iconic moustache.

The bhangra musicians often played at weddings, and the music was so popular that the events were also frequented by strangers who wanted to dance. Back then, girls were not allowed to go out in the evenings, so separate clubs were arranged during the day, which led to a lot of skipping school. The girls had to hide their colourful Indian outfits under their strict school uniforms, so they could quickly tear off their school clothes as soon they arrived at the disco. Thinking about how conservative interpretations of Islam have taken such a central role among Muslims in Britain in recent years, it's quite incredible to watch the dance scenes in *Pump Up the Bhangra*, with Muslim boys and girls dancing close together. The change took place almost overnight, and long before 9/11. I remember how some of the girls in my circle of friends went from being alcohol-drinking party girls to suddenly covering up and never going out any more. I couldn't understand it, but Salman Rushdie's novels had got young British Muslims to take a good look in the mirror. They wanted to be ambassadors for Islam. To stop hating themselves. Even though I was in outsider in the Asian community, I was deeply fascinated by the youth culture in Southall. Probably because it represented a community I would never have access to. I received snippets of information from my cousins, who shared their coarse stories with me. They told me about gangs, about tough guys in leather jackets driving around in sports cars – preferably BMWs – and about secret relationships that transcended castes and religions; secret desires that remained hidden from their parents and beautifully captured in Gautam Malkani's brilliant novel *Londonstani* (2006).

When I'm back in the apartment after my trip to Southall, I flip through the pages of the book *Asian Britain: A Photographic History* (2013). I've looked at it many times before. It is my history I see in the images contained within it – my heritage. I turn the pages, past photographs of Lascars, nannies, Indian soldiers during the world wars, Indian restaurant owners, investors, newspaper reporters, lawyers, cricketers, authors, politicians, demonstrators, industrial workers, teachers, doctors, bus drivers, musicians . . .

London is brimming with repressed stories that can ultimately change our view of the colonial past. I suspect that there are many connections to today's London that have been neglected in the story that has been written so far. Luckily, things are changing. I also find images from Veeraswamy – London's first truly fine Indian restaurant. The photographs from the restaurant's first year show refined men in suits and women in dresses and elegant saris, standing along-side London's lords and ladies. The Indians are solemn, as custom often demanded at the time. Today, I don't think they'd be able to stop smiling if they could see how successful their descendants have become in London. And one of them has even become London's mayor.

In the footsteps of Sadiq Khan

'Welcome to Taj Stores', 'Geeta Sarees', 'Halal Meat and Poultry', 'Ambala Sweets' – the shopping streets in Tooting, south London, are full of shop names that leave no doubt. This is where you come if you're looking for food, gold jewellery or clothes from the Indian subcontinent.

I've lost count of how many times I've wandered up and down Tooting Broadway and Upper Tooting Road with my mother as she inspects and smells bunches of coriander, or carefully squeezes pomegranates, wrinkling her nose; as she examines mooli (long white radishes), orders the butcher to cut the meat into manageable pieces, sniffs mangoes or asks the women behind the glass counter at Ambala and Pooja Sweets to fill small boxes with Pakistani confectionery – gulab jamuns, jalebis and habshi halwa. She feels at home among the population here, which includes Tamils, Pakistanis and Indians. Tooting is not like Southall. Here, the energy is palpable. And not least, there are many Kenyan Asians in Tooting – the minority to which we belong.

The numerous Indian restaurants here are the reason that Tooting Broadway is referred to as the 'curry mile' among those in the know.[1] For the enthusiasts and connoisseurs, there is even a dedicated club: the Tooting Curry Club. Nowhere else is the regional culinary diversity that India represents as visible as it is in these streets. Here you can find ingredients from almost every nook and cranny of the Indian subcontinent, in large, well-maintained grocery stores. One of the oldest is Patel Brothers, on Upper Tooting Road. Ten-kilo bags of rice, chickpeas, lentils, onions and an abundant selection of spices lie spread throughout the simple shop.

The shop opened after the family left Uganda in 1973, when President Idi Amin had had enough of the Indians. An unconfirmed version of the story posits that Amin wanted to marry one of the richest people in Uganda, an Indian woman, but she refused; Amin reacted by throwing the Indians out of the country. Broken-hearted or not, in August 1972 Amin began an economic war on the around 100,000 Indians who had been living in Uganda for several generations, ever since the country was a British colony. The Indians were enterprising businesspeople, and important for the country's economy. But this didn't prevent Amin from ordering the expulsion of 50,000 of them. Horror stories of how the Ugandans turned against the Indians, and of hate seething in the country, are rife. Since many of the Indians were British citizens, London became a natural place to go. When the Patel family arrived in the city, there were hardly any shops here selling Indian goods. They worked from morning to night, importing everything they sold directly from India. After a few years they were able to expand their shop, and Patel Brothers became a Tooting institution.

I look out of one of the large windows from the shop. Right across the street are four family-owned shops that have recently closed for good – the buildings that house them are going to be torn down. The developer who purchased the premises is going to build a housing complex here. Small shops are vanishing, only to be replaced by generic chains – but there is hope. American Express, of all companies, has started the Small Stores campaign to stimulate the economy in the neighbourhood: when spending £10 or more in a local shop, American Express card users get £5 back.

'One of the world's coolest neighbourhoods' said the staff at *Lonely Planet* of Tooting in August 2017. Commentators in British newspapers went crazy, raving to their readers about how they lived there, or had long since known that Tooting was a great place. For some of us, this enthusiasm only confirmed what we had always known: south London *rules*. The districts south of the Thames have long been the capital's best kept secret, with Tooting as the jewel in the area's crown.

South London has more parks and green areas than the north of the city. One of the most interesting is Crystal Palace, which reportedly contains the world's first dinosaur statues, dating from 1854. Here you will also find Britain's largest and oldest outdoor pool, Tooting Beck Lido. The streets are fairly plain, but the smell of freshly ground coffee has grown stronger in recent years. Not far from Patel Brothers are several of the restaurants that Tooting is known for: at weekends there are long queues outside Dawat, Lahore Karahi and Spice Village, large, cafeteria-like premises where families gather. All the restaurants are in the same street, just a short stroll from the council estate where Mayor of London Sadiq Khan grew up – the Prince Henry Estate. And in case you were wondering, the Mirch Masala restaurant is Khan's favourite.[2]

The election of Sadiq Khan as London's mayor in 2016 was in my teary eyes an event just as huge as when Barack Obama was elected president of the United States. Of course, Rotterdam can boast being the first European city to elect a Muslim mayor, but London is, after all, the centre of the world. Khan is a child of London's shabbier streets. Unlike the city's previous mayor, Boris Johnson, who attended Eton and Balliol College, Oxford, having come from an affluent background, Sadiq Khan is the son of a Pakistani bus driver and a Pakistani seamstress. Khan beat Conservative candidate Zac Goldsmith, who like Johnson was Eton-educated and wealthy.

During the election, Goldsmith went after Khan's background hard, claiming he was a Muslim extremist who couldn't possibly unite London's population. But Goldsmith was wrong. London's residents would not succumb to fear. Instead, they supported Khan. With a political project that emphasised the construction of more afford- able properties for ordinary Londoners, improved transport and inclusivity, Khan won the election.

Sadiq Khan's childhood on the council estate in Tooting likely made him acutely aware of the kinds of challenges London struggled with throughout the 1970s and over the years that followed. During Khan's adolescence, his family was subjected to racism, and so he joined his local boxing club. After finishing high school he consid- ered becoming a doctor, but ended up studying law at North London University. He began his career as a human rights lawyer. I can just imagine the young Khan on the streets of Tooting. Perhaps he too was walking down Tooting Broadway on one of the occasions my sister and I had reluctantly been dragged there to visit my parents' friends and their children. Maybe Sadiq and I would have been friends had I grown up here. But there still would have been one significant difference between us, beyond which restaurant in Tooting we hold in highest regard: Khan was born in London, while I was born in Nairobi.

Is there a single street in London that doesn't contain a story from the British Empire? The houses in Tooting are full of them, and some of these stories are about Kenya. They're about people and their identities – my own identity included. My grandparents had no idea of the challenges those who left India to work in Kenya would have to face, nor how British immigration policy would have such far-reaching consequences for the family in the years after they passed away. But our lives have been shaped by the political deci-sions of the British.

Ever since the East African Protectorate was founded in 1895 by British merchants, and later transformed into the Colony and Protectorate of Kenya in 1920, the British in Kenya had estab-lished a close connection to India through the British East Africa Association. The following year, in 1896, they moved their head-quarters to Mombasa, crossing the Indian Ocean with hundreds of Indian employees who settled in Kenya. In 1896, the British government began to build railways along the 582-mile stretch from Mombasa to Lake Victoria. The railway line was completed in 1902, and named the Uganda Railway because it linked Uganda to the rest of the world. The British needed the Indians to construct and manage railways throughout East Africa.[3] Over 30,000 Indians, or 'coolies', as the British so contemptuously called the workers, came to Kenya. The Indians were not unfamiliar with Africa's east coast – they had traded in the area themselves, long before the arrival of the British. The period the British spent in Kenya is unfortunately yet another appalling chapter in British history.

In the book *Britain's Gulag: The Brutal End of Empire in Kenya*, by Harvard professor Caroline Elkins, British rule in Kenya is examined under a microscope. It reveals that the British not only had financial motives in the area, but that they also believed they had a moral responsibility to save the souls of the African people. The mentality of those in power was completely in line with perspectives of the day: the British were superior rulers, while the Kenyans were inferior and uncivilised. The British colonial powers were especially hard on the Kikuyu, the largest ethnic group in the country, who lived in the lushest areas near Mount Kenya. The Kikuyu were known for their rich cultural heritage and clan system in which everyone was deemed equal, but when their areas were occupied by British settlers, the lives of the Kikuyu were drastically changed. The British had the idea that the various regions should be led by different chieftains – a system that was completely alien to the Kikuyu and which created significant internal conflicts. The chieftains were tasked with recruiting workers and collecting taxes. The British ruling class in Kenya had little respect for the Kikuyu, and mocked the rituals they had passed down for generations. As the years went by, the appalling treatment of the Kikuyu people escalated. A number of attempts at rebellion against the British were made. In 1944, political organisation the Kenya African Study Union (KASU) was founded, and later became the Kenyan Africa Union – the precursor for what would become known as the Mau Mau movement.

Two important events took place in October 1952. On 3 October, Mau Mau rebels are said to have killed an Englishwoman, Mrs A. M. Wright, at her home in Thika, not far from Nairobi. Four days later, on 7 October, Senior Chief Waruhiu – one of the most ardent supporters of the British – was murdered in his car. The rounding up of 1.5 million Kikuyu people followed. The British established prison camps, where torture was widespread, and at least 100,000 Kikuyus died as a result of sexual violence, starvation, disease or exhaustion. The witness testimonies Elkins has gathered are horrifying. But the conditions at these camps would remain a British state secret until as recently as 2011 – all the official documents were hidden away at the Hanslope Park colonial archives in Buckinghamshire.[4]

Caught up in the midst of all this were around 200,000 Kenyans of Indian descent – a group with significant ethnic and religious diversity. Hindus. Christian Goanese. Sikhs. Muslims, from several schools. Gujaratis and Punjabis. But common to all of them was that they were referred to as Asians, since they were no longer Indians, and were an integrated part of the Kenyan workforce. They worked in the business sector, and were teachers, bureaucrats and doctors – like my father and his eldest brother. My dad worked at the Aga Khan hospital in Nairobi, where in the early 1960s Asians made up a third of the population, and he had travelled all around Kenya, helping the sick and welcoming new generations of Kenyans in the villages.

Hearing my parents speak about the years they spent in Kenya is like listening to a radio programme from a bygone era that almost seems made up. The English, Asians and Kenyans lived completely segregated. There were barbed-wire fences between the various areas in which they lived. People didn't mix. The racism was real.

My father remembers the Mau Mau uprising well. He supported the Kenyans, and my father's eldest brother, who was also a doctor, was tasked with inspecting the prison camps and had to warn the British that typhus had broken out. There were many years of unrest and violence. In 1963, Kenya finally became independent, and then the Asians were able to choose whether they wished to take Kenyan or British citizenship. The country's new prime minister and later president, Jomo Kenyatta, demanded that the Asians decide once and for all – were they British, or Kenyan? As part of Kenyatta's Africanisation policy, he informed the country's residents that Kenyans would be prioritised when jobs were filled. Property could be confiscated. Asians who chose to remain faithful to the British Queen risked losing their jobs and their homes. In 1967, Kenyatta decided that Asians who did not have Kenyan citizenship could not take their right to remain in the country as a given, even if they had been born there. Most of the Asians wanted to go to Britain. They were nervous about what might happen to them, now that Kenya had attained independence. Many British politicians probably choked on their tea when they realised that close to 120,000 Asians were now on their way to the heart of the Empire.

Labour Prime Minister Harold Wilson immediately implemented measures to prevent the Asians entering Britain, despite their British citizenship. An additional entry document would be required, and these would only be distributed in restricted numbers. These restrictions would not apply to the white settlers, however, who understood that their time in Kenya had come to an end.

The British sent a delegation to India in an attempt to convince India to take the Asians from Africa. But the Indians refused. We were British, not Indian.

BBC news broadcasts showed thousands of Kenyan Asians at the airport in Nairobi, ready to travel to London. In March 1968, the home secretary at the time, James Callaghan, suggested tightening the Commonwealth Immigrants Act of 1962 even further. The new amendments would prevent immigration from what the government referred to as 'the new Commonwealth countries'. Australia, Canada and New Zealand were classified as 'the old'. Several commentators suggested that these changes were racist. For the Asians in Kenya, the change in legislation caused chaos. Many who arrived in London were immediately deported, supposedly because their paperwork was not in order. They were sent to countries like Uganda or Tanzania, and risked being put in prison if they returned to London. Huge demonstrations against what many believed was a racist legislative amendment took place outside Downing Street.[5] But nothing helped.

I was born in Nairobi that year. My parents had good friends among the Kenyans, and my father was coming to the end of his training as a junior doctor. My father's eldest brother had become Jomo Kenyatta's personal doctor at this time, and my dad would step into the role whenever my uncle travelled to London to attend conferences. My uncle was present when the current president of Kenya, Uhuru Kenyatta, was born in 1961, and my dad once cared for him when he had a throat infection.

In 1970, we travelled to Britain because my father was going to undertake his postgraduate training there. We stayed. And forever became Kenyan Asians. And British.

In Kenya, the Asian population shrank dramatically, from almost 200,000 in 1963 to 78,000 in 1979.[6] Those who stayed continued to be an important part of Kenyan society. On Mombasa's sandy beaches, on plantations out on the plains and in small houses all over Nairobi, memories of a happy life were left behind.

'Choose me, Jyoti! And I promise you that our life will be the most amazing adventure!'

A young Indian man is staring deep into the eyes of the woman in front of him, there on the street in the city of Ahmedabad. She has to choose who she will marry, and she chooses him – Rasik. Together, they cross the Indian Ocean and settle in Kenya, where they enter into a successful collaboration with David, a young Kenyan from the Kikuyu tribe, who isn't permitted to own land or trade in goods because of the laws introduced by the British settlers. At first, everything goes well. David, Rasik and Jyoti form a trio, one that makes life work. But when David joins the Mau Mau uprising, the Kenyan liberation movement, the dream turns into a nightmare. Close friends become enemies. Rasik and Jyoti travel to London, where they have to start all over again – this time facing new challenges.

Witnessing a play that captures what could have been my parents' life is rare, even in London. I'm at the Bush Theatre in Shepherd's Bush, west London, watching the play *An Adventure*, written by up-and-coming dramatist Vinay Patel. Jyoti and Rasik struggle with homesickness and discrimination at their workplaces. Jyoti becomes a union activist, one of 'the striking women in saris', as the media referred to them when they stood outside the factories in the 1970s. Jyoti's husband tries to move up the ranks at his job by becoming as English as possible, but it doesn't help. Their amazing adventure ends with a journey back to Kenya to see David again, and the reunion is a painful one.

Until now, I've mostly looked to journalist and author Yasmin Alibhai-Brown for inspiration. She is of Ugandan Asian descent, and has written a beautiful memoir of her childhood, *No Place Like Home* (1995). She's been the only person who understands where I actually come from, and I've had the pleasure of meeting her several times. I've always felt reassured, and even proud, after speaking with her. We see eye to eye on so many issues, being liberal, secular, Muslim women working in the media.

'I've had so many comments from people who have seen the play. They tell me that they find parallels to their own lives in it. They're so happy and grateful,' says Vinay Patel.

'I can totally understand that,' I say to Vinay. 'I saw my own family's history there, and I don't think that's something I've ever seen on stage before. We Kenyan Asians live a somewhat invisible life. We don't fit into the usual pigeonholes people tend to operate with when they think of people from the Indian subcontinent.'

I feel that I've finally met somebody who understands who I am. I don't need to explain anything to Vinay, as I often do when I meet other immigrants from India or Pakistan. A lot of people know that there are Indians in South Africa and Uganda. But Kenya?

We're sitting in the British Film Institute's cinema in the Southbank Centre, just beside the Thames. Around us buzz famous and lesser-known film directors and film geeks. The BFI's annual London Film Festival is in full swing, and all the film industry's elite are here. Vinay also dreams of writing for film one day, but for now, he has enough to do – on 11 November 2018, his episode of *Doctor*

Who aired on the BBC. He was the first person with an Asian background to write for the legendary British sci-fi series.

'When I started working on the play, I had to take a deep dive into my family's history. It was painful for everybody. My grandparents came here with nothing, and had to start all over again. They were spat on, and even those on the left, who were supposed to be their allies, refused to serve them when they went to the local pub. They had nothing. They carried this pain with them, and my parents observed it,' says Vinay, who is now thirty-six.

He grew up in Bexley, in south-east London, where his parents run a pharmacy. It was expected that he would take the business over, or become a doctor, but Vinay wanted to read books and watch *Star Trek* – not Bollywood movies. Reluctantly, Vinay's parents accepted his plans to study at the Royal Central School of Speech and Drama, and when his work was shown on the BBC they were bursting with pride.

'I have friends who have taken their parents to see *An Adventure*. Their families became closer afterwards. We simply have to have this conversation – I now understand why my grandmother had her rigid attitudes about Black men, and I almost forced her into having a pretty difficult conversation about prejudice when I wrote my episode of *Doctor Who*, seeing as it was about the partition of India and Pakistan. That's how we can move forwards,' Vinay says.

He speaks quickly and enthusiastically: about his need to make stories from the age of colonialism into normal stories that affect everybody, not just those who come from the subcontinent; about the importance of diversity in the type of stories that are told; about raising up new young talents; and about his childhood in Bexley, where he was almost the only person to come from an Indian-Kenyan background.

I have to ask him about *EastEnders* – the London series of all London series. Around 6,000 episodes of the show have aired since

1985. Yesterday's episode is fresh in my mind as I sit there with Vinay. One of the main characters was pregnant and felt unwell at the local Boots, where she was assisted by an older, extremely motherly Indian woman who taught her some breathing techniques. Really? Do all Indian women have to have some innate knowledge of yoga? Vinay laughs as I recount the episode. *EastEnders* has received a lot of criticism for its stereotyped representations of minorities over the years.

'I know exactly what you mean! But at least we can say that we've come a little further than when we thought it was terrific if the credits included an Asian name – no matter what the person had done. Even if it was being responsible for the catering!' Vinay chuckles.

I take his point, but wrinkle my nose anyway.

'I was at least happy to see an Indian in the *Patrick Melrose* series, that was fantastic. It made it more believable. We were after all part of London life back then,' I say to Vinay.

Prasanna Puwanarajah, who is of Tamil descent and plays Johnny Hall, Patrick Melrose's close friend in the series, is a close friend of Vinay.

'He trained as a surgeon before he became an actor. His father is a dentist and his mother a psychiatrist. At first, he was only given roles as a doctor or a terrorist. But now he's managed to break out of that pattern, and plays pretty much everything.'

Benedict Cumberbatch – perhaps the most quintessentially British actor of recent years – who plays Patrick Melrose hasn't had to struggle against such limitations. He's even played a character with the curious name Khan Noonien Singh in the sci-fi series *Star Trek*.

The sun dazzles me as I leave the dimly lit BFI café after my conversation with Vinay. I walk over to Waterloo Bridge and look down at the Thames, which is dark blue and beautiful today. I can hear the Kinks' 'Waterloo Sunset' at the back of my head and see if I can see

Terry and Julie. There are several hundred thousand of us who are connected to those first civil servants who worked for the East India Company. Our lives have been shaped by British imperialism, and later by passionate nationalists. Revolutions and rebellions. Our parents conquered London's streets. For us. We are now one with the city.

We are London.

Arab London – Edgware Road, Knightsbridge, Wembley

The Arab and the princess

'Dodi was a hero!'

Young Egyptian feminist Sana eyes me with her penetrating gaze. She takes out a packet of tobacco and rolls what might qualify as the world's thinnest cigarette, twists around on the floor in an attempt to find a comfortable sitting position on the rug in front of me, then lights up. I'm sitting on a sofa in a small, north London apartment inspired by Scandinavian minimalism. Sana is slender, her hair pulled back into a large ponytail. Over her fitted, sleeveless linen dress she wears an oversized woollen cardigan, which constantly slips off her shoulders.

'He was an idol for the Egyptian and Arab working class in this country. They were so proud of him. He was an Egyptian man who had managed to get one of the colonial powers' own daughters. When Al-Fayed was given the cold shoulder by the British upper class, the colonial powers revealed their arrogance and racism once again. That's why the story is so much more than a sad tale about a princess. It did irreparable damage to the relationship between the Egyptians and British. You have to look at the love story from that perspective – their relationship threatened the monarchy,' Sana says.

Mohamed Al-Fayed and his son Dodi are symbols of the tense relationship between Britain and Egypt, between British aristocrats and Egyptian nationalists; the leaders of empire and the children of empire. Film producer Dodi and Princess Diana got together in 1997, and their relationship created a certain furore because Dodi was seen as a playboy. He was also Muslim, and therefore not suitable marriage material. Was their love the consummation of the close ties the British have always had to Egypt?

The Suez Canal was of strategic importance to the British Empire, and British archaeologists had long been fascinated by Egypt. Clear signs of this obsession can be seen all across London, not only in the British Museum, which contains the largest collection of ancient Egyptian relics outside Egypt, but also in Camden, where the entrance to Carreras Cigarette Factory is guarded by two black Egyptian cats. On Victoria Embankment is Cleopatra's Needle, a 21-metre-high granite obelisk. The monument was a gift from the Egyptian King Muhammad Ali in 1878, and later flanked by steel benches shaped like camels. At Holborn Underground station, passengers are greeted by murals of Egyptian mummies. Egyptology was hugely popular among the Victorians, and the Arabs were studied through a prism of titillating exoticism and fear. This is a state of affairs that hasn't much changed, and which has shaped the relationship between the British upper class and Mohamed Al-Fayed.

We are far from the extravagance of Harrods, the popular department store in Knightsbridge. Should you have millions in the bank, Harrods is able to cover all your needs – everything from exclusive perfumes and diamonds to extravagant apartments in Dubai. Millions of customers spend their money at Harrods each year. Some even spend hundreds of thousands of pounds on a single ring or a handbag from Hermès. Others display their wealth outside the store – on Brompton Road. When young men from the Arab states of the Persian Gulf come here to party, or celebrate the Muslim festival of Eid, the areas of Knightsbridge, Kensington and Mayfair are thick with luxury cars. The vehicles are flown in on special planes that have space for these motorised gems. The most luxurious of them are covered in Swarovski crystals or in rose gold.

Ever since Harrods was founded in 1834 by Charles Henry Harrod, the store has, to borrow a cliché, focused on offering its customers a unique experience. The department store was long regarded as a British treasure, right up until 1985 when the cash-rich Egyptian Al-Fayed brothers acquired House of Fraser, the company that owned Harrods. The beloved British department store was suddenly in foreign hands. Arab hands.

The acquisition of Harrods sent shockwaves through the British establishment, but it was simultaneously Mohamed Al-Fayed's ticket into British society and the royal family. At the head office from which he ran the company hung four royal seals, which confirmed the royal family's close ties to the institution. Harrods also sponsored the Windsor Horse Show, where Prince Philip was both president and a rider. Al-Fayed would now be able to sit beside the Queen in the royal box. The son of a teacher, raised in a family of modest means in Alexandria and mocked by the British press for having decorated his name with the prefix 'Al-', was finally where he had always dreamed of being: among the truly rich. All the years of hard work and countless hours spent devising new strategies to move up and get ahead had finally paid off.

With the charismatic Mohamed Al-Fayed at the helm, Harrods was transformed. One hundred years after the first escalator in Harrods had been switched on, the Egyptian Escalator began to move. The escalator, located at the centre of the department store, is a tribute to Egyptian mythology. A dedicated Egyptian Room, which contains several busts of Al-Fayed, was also built. The work is said to have cost Al-Fayed over £35 million.

Both the Egyptian Room and the Egyptian Escalator now have listed status. I never know whether to laugh or be impressed on the occasions I take the escalator, because it's easy to see the vulgarity in such excess. But Al-Fayed is so much more than an Egyptian businessman with questionable taste.

Sana tells me that her mum moved back to Egypt.

'My mum couldn't handle living the hard life alone. She grew up wealthy. Egyptians like to be comfortable – that's why Mum moved home. Egyptians in London always move back, because they don't want to be British. Since Egyptians generally have a high level of education, they have plenty of options. They go home at least twice a year on holiday and then eventually retire there, where they live the good life with their own chauffeurs and a big social network. Egyptians are pretty bourgeois,' says Sana.

Britain – along with much of the world – was struck by shock and consternation when on 31 August 1997 the news broke that Princess Diana and Dodi had been killed in a car accident in the Pont de l'Alma tunnel in Paris. They were being pursued by paparazzi; their driver, who apparently lost control of the car, was also thought to have been intoxicated. Everybody cried. I cried. But few of us spared a thought for Mohamed Al-Fayed, who had lost his son. Dodi was buried in a quiet Muslim ceremony and interred on the family's estate in Surrey, where Al-Fayed has erected a memorial to his son.

A short time after the tragedy, Mohamed Al-Fayed made it clear that he simply did not buy the accident theory. He thought the couple were the victims of a planned murder. The reason for this? Their relationship was burdensome for the British royal family and the British government.[1] Even the prime minister at the time, Tony Blair, is said to have been worried about the blossoming love affair between the couple. The relationship between Mohamed Al-Fayed and British high society was already far from cordial. He had twice been refused British citizenship, mainly because he had paid Members of Parliament to ask questions in the House of Commons on his behalf. The 1994 'cash for questions' scandal, as it became known, resulted in two Conservative MPs being suspended. The relationship turned stone cold. The royal family stopped shopping at Harrods, while Egyptians in London were furious at how Al-Fayed was treated by the English royals. In 1998, British journalist Tom Bower published the unauthorised biography *Fayed*, in which Dodi and Al-Fayed are depicted as unrestrained and vulgar playboys. According to Bower, Al-Fayed practically manipulated his son into pursuing Diana. Sana tells me that she feels sick to her stomach when she thinks about the story.

'Al-Fayed was no saint, but the way the tabloids treated him was just beyond the pale, and totally in keeping with the British view of Arab men as fawning and untrustworthy. This has deep roots in colonialism.'

At the time of writing, eighty-eight-year-old Al-Fayed has completely withdrawn from public life.

Sana has real grassroots experience. When the political movement that would later become known as the 25 January Revolution broke out in Egypt in January 2011, Egyptians in London mobilised in solidarity with their countrymen. Hundreds of Egyptians who had had enough of President Hosni Mubarak's endless regime gathered outside the Egyptian embassy in Mayfair to show their disgust. Egyptians from different backgrounds gathered to protest together, forming a community Sana had never experienced before. After Mohamed Morsi, who won the presidential election in 2012, became the victim of a coup d'état, many members of the Muslim Brotherhood were granted political asylum in Britain. In London, they mostly keep a low profile.

I am very intrigued by Sana's analysis of Dodi and Diana, and the way she describes the Egyptians. The ones who live in London are a very multifaceted group. She rejects so many stereotypes. Or am I just experiencing my own preconceptions of who Egyptian women are?

When I studied international relations at the London School of Economics in the late 1990s, there were very few lecturers besides white English men in suits. Nor were there many others on the course from Muslim backgrounds. Those of us from Muslim families conspired together, casting meaningful glances at each other whenever Islam appeared on the syllabus. We missed learning more about political Islam and the complex relationship between Egypt and the British Empire. We rarely heard about the role of Egyptian women who were later to be highlighted during the revolution in 2011, nor did we delve into the Muslim Brotherhood and their important legacy in Egypt. But that was before 11 September 2001, when a new world order took over. Little did we know the kind of future that awaited us: a time when Islam would suddenly define us in a way we really did not like.

The political unrest in the Middle East has constantly crossed national borders, and caused both explosions and riots on London's streets. There are few places you can go that capture the Arabs' history in London better than Edgware Road and nearby Bayswater.

The scent of roses

Marble Arch – a real arch of marble, inspired by the Arch of Constantine in Rome. But no matter how beautiful and magnificent Marble Arch may be, it cannot hide the fact that the area is one of London's busiest junctions. Even in the surrounding park it's hard to escape the noise of the buses and cars. Here, touristy Oxford Street meets filthy-rich Park Lane, which again meets cosmopolitan Bayswater Road – the entry point to one of the oldest Arab districts in London.[1]

The smell of sweet tobacco and cardamom is a strong presence here. Young Arab men wearing Adidas sweatpants and Gucci caps saunter down the street, which is full of Arab restaurants, the tables outside them busy with activity around the water pipes. My gaze constantly encounters posters of Mohamed Salah, the Egyptian Liverpool player, along with advertisements for hair salons for women only. At the hotels in the area, parties exclusively for Arab women are held, with female DJs.

Dusk has fallen by the time I walk past the neon signs that shine from the cafés. Edgware Road is like a condensed version of the Middle East. Here you'll find people from Morocco, Iraq, Algeria, Turkey, Syria and Egypt side by side, with all the tensions this brings with it. London is where major international political conflicts play out at street level, not just in the empty phrases spoken around negotiating tables in expensive hotels. All this is naturally linked to British wanderlust.

The imperialistic tentacles of the British didn't just reach the Indian subcontinent, Caribbean and Africa – they also twisted their way through large parts of the Middle East: Egypt, Iraq, Kuwait, Qatar, Yemen, Bahrain, Muscat, Oman and Jordan. The diplomatic ties to Syria, Iran, Lebanon, Turkey and especially Saudi Arabia have always been close, but rarely problem-free. A dramatic situation arose when the British suggested giving the Jews their own homeland in Palestine – in all likelihood because they didn't wish to settle them in their own country. The establishment of the state of Israel in 1948 has been an ongoing source of conflict, to put it mildly, and Israel's existence goes to the very heart of British politics. Mayor of London Sadiq Khan has had to tolerate significant criticism for his sympathies for and connections with Palestinian freedom fighters – something that has caused deep divisions within the Labour Party. Britain's close links to Palestine have also resulted in a significant number of Palestinians settling in London.

'Shisha?' a waiter tempts me, showing me a water pipe. I shake my head, returning his smile as I continue down the street. The shisha cafés in London are meeting places for Arabs young and old, but there are strikingly few women to be found at them.

As the smoke seeps out, tips are shared about how the tobacco is best enjoyed. Is it best to use ice cubes or rosewater in the pipe? Is traditional or modern tobacco best? Strangely enough, young Arabs often find that their parents more easily accept them smoking shisha than ordinary cigarettes. Smoking a shisha is regarded as an authentic activity, and Arab parents prefer that their children hang out at these cafés rather than go to nightclubs.

But the tradition of smoking shisha and drinking coffee hasn't always been seen as acceptable. When the cafés appeared in Cairo,

Baghdad, Damascus and Medina in the 1400s, they were controversial. Scholars wanted to ban the drinking of coffee, which they believed intoxicated people, and wished to close the cafés, which they believed encouraged immoral behaviour. When they realised that this would be impossible, the scholars began to frequent certain cafés in order to give them their blessing. They are now an integrated part of Arab working-class life, and provide an alternative to the pubs Arab men rarely visit – not necessarily because they serve alcohol, but because the pubs are the home of the white working class.

The women in Edgware Road reflect the diversity of Arab women in London and the Middle East: emancipated, liberal, conservative, religious – all of them are here. Women in niqabs and floating black abayas that cover their entire bodies walk alongside those who are heavily made-up. But the belly dancers in the restaurants on Edgware Road are not Arab – it is European women who swing their hips, fulfilling the clichés promoted by the films of Hollywood, where since time immemorial dreams of harems have perpetuated views of 'us' and 'them'.

I make my way to Green Valley, an Arabic supermarket just around the corner. The shelves are full of fruit and vegetables that are difficult to find in Norway. In a corner of the shop a young man stands behind a glass counter, selling variants of Arabic coffee with cardamom, *kahwah*. The smell is alluring. I also discover a pick 'n' mix stand, but rather than being full of mass-produced jelly sweets this one features Turkish confectionery in kiwi, banana, mint and strawberry flavours; nougat dipped in honey and almonds, pistachio and walnuts.

I catch myself becoming rather dazzled by all the wealth I see along Edgware Road, but if you look closely, you'll notice that this part of London is not completely free of poverty. The black market is extensive. Those who work on Edgware Road as waiters, dishwashers, refuse collectors and cooks are part of the casual economy upon which London is so dependent. A number of the men are refugees from the civil wars in the Middle East. The men are often single, and live together in small apartments a little north of Edgware Road.

The sound of sizzling meat hits me as I walk through the door of Maroush Express. The young men in their white uniforms behind the counter are working quickly with the meat being grilled. Enormous bowls of salad stand ready to be arranged and served. Every Middle Eastern culinary classic you could wish for can be had here: hummus, tabbouleh, kibbeh, falafel, soujouk. The premises have been decked out with a few rows of red sofas, tables in various colours and simple wooden chairs – you're not supposed to stay here very long. At one of the tables sits the Palestinian-Egyptian-British film director Saeed Taji Farouky.[2] He's a gentle, pensive young man in his thirties. Saeed grew up in a wealthy Egyptian-Palestinian family, with parents who made sure that he was born in London – they wanted their son to be a British citizen, and insisted that he speak English rather than Arabic early on to ensure that he would be fully integrated. Saeed's parents had grown up in Egypt, and it wasn't until he was around ten years old that Saeed learned he was actually Palestinian.

'My father didn't want to trap me in Palestinian nationalism. I'm glad he made that choice because I've never been a nationalist, and nor would I have enjoyed being raised as a hardcore nationalist. I was able to choose for myself. Nor were my parents very concerned about their Arab roots, and religion meant very little to them. My Egyptian mother came from an extremely liberal, intellectual family. When I went to nursery school, I realised that my Arab friends came from homes where there was much more focus on preserving what was Arabic. They spoke Arabic together, ate Arabic food, and the interiors of their homes reflected their roots. You know, the low sofas, thick rugs and gilded coffee pots? Clichés, but still necessary reminders,' Saeed says.

These homes. Tiny treasure troves. Insignificant things to some; symbols of destiny and hope for others. But although his childhood lacked Arab influences, as an adult Saeed has spent a lot of time in places like Cairo, Jordan and Morocco, where he learned to speak Arabic fluently and became more confident in his Palestinian identity.

'I felt that I had to explore that part of my identity, and now I feel a strong natural connection to my Arab background. I've become an activist, for better or worse. Even though I was born in England, I'm not English – I'm Palestinian. For me, being English is about a culture, and I feel alien in the English culture. But the Palestinian, the Arab culture on the other hand – that's where I feel at home. I've also noticed it in my work as a film director. I tell stories in a different way, taking inspiration from an Arabic narrative tradition,' Saeed says.

Saeed belongs to a long history of Arab immigration to London. The first Arabs are thought to have come to London at some point in the early 1800s. This was when Yemenis and Somalis from the coastal towns found their way to England. Later came the Egyptians, who after Britain took control of Egypt have always had close ties to Whitehall. Like those from the other colonies, Egyptian intellectuals flocked to London as early as the turn of the last century in order to get an education. At the same time, the rebellion against the British in their homeland became more organised, and in 1919 the Egyptian Revolution took place.

In 1933 the Arabic Cultural Association was formed, where diplomats and Orientalists – as it was acceptable to call oneself back then – met to cultivate the Arab cultural scene. Throughout the 1930s and parts of the 1940s, there was a buzzing intellectual scene among the Arabs in London, and the University of Oxford had its own Anglo-Arab Union. The Arab–Israeli conflict of 1948 would show just how dependent Arab leaders were on the British ruling class, who to varying extents had used them as yes-men. This dependence also became more visible as anti-colonial forces began to gather strength, and the Israeli–Palestinian conflict became evident on the streets.

One person who captured this unique time when intellectuals from the Arab nations came to study in London, and especially at Oxford and Cambridge, was Sudanese author Tayeb Salih, who wrote the novel *Season of Migration to the North* (1966, translated into English three years later). The book's protagonist, a poet educated in Britain, returns home to his village where he meets a mysterious new resident, Mustafa Sa'eed. He's been in London for a long time, associating with the British elite – with catastrophic consequences. The novel is a gripping depiction of the British colonial powers and the burgeoning nationalism among those in the midst of empire.

The role of the British in the establishment of Israel also meant that London was marked by the political fronts in the Middle East. In 1969, the Popular Front for the Liberation of Palestine (PFLP) began a series of bomb attacks against Israeli and 'Zionist'-owned shops in London. In July, a bomb exploded outside Marks & Spencer on Oxford Street. The following month, the offices of the Zim Israel Navigation Company on Regent Street were struck by a blast. And the attacks continued. Throughout the 1970s, the British and residents of London were hit by a number of riots and explosions linked to conflicts in the Middle East.

Another factor would also come to mean much for the close relationship between Britain and the Arabs – the discovery of oil in 1938. The ruling families in Kuwait, Bahrain, Qatar, Saudi Arabia and the United Arab Emirates all had close ties to London, and the city became a natural place to invest money. Arabs from the Arabian Peninsula became known by the Arabic term *khaleeji*.

Unlike the intellectual Arabs who arrived in the early 1900s, and who had fortified their position among the British through exclusive clubs and dedicated newspapers, the *khaleeji* stood out. They didn't intend to settle permanently in London, and had no intention of adapting to fit in. The first generation had dressed in Western clothes, in suits and trouser suits. But when the oil sheiks and their wives came to London in the 1970s, they wore traditional tunics. The women were covered from head to toe, their faces included, which attracted attention among the residents of London, who at the time were not used to seeing women covered in this way.

The Arab families spent enormous sums of money in London's fashionable districts. The men became notorious for their aggressive sexual behaviour in London's casinos and nightclubs, which confirmed existing prejudices held among the British that the Arabs were relatively uncivilised. In the newspapers, the Arab sheiks were constantly mocked. They established their own hospitals, including the exclusive Cromwell Hospital in South Kensington, which with its blue-tinted windows is impossible not to notice. At the exclusive doctors' offices in Harley Street and St John's Wood, famed for their medical expertise, the owners employed their own Arab doctors.

At some point, British universities discovered that they could also recruit students from the Gulf states – for significant sums of money. The Arab student community, which had previously mainly consisted of students from Iraq, Egypt, Palestine, Jordan and Syria, was thereby expanded with young Arabs who were not quite as interested in Marxism or post-colonialism as they were in partying and expensive cars.

The 1970s were not only characterised by the gleeful spending of oil money, but also by political positioning. Intelligence services from various Arab states would eventually wage war on each other on London's streets. Yemen's former prime minister was murdered outside the Lancaster Gate Hotel in 1977, and two Syrian embassy employees died when a Volvo exploded on Stafford Street near Piccadilly Circus, on New Year's Eve that same year. The vehicle's roof was blown off, and the two men were found burned to death inside it. A couple of days later, the Palestine Liberation Organisation's representative in London, thirty-six-year-old Said Hammami, was shot and killed at his office in Mayfair.

In the 1980s, Libyan dictator Muammar Gaddafi began hunting his political enemies in London, and in April 1980 two men shot and murdered Libyan journalist and dissident Mohamed Mustafa Ramadan near Regent's Park Mosque. One of the most shocking events took place when a bomb exploded at a newsagent's in Queensway, Bayswater, which sold Arabic newspapers. A few minutes later, another bomb exploded in front of L'Auberge, a nightclub whose owner was Lebanese. A third bomb was discovered in Kensington Road, and later in the evening yet another bomb was detonated in Queensway. Nobody was charged for these crimes, but the evidence pointed to Libyan terrorists.

Saeed's father kept a low profile during this period, and stayed out of politics.

'He also raised me to lie low, said that we should choose the path of least resistance. I think that was because of his background as a refugee, and the fact that he had experienced two wars in Egypt and the civil war in Lebanon. He didn't want us getting involved in dramatic events, and worked hard to ensure that we could live in safe surroundings. But I'm not afraid to raise my voice,' says Saeed, who now sits on the board of the Arab British Centre (ABC). The centre, situated just a few minutes from Fleet Street in the centre of London, opened in 1977 on the initiative of the Council for the Advancement of Arab British Understanding, after several years of unrest following the establishment of Israel. In 1989, the centre became politically neutral.

The Arab British Centre has to constantly work hard to secure financial funding. Arabs from the various states are not necessarily interested in supporting each other, and the revolutions in the Arab countries have made forming a community complicated. Those from the United Arab Emirates and Saudi Arabia have apparently stopped shopping at Harrods – or 'Harrabs', as the department store is also known – because it is now owned by businesspeople from Qatar. Instead, they now shop at London's two other exclusive stores: Harvey Nichols and Selfridges.

Everything relating to Arab high-level politics is controversial – not just Palestine. The Arab Spring, the wars in Syria and Iraq, the founding of IS – all of this has contributed to making life for Arabs in London more difficult. Saeed is also worried about increasing nationalism, and believes that this is why there is no environment in which Arabs can gather and help each other in London. The ideology of Pan-Arabism that filled the Arabs with visions and hope in the 1960s is now dead.

The Israeli–Palestinian conflict is just one of many inflamed wounds in London. Saeed can't even bear to comment on it. The war in the Gulf in 1991, and again in 2003, also had massive consequences – politically, but also for the composition of the Arab population in London. Immigration from Iraq increased significantly. Around 10,000 Iraqis obtained British citizenship in the eight years between 1992 and 2000 – a doubling of the figure from the previous thirty years.

The myth of the Arab man as terrorist gained a foothold. In the 1980s, Arab men in black suits and Arab sheiks began to appear as Libyan or Iranian agents in the most innocent of films, and this stereotyping continues today. After the terror attacks in New York and Washington on 9/11, the situation for Arab men worsened even further. Saeed was often stopped by the police; offensive remarks were thrown at him whenever he took the Underground.

'Because I work as an independent film director and am therefore shielded from a normal working life, I'm luckily spared much of the racism that I know goes on in workplaces, or where people do a lot of networking,' Saeed says.

Out on Edgware Road, we part ways. Sirens howl relentlessly as I make my way towards Bayswater Road, which runs alongside Hyde Park. Not far away is Holland Park, another green oasis where peacocks wander freely and which features two Japanese gardens, often enjoyed by the area's rich Arabs.

Close by is the Leighton House Museum, built in the 1860s by Victorian artist Lord Frederic Leighton. Leighton was so smitten with the Arab aesthetic that he constructed the Arab Room, a luxurious tribute to Islamic architecture. The music video to 'Golden Brown' by the Stranglers, from 1981, was partly recorded here – as was that for Spandau Ballet's huge hit, 'Gold'. Halfway through the music video, vocalist Tony Hadley can be seen playing with golden water from the pool in the centre of the room as he sings: 'Gold!' It must have struck a certain chord with London's Arabs as they strolled past, just outside.

Holy war in London

Tavistock Square in Bloomsbury. A classic piece of London, with a park surrounded by stately houses from the early 1880s. Charles Dickens lived here while writing *Bleak House, Hard Times* and *Little Dorrit.* At the square's centre, a statue of Mahatma Gandhi has been erected. Gandhi witnessed many bloody misdeeds in his fight against the British, but he would probably have collapsed in horror had he witnessed what took place in Tavistock Square on 7 July 2005.

Eighteen-year-old Hasib Hussain had left his hometown of Leeds early that morning, together with three other young men. To all appearances, Hussain was an ordinary teenager, interested in cricket and computers. Like many other Pakistani immigrants in the area, his parents were low-paid workers, proud of their roots. Nobody noticed anything strange about Hussain as he arrived in King's Cross station together with his friends. Each of them was carrying a rucksack. After arriving at the station, they went their separate ways. Hussain is thought to have taken the number 30 bus towards Euston. When the bus drove into Tavistock Square, it exploded right in front of the premises of the British Medical Association. Footage from surveillance cameras inside the building shows people running into the premises in terror just seconds after the blast, which left thirteen people dead. The bomb was one of four that would be detonated over the course of an hour that morning.

Thirty-nine people died after suicide bombings on the Underground at Aldgate, Edgware Road and King's Cross. With the addition of the thirteen individuals who lost their lives in Tavistock Square, a total of fifty-two people died in the attacks. Seven hundred were injured. Political commentators pointed to Britain's role in the Iraq War as a triggering factor.

Two years earlier, on 15 February 2003, almost a million people had marched through London's streets to demonstrate against the war. I was there, too. With my husband I walked beside pensioners, single mothers, bearded Islamists, families with small children, nuns – an extraordinarily varied crowd of people. The atmosphere was calm. And perhaps this is why I've never quite got over the terrorist attacks that took place in London two years later. It seemed so unthinkable that anyone would choose to attack residents of London – a city where hundreds of thousands had stood united against the war.

In the neighbourhood of Wembley, in north-west London, sat a former jihadist, a holy warrior who had fought in the Afghan mujahideen to drive out the Russians, who had occupied Afghanistan since 1979. He was contemplative. It was time to make his voice heard. He wanted to caution his fellow believers against listening to the fanatical voices of Islamic extremists like Syrian Omar Bakri, British-Pakistani Anjem Choudary and Egyptian Abu Hamza. These men used their freedom of speech to spread hate, attracting young Muslims searching for greater meaning in their lives to a mosque in north London: Finsbury Park Mosque.

The clouds are heavy as I take the Overground to Wembley one day in October. I prefer to take the Overground trains rather than the Tube whenever I can, to see more of the city. As I approach Wembley,

I catch sight of the new stadium that opened in 2007: elegant modern architecture with an iconic arch. I miss the old one, which had two beautiful white towers with cupolas and flags on the top. But England needed a new stadium. One of the towers has since been placed on a housing estate in Neasden as a memorial.

Outside Wembley Central station towers a modern apartment complex, clad in cheerful colours. Just next door I find a world-famous Indian astrologist who can offer solutions to all your problems, be they in your marriage, relating to the presence of magic in your life or a lack of education. *One Hundred Percent Satisfaction Guaranteed.*

I quickly recognise Abdullah Anas in the square outside the station, even though the photograph of him I've seen in his recent autobiography is over twenty years old.[1] Anas came to London in 1995, after he accomplished what he refers to as his mission: driving the Russians out of Afghanistan. He had come from Algeria as a young man, ready to face the Soviets, one of many thousands of Muslims who came from all across the world to fight beside the Afghans. Anas fought with Osama bin Laden, Mujahideen leader Ahmad Shah Massoud and Abdullah Yusuf Azzam, who later became his father-in-law. But unlike bin Laden, Anas didn't want to participate in the holy war. When civil war took over, and the Taliban was established, Anas no longer wished to be in the country. He was frightened at the way things were going, and thought the holy war the Taliban and al-Qaeda wanted to fight was unacceptable. He randomly chose to seek asylum in London and not Paris, which would have been a more natural choice since Algeria had been a French colony. Anas believes this turned out to be a blessing.

'In the Koran, it says that Allah has made us different because we shall learn from each other. When I read the Surah, I couldn't imagine that such a place existed. But when I came to London, I realised that this was where everything the Surah represented could be found. In London, people from all over the world live side by side. Even enemies live right next door to each other, socialise with each other. What other city can lay claim to such diversity?'

Anas enthusiastically throws his arms wide.

'I don't see even a hint of this in the capitals of Muslim countries, in Riyadh or Doha,' he adds, eyebrows raised.

Anas believes that equality before the law is what enables people to live in relative harmony. He isn't naive, and emphasises that injustices exist and that problematic judicial decisions can be made, but in principle everyone is equal. Coming to London was challenging, but Anas says that he quickly discovered a buzzing Muslim community, and mosques where he could feel at home. The fact that he was a returned holy warrior also gave him influence, and he remained engaged in political activism. He put down his weapons and demonstrated alongside Jews and Christians in protests, including those against Israel's war on Palestine.

'I've both participated in and witnessed historical events, lived in closer proximity to them than others,' Anas explains, rattling off a list: the Soviets withdrawing from Afghanistan, the establishment of the Taliban and al-Qaeda, and the dissolution of the Soviet Union.

Two days before 11 September 2001, his close friend Ahmed Shah Massoud was killed, in all likelihood at the behest of Osama bin Laden, who had come to disagree with his spiritual advisor.

'I sat in London, deep in grief. I had my suspicions that something terrible was going to happen, and when the twin towers fell, I knew that a new era was dawning,' Anas says.

Anas found the situation extremely challenging. Muslims in London praised Osama bin Laden for his attack on the US – many saw the attacks as a political act, not a religiously motivated one. The war subsequently waged on Afghanistan by the US and their allies was awful. Innocent men were sent to the Guantánamo Bay Detention Camp.

'I gave speeches in the mosques, where I tried to explain, especially to young Muslims, that it was possible to criticise America's war *and* reject al-Qaeda's dangerous war packaged as religion at the same time. After all, I knew what I was talking about. I had been a warrior myself. But I found myself in an impossible situation. I risked being arrested and sent to Guantánamo. I was a former friend of bin Laden. Many Muslims called me a traitor and a coward.'

Anas is convinced that lack of knowledge and life experience is what leads young men and women into the arms of radical forces. He thinks it is striking how little young Muslims in London know about their own cultural heritage and Muslim history, and strongly opposes preachers who glorify the past and mythologise the caliphate and sharia law while holding forth on how oppressed Muslims are.

'London is a city in which the vast majority of Muslims can practise their religion in peace. In Muslim countries, they are killing each other. Even Omar Bakri, who was deported to Jordan, is still fighting to return to London! How come he can't just stay in Jordan – a Muslim country – if he's so dissatisfied with the state of things in London? These radical Muslims have no solutions to the huge problems we're struggling with: poverty, war, illegal immigration,' says Anas.

The British authorities report that there has been a dramatic increase in hate crimes against Muslims in London, and in Britain in general. Women are spat on and accused of hiding bombs under their clothes; older Muslim men are attacked by gangs of youths. And Arabs and Muslims remain the chief villains in TV series, most recently in *The Bodyguard*, one of the UK's most watched series ever. I think of Anas's five sons. The oldest two are in their early twenties. Imagine growing up in London, in such a volatile situation – and with a father who fought with the mujahideen in the holy war to boot. A grief-stricken expression crosses Anas's face when I steer the conversation to these challenges. His sons have told him how fellow believers refer to their father as a traitor, and about how they have been bullied. But now that they have read their father's autobiography they are proud of him, and follow his personal philosophy.

'They appreciate London and the opportunities here. My sons understand that this is a city where Allah's word truly manifests itself. If it were up to me, I would implement London's ideals as the template all over the world. I can understand how the average non-Muslim resident of London might feel uneasy and afraid when preachers come along, threatening to turn London into a caliphate. Supporters of this ideology make life difficult for their fellow believers. Don't they understand that?'

Few other religious groups in London are as intensely polarised and marked by major international conflicts as the Muslims. Britain's significant role internationally leads everyone to London. The city is not a neutral area. In 2003, television channel Al Jazeera established themselves in the city. The channel is financed by Qatar, and today has several hundred employees in London, including the cream of British journalists. Arabs in London also have a number of other television channels they can watch – Al Jazeera's main competitor, Al Arabiya, is financed by the Saudi royal family. Abdullah Anas has also taken up the fight: in 2011, he and several other wealthy businesspeople started the channel Al Magharabia, which is based in Wembley, and mainly focused on North Africa. Anas refers to himself as the channel's founder and political advisor, and is proud that the channel has become one of the most popular in Algeria.

We part ways on a busy Wembley street. A group of young boys in school uniforms storm towards me. They laugh, satisfied, clearly up to some tomfoolery or other. A woman in the doorway of a nail salon shakes her fist at them, but laughs at the same time as she kicks away an empty drinks bottle the boys appear to have thrown against the windows. I continue past shops selling Lebanese food, an office with job advertisements for Romanian workers, Somali women with prams and small, grey-haired elderly Indian women in saris. Outside a pub sit three older white men, their faces deeply furrowed. I remember Wembley from the 1980s. There were not so many Somalis or Romanians here then. Mostly Indians. Back then there was still a branch of Woolworths – the chain of retail stores that went bankrupt in 2008 – on Wembley High Road. I bought New Order's album *Power, Corruption & Lies* there in 1983. London was starting to change after the extensive economic measures introduced by Thatcher's government. Nobody was concerned with religion. But this would change drastically over the years that followed.

It is 17 June 2017: Seven Sisters Road, north London. Just after midnight. Several hundred Muslims are on their way out of Finsbury Park Mosque and the Muslim Welfare House after *tarawih*, evening prayers during the fasting month of Ramadan. Out of nowhere, a van hurtles on to the pavement and into the crowd. Total chaos ensues. Grandfather and father of six Makram Ali, originally from Bangladesh, dies instantly of his injuries. A dozen or so others are injured. Darren Osborne, a father of four in his late forties, is later arrested for the crime. According to witnesses, he shouted, 'I'm going to kill all Muslims,' as he ploughed into the crowd.[2] Just thirteen days earlier, Muslim extremists had murdered eight people in Borough Market beside London Bridge; forty-eight people were injured. The sickly feeling that somebody had taken the Old Testament expression 'an eye for an eye, and a tooth for a tooth' literally began to creep in.

High up on the exterior of Finsbury Park Mosque hangs a huge banner. The message that is written there, in all the colours of the rainbow, is the one that Abdullah Anas referred to when we met: '. . . and we have made you into nation and tribes that you may know each other, Qu'ran 49:13'.[3]

The mosque looks well maintained, but it hasn't always been this way. Once, many of the windows here were broken, the brick covered in moss and litter scattered about outside. Inside, there is space for 2,000 worshippers spread over the building's five floors, but in the early 1990s there were hardly fifty people who came here. Instead, most of the Muslims in this neighbourhood prayed in the Muslim Welfare House mosque nearby, terrified of the leaders at Finsbury Park Mosque. For several years, the mosque was led by Egyptian-born Abu Hamza al-Masri, and functioned as a refuge for terrorists.

Abu Hamza came to the UK as a student in 1979. Back then, there was little to indicate that he would become one of Britain's most despised Muslims. He became a bouncer at a strip club in Soho, before turning to Islamism when the war in the Balkans broke out. He then went to Bosnia and fought against the Serbs, side by side with the other holy warriors. He is said to have lost his hands in a training exercise with the Pakistani military in Lahore. The warrior then returned to London with big ambitions.

Finsbury Park Mosque was originally founded by the local Bengali community who wanted a place to worship. After gathering financial support, which included a contribution of over £1 million from King Fahd in Saudi Arabia, the mosque as it stands today opened in 1994. Exactly why Abu Hamza was invited to become the mosque's imam is unclear, but by 1997 he had taken control and introduced a strict regime. People he didn't trust were shut out, and when the mosque's council tried to remove him, he responded with violence. Once a lively and popular institution, the mosque was transformed into a base for al-Qaeda extremists. In 1998, the council went to the police in an attempt to throw Hamza out. But despite an eviction order being issued, nothing was done and Hamza continued his autocracy. On the first anniversary of the 9/11 terrorist attacks, Hamza arranged the conference 'A Towering

Day in History', to remember the terrorists who had carried out the attacks. Several of the UK's most notorious extremists attended, including Anjem Choudary and Omar Bakri Mohammed. A team of 150 police officers stormed the mosque after plans to commit a biochemical attack on the London Underground were discovered, and the arrests of seven men at the mosque meant that the council finally managed to remove Abu Hamza. But Hamza wouldn't be stopped – he began holding prayer meetings outside the mosque instead. It was disheartening to see the former warrior standing on the street, giving aggressive speeches to audiences of young Muslim men who seemed fascinated by his hateful rhetoric. In 2004, Abu Hamza was finally arrested under the British Terrorism Act, and after several court cases he was deported to the US in 2012, charged with kidnapping and inciting holy war. He was sentenced to life in prison, without the possibility of parole.

'What's done is done. Now we have to look forwards,' says Mohammed Kozbar, leader of the council at the mosque.

I'm sitting in his office on the first floor. The building is quiet. Finsbury Park Mosque has been transformed into a liberal, open institution, focused on building bridges with the local community and the Orthodox Jewish neighbourhood of Stamford Hill close by.

'A new age has dawned. We Muslims must open our doors, and teach people about our religion. Withdrawing, isolating ourselves and becoming sceptical when we are threatened is not a feasible strategy,' Kozbar says.

Kozbar is a soft-spoken, calm man, wearing suit trousers and a shirt. No tunic. No prayer cap. Kozbar came to the UK from Lebanon as a student in 1990, and was part of the group who took control of the mosque in 2005, determined to introduce a completely different regime than that implemented by Abu Hamza and his followers.

'We are a centre for the entire neighbourhood. Every week we have a day dedicated to the homeless, "Meals for All", where we give those in need free food, and they can stay here and keep warm,' he says.

Kozbar has studied the charitable work carried out by Christians and Muslims – the two groups have much in common. It is not without reason that socially engaged souls have always sought out churches and mosques, and found meaningful work among their local communities. I'm familiar with the mosques' solidarity work. Muslims must give *zakat*, around 2.5 per cent of their income, to those in need, just as practising Christians pay tithes to the church. But the contrast between how Islam is perceived and how the religion is practised is colossal – both within the Muslim world and in the West. It's almost irritating how Muslims almost have to insist that they love their neighbours, I think, as Kozbar tells me about all the charitable work the mosque is doing. In 2008, the mosque was awarded the 'Best Islamic Centre in Europe' prize by IslamOnline, the world's largest Muslim website. I note that Kozbar doesn't pepper his speech with Muslim phrases like *inshallah* and *mashallah*, as I've always experienced when speaking with other mosque leaders. It feels liberating.

'When the extremists were here, they weren't just a burden for ordinary Muslims, they also ruined the neighbourhood. The police were here all the time, as were photographers from the press. It was an uncomfortable phase. We unfortunately received a lot of hate mail, and in 2011 we even got some unidentified white powder in the post and had to evacuate,' Kozbar tells me.

The following year, Kozbar received the Courageous Citizen Award from Islington Council. But the legacy Abu Hamza left behind would continue to plague the mosque. Over thirty-five of the individuals now imprisoned behind the barbed wire fences at Guantánamo Bay are said to have stayed here in the mosque during its worst years. One of them was Richard Reid, who also frequented Brixton Mosque. He was caught when he tried to blow up a plane from Paris to Miami using explosives hidden in his shoes. In November 2015, somebody tried to burn down the mosque, and the following year rotten pork was thrown at the building. In 2016 the Muslim Council of Britain started the 'Visit My Mosque' project, a day where anyone who wished to do so could visit a mosque and learn about Islam. The event was a huge success. Finsbury Park Mosque also won the Visit My Mosque prize, which was awarded in Parliament. The mosque's work is unrivalled within British Islam.

I have noticed that Kozbar often appears in the media as the mosque's leader, and regularly has to stress that the days of Abu Hamza are now far behind them; that the mosque is no longer a base for terrorists.

'Don't you get tired of it?' I ask Kozbar.

He smiles.

'Unfortunately, we've ended up in a position where terrorists have kidnapped our religion – you'll notice I don't call them Muslims. We have to emphasise our positive stories in our encounters with the media, we have a duty to change the impression people might have of us,' he says.

After the terrorist attacks in 2017, both Prime Minister Theresa May and Labour leader Jeremy Corbyn, who lives in the constituency, came to Islington to show their support. London's Chief Rabbi Ephraim Mirvis condemned the acts of hate using strong words. The rabbi had just finished an interfaith *iftar*, the daily meal that breaks the Muslim fast during Ramadan, in his home when he heard the news. Kozbar points out that both anti-Semitism and Islamophobia have recently increased in scope, and that the Jewish and Muslim communities must work together to tackle the spread of hate.

I see that worshippers are now coming in to pray. They are from many different countries around the world – here there are Iraqis, Albanians, Somalis, Kurds, Turks, Algerians, Bengalis. Kozbar is eager to highlight the women in the mosque. The Sisters Committee holds regular meetings with the women's group at the local church. He continues to rattle off details of all the different events they organise; the youth club is popular, too. I almost want to say: 'Stop, it's OK – I can see that you run a fantastic mosque!'

Kozbar and I walk down the carpeted stairs to the exit, which is full of men. They look at me a little strangely – I'm supposed to be in the women's section. Finsbury Park Mosque is, after all, a conservative mosque. There will be no feminist revolution taking place here any time soon. But they smile at me. Kozbar believes there's a long way to go before women and men will pray together.

Thinking about the quiet revolution that is happening in so many Arab countries around the world, and in some of the Muslim communities here in the city, I leave the mosque feeling a touch hopeful. It wouldn't be so surprising if something was brewing. Perhaps it isn't unthinkable that there are women sitting not far from here, behind the net curtains, planning a revolution at this very moment? I would support them wholeheartedly.

Russian London – Mayfair, Kensington, Knightsbridge, Bloomsbury

The revolution in Dior

'Welcome, Nazneen!'

The Russian Debutante Ball's PR manager, Charlotte Ellis, is geniality itself as I give her my name.

'Here's your ticket!' she says, handing me an envelope. She is a glamourous woman with long, blonde hair and a lovely smile. I'm finally going to party with some of London's wealthiest at the Grosvenor House Hotel.

London has always been the playground of the rich and famous. The world's flushest buy houses and apartments in Knightsbridge, Mayfair, Belgravia, Kensington, Brompton, St John's Wood and Chelsea. They stay at exclusive hotels like Grosvenor House, the Savoy and the Ritz, sip drinks at Claridge's and the Sanderson Hotel, and drive around in Bentleys, Bugattis, Porsches, Ferraris and Rolls-Royces.

Every year, the *Sunday Times* newspaper publishes the *Sunday Times* Rich List – a list of the 1,000 richest people resident in Britain, measured in net income. It has revealed that London is the city in the world with the most billionaires, so perhaps the streets here really are paved with gold? Moscow is in second place, while New York takes third. A significant number of these billionaires are not British by birth, but Indian, French, American, Nigerian and Russian – that is, from the former Soviet Union. In 2020, Alisher Usmanov, who was born in Uzbekistan, came in seventh place. Roman Abramovich found himself in twelfth place. Both are assigned the umbrella label of 'Russian'.

The large, white stucco houses and townhouses in Mayfair and Belgravia spanning several floors hide generous residences. Many years ago, I interviewed British politician Michael Heseltine at his home in Belgravia, one of London's most exclusive addresses. He probably has several homes, come to think of it. The meeting took place in the library – the room had a glass roof and extended out of the main building. The walls were also glass, providing a view of the well-maintained garden. The floors were covered by thick Persian rugs, and there was art everywhere. It was extravagant. At the start of the interview I had problems concentrating, because I really wanted to ask him for a tour of the house instead of having a boring conversation about British politics. In the 1950s and 1960s, it was the Americans, the French and members of English high society like Baron Michael Heseltine who owned these houses. They still live here, but they now have new neighbours – Gulf sheiks with oil money moved into the well-kept houses and gardens in the 1970s and 1980s.

In the 1990s more new occupants arrived – and some of them spoke Russian. Until this point, there had been few Russians in London, and those who did live in the city mainly worked for the Aeroflot airline and the Bank of Moscow. In 1991, just 100 visas were issued to Russian citizens.[1] Today, it is estimated that almost 300,000 people with a background from the former Soviet Union live in Britain or, more precisely, in London.[2]

The Russians have fascinated me ever since I started hearing Russian being spoken on the escalators of Harrods and Harvey Nichols in the mid-1990s. I would turn to see tall, slim women in Versace dresses, carrying expensive handbags. They were different from the wealthy Arabs I had observed in the 1980s – the Arab women were often hidden by niqabs and abayas, and their wealth was only visible when they tried on shoes, when you might see expensive Chanel, Gucci or Versace heels and delicate feet. It soon became apparent to everyone in London that Russian couples were not just visiting Knightsbridge to shop for haute couture. The Russians were also beginning to invest heavily in London's property market. The city was soon nicknamed 'Moscow-on-Thames' and 'Londongrad'. What on earth was going on?

As the Soviet Union collapsed, and Russian statesmen Mikhail Gorbachev and Boris Yeltsin pursued their dreams of a capitalist Russia, British politicians had a vision. London would become the finance capital of the world, and newly rich Russians were coaxed to the city with tax breaks. In New York – which otherwise would have been a natural place to go – foreign investments were strictly regulated. By allying themselves with Boris Yeltsin, Russian businessmen could become filthy rich. They then became known by a designated term: *oligarchs*. Not only did they become owners of Russia's natural resources – which represented inconceivable wealth – but the oligarchs also obtained significant political power. But the money had to be invested in new projects, and many wanted to place their wealth somewhere other than Russia, where it would be safe. For the richest Russians, London appeared the perfect place to invest their funds. It wasn't far by plane, and had plenty of airports for private jets. In London, they would never risk having their properties confiscated by the state – a slight increase in tax was the worst that could happen.

For unassuming Brits, the vulgar displays of wealth performed by the Russian nouveau riche were shocking and confusing. How could it be that the Russians, who had previously had to stand in hour-long queues to buy bread, were now throwing millions of pounds around in wild bidding wars and securing themselves London's most expensive properties? Their desire to show off led to the resurrection of old Russian traditions, such as the Debutante

Ball at the Grosvenor, where I'm now wandering around beneath the lavish chandeliers.

The tradition of the debutante ball was originally established in England, and a debutante is a young woman from society or the aristocracy who has reached a certain level of maturity and is therefore ready to be introduced to the world. Wearing white ballgowns, the debutantes would remind society at large that they were ready to marry. It was King George III of Great Britain who arranged the first debutante ball in 1780 – Queen Charlotte's Ball – in honour of his wife. Debutante balls also became popular among the aristocracy in Europe and Russia, where the tsars spearheaded society life. But with the Russian Revolution, the tradition of the balls came to an abrupt end. Interest in the tradition first reappeared after the fall of communism towards the end of the 1990s, when newly rich Russians were able to show off their new material wealth without shame.

Three young women in white ballgowns run past me on the thick carpets, bursting through a gilded door just beside the entrance to the ballroom. In the dressing room a dozen or so girls are buzzing around – some flicking powder brushes carefully across their faces, others trying to help each other attach flowers and do up the tiny buttons on their dresses. One of the girls is wearing a white T-shirt with the word 'Feminist' on it over her ballgown. I guess she'll have to take that off before she makes her entrance in the ballroom.

If you want to appear as a debutante here at the ball, it isn't just a case of buying a ticket. First, you have to write an application. If you're a woman, you have to be under twenty-eight years old, while the men can have turned twenty-eight, but shouldn't be too much older. Everybody has to be unmarried. You should be a student at a university or have a permanent job. In addition, you must have acquired an elementary proficiency in dance – especially the waltz. Once the applications have been submitted, a first screening of the candidates is performed, and then you may be called to an interview at which your education, appearance, manners and language skills are assessed. These interviews take place at a distinguished church in Chelsea. Should you manage to make the cut, your entry ticket will cost you £250. You can then look forward to an evening where members of British and Russian high society sip vodka as they mingle.

There's still just under an hour to go until the debutante couples will walk down the beautiful staircase into the ballroom. The young women are all allocated a partner. There have been problems finding enough men to sign up to the balls in recent years, so the organisers have recruited some British soldiers to step in.

On the piazza, located one floor above the legendary ballroom, people in ballgowns and tuxedos sashay around. Lots of champagne is being served. Tense waiters offer painstakingly crafted canapés. A small queue forms at a photo wall, on which all the event's sponsors are listed. The wall also features illustrations of the lavish towers over Saint Basil's Cathedral in Moscow, and London's Big Ben. An older British gentleman with a roguish gaze sidles up to me and whispers:

'Aren't they all simply enchanting?'

A tall blonde woman, who has been a little overenthusiastic with the blusher and is clearly refusing to accept her real age, sashays past us in a slinky pastel-pink evening dress covered in sequins. The man nudges me.

'Did you see her? She's marvellous. Absolutely marvellous. Russian women are marvellous!'

I can do nothing but agree as I stand there watching the guests with him. Russian women are in a class of their own, says the man, because in addition to being charming they are also extremely well educated. The marvellous woman he pointed out, however, is not Russian – she's a lesser-known British actor. I don't have the heart to tell him.

As I admire all the beautiful dresses that pass by, I notice that the photographers are growing restless. They are gathering, ready to pounce. An older woman glides graciously into the room, wearing a tight-fitting lace dress. The photographers run after her, and I quickly realise why the press are reacting – it's sixty-seven-year-old Princess Olga Romanoff, great-granddaughter of the tsar's sister who managed to flee Russia during the revolution. She is the ball's patron. A crowd gathers. Everybody wants to be photographed with Princess Olga. Then Admiral Lord West – also a regular guest – has to be photographed. It doesn't take long before he has four young women on either side of him, all fighting for the camera's favour. Stomachs in. Chests out.

The Russian Debutante Ball in London was first arranged in 2012 on the initiative of Austrian-Russian couple Dr Alexander Smagin and Dr Elisabeth Smagin-Melloni, who have arranged similar balls in Moscow, Vienna, Paris and Tel Aviv. Elisabeth is a former professor, a smart, small and intense woman in her late fifties. She explains that the balls in Vienna are an important part of society, and that most occupational groups have their own: the plumbers' ball, the doctors' ball, the carpenters' ball . . . She makes no attempt to hide the fact that networking is one of the ball's most important objectives, and emphasises the ball's safe social framework.

She and her husband arranged their first ball in Moscow in 2003.

'The Russian girls we spoke with then said that we should organise similar balls abroad because wealthy Russians now live in Paris and London, and especially here because the British have the impression the Russians are unsophisticated, vodka-drinking hooligans,' Elisabeth says. She and her husband therefore decided to showcase the very best of Russian culture during the ball.

Over the loudspeakers, an ingratiating voice requests that we take our seats. We head down the stairs, into the ballroom. A three-course meal will keep us going throughout the evening. Everything has been carefully planned down to the finest detail, with small flower arrangements and candles. Later, chamber orchestra the Russian Virtuosi of Europe and the Len Phillips Big Band will play. We'll also see dancers from the Bolshoi Ballet in Russia perform.

A short time later, we have to stand as Princess Olga takes her place, before the ballet dancers perform a short piece from *The Nutcracker*. The lights are dimmed, and to classical music fifty debutante couples make their way down the stairs and into the ballroom. The young women glide, skilfully guided by their escorts, treading with grace and charm. Jewellery and pearls glitter, as do jewelled tiaras and designer dresses. It looks like a scene from a Leo Tolstoy novel, but this is reality in London – for a select few.

The year is 1902. A young man is on his way out of the front door at 30 Holford Square in north London, perhaps with a particular spring in his step. He isn't very tall. His hair is thinning. Spring is in the air, and the daffodils are blooming in London's parks. Perhaps he walks with his friend, the Marxist Henry Quelch, or with his young wife, Nadezhda Krupskaya. The couple have recently arrived in the city, and will pave the way for a historic world event. The young man's newly adopted pseudonym will spread to every corner of the globe. In just a few years, everybody will know about Vladimir Ilyich Ulyanov – Lenin – and the Russian Revolution.

Lenin seemed to enjoy London. In the years between 1902 and 1911 he visited the city several times. He originally came to Britain's capital because he wanted to study at the renowned British Library. Today, the library is located in a modern, red-brick building at King's Cross, but in the early 1900s it was part of the British Museum, which is situated in Holborn. During his visits, there was one place in particular that Lenin used to go: the Crown and Anchor pub in

Clerkenwell Green – although scholars disagree about whether it was in this pub that Lenin met Stalin for the first time. The pub is now called the Crown Tavern, and has become popular among those with left-wing sympathies.

There was a number of radical Russians in London, all with revolution on their minds, even before Lenin's time. In 1886, British Charlotte Wilson and Russian Peter Kropotkin founded the anarchist newspaper *Freedom Press* in Whitechapel. Later, the premises also became a publishers, bookshop and printers, as I mentioned earlier, as well as a meeting place for all those with anarchist sympathies. The godmother of Russian anarchism, Emma Goldman, also enjoyed frequenting the *Freedom Press* premises in the 1920s, after she was deported from the USA.

I dread to think what the anarchists would have said about the ball I'm currently attending. Maybe they would have stormed the hotel, waving black flags and shouting out slogans. As we clap for the couples and watch their cheeks flush, I can't help but think about the exhibition entitled *Russian Revolution: Hope, Tragedy, Myths* (2017), which I visited at the British Library. I hardly think the intention was for the revolution to result in debutante balls in London or Russians buying up enormous properties here. Photographs of the Russian royal family, with Tsar Nicholas II sitting with his wife Tsarina Alexandra, were on display at the exhibition. At the start of 1917, the Romanov dynasty consisted of thirty-two men. Thirteen of these were killed during the revolution. The Romanov family was executed in Yekaterinburg in July 1918; the remaining members of the dynasty fled and settled mainly in France, but also in London. Russian history in London is full of contrasts: from passionate communism to shameless decadence.

'There aren't exactly many oligarchs here – the real oligarchs shy away from publicity,' Charlotte the PR manager whispers to me as we eat profiteroles filled with mint cream for dessert.

The closest we'll get tonight is Natalya Rotenberg, who is radiant in a beaded, bottle-green mermaid dress. She's so beautiful that I can do nothing but stare – she almost looks like a Barbie doll. Rotenberg became famous when she divorced businessman Arkady Rotenberg, Vladimir Putin's judo partner of ten years. He refused to pay her divorce settlement, and the conflict led to major headlines in the press.

'Come on, let me introduce you to Princess Olga,' Charlotte says, taking me by the hand.

Charlotte's friendliness surprises me. It turns out that she's actually Hungarian. She leads me over to the table where the princess and her husband Admiral Ionnides are sitting. The princess turns out to be free of the rhetorical acrobatics I'm used to from the British upper class, and answers all my questions in a strikingly straightforward way. She's just published an autobiography, in which she talks about her eccentric upbringing on the Provender House estate in Kent, which was built in the 1200s. Olga – as she insists on being called – says that the reason she published the autobiography wasn't just because she had so much to say: she also needed the money.

'The house was in need of maintenance. I didn't want water dripping down over my head,' she says. She bats away my question about how it must have been sad to sell her inheritance.

'What am I going to do with it when the house falls down?'

She doesn't have especially warm feelings towards Russia.

'I've been there a couple of times. It's fine.'

And when it comes to the Russians in London, she doesn't have much to say, even though she's part of the Romanov family.

'They're a nice bunch, but not close friends.'

Princess Olga is measured, calm and laconic on the evening I meet her, but in a documentary that aired on British TV she cried when she was interviewed about her family history. In the interview, she stressed that it was actually British King George V's fault that the

Russian royal family was killed. Historians have long claimed that it was British Prime Minister Lloyd George who didn't want the Russian royal family in the country, but Olga believes it was the king who withdrew his offer of asylum because it would have been 'inappropriate' to have the family in England.

The neatly styled hair of the young women is becoming dishevelled and the dancing noticeably more unrestrained as I leave the ballroom long after midnight. I end up talking with a young couple who are taking photos of each other. He's tall and dark, she blonde – and of course astonishingly beautiful. They tell me that they met on a plane from Moscow to London. He works at an investment bank, while she's studying economics.

'I love London. I love the safety this country offers us,' the young man says, as the woman drapes herself around him, entranced.

His English is almost parodically correct. I have to ask him about the revolution – after all, it isn't every year that a revolution celebrates its hundredth anniversary. He waves my words away.

'A tragedy, if you ask me. That's all I have to say on the matter,' he says, and smiles. A slightly older woman in a far-too-tight sequined gown jostles past us. She's on her way to the exit, her sequined dress slowly creeping downwards, and she's doing everything she can to keep the top part of it decent.

As I leave the party, I pass some young couples in the hotel lobby, who are most likely Arabs. The women all look like Kim Kardashian. I am struck with a certain sense of melancholy at the fact that I will never be the kind of person to attend such balls on a regular basis.

Nights in London have a special aura, filled with promises of excitement and glamour mixed with a sense of desperation and melancholy. I enjoy the sight of the cars' red tail lights as they tear through the dark. What stories are playing out in the back seats or in the thoughts of the drivers? A small group of Russians stand next to me as they wait for their chauffeur, their dresses glittering in the darkness. The scene feels like a dream, and this is precisely what the ball is: a dream for the wealthy, and for those who make the cut. The Russians I have mingled with this evening make up only a tiny fraction of those who live in London – not all Russians in this city have lives like this. There are some who are childminders, tradesmen or Uber drivers. But it is the richest Russians who have changed London's cityscapes with their extravagant dreams. I hail one of the black London cabs, and am soon on my way through the city streets.

The taxi drives down to Wellington Arch, and turns towards Knightsbridge. At Hyde Park Corner, where we turn off Piccadilly, there's an underpass where I always see beggars and homeless people. I think of the overwhelming divides between rich and poor in London. And the differences only continue to grow. According to official statistics, the number of homeless in Britain has increased by 169 per cent since the autumn of 2016. This is such a marked increase that it's noticeable even without reading any statistics. I see more and more homeless people in shop doorways, in areas where until fairly recently I had never seen any before.

If you'd like to obtain an insight into the lives of the less fortunate, you can watch the programme *Can't Pay? We'll Take It Away*, where bailiffs turn up at the doors of people who haven't paid for certain products or their rent. They either have to give the bailiffs the property they haven't managed to pay for within an hour, or settle their debt within the same timeframe. Those who haven't paid their rent are forced to leave the property, taking only their most necessary belongings with them. One night I watch an episode in which an older man is thrown out of a room of no more than ten metres square. He has no hot water, no stove, and the place is crawling with cockroaches. As the bailiffs help the man pack up his things, they discover that he's a former well-known actor who is struggling with his health. But despite his health problems, the man is evicted. These kinds of problems are hardly experienced by those who frequent the neighbourhoods of Knightsbridge, Brompton and Kensington.

Soon the taxi arrives at the junction where Brompton Road meets Sloane Street. I look out at the Mandarin Oriental Hyde Park, a baroque-inspired, five-floor luxury hotel, built of brick and with large bay windows. I haven't been there yet, but dream of eating in the hotel restaurant – Heston Blumenthal's Michelin-starred Dinner. Next door tower four ten-storey apartment blocks in steel, glass and concrete: One Hyde Park. One of the world's most expensive housing complexes, if not the most expensive of them all. The prices of the apartments start at £20 million. The most expensive advertised on the open market had an asking price of £75 million.[3]

Candy Property and the prime minister of Qatar are behind One Hyde Park, with the latter owning the finest apartment there, a triplex. The residents here could have made up the cast of a bad thriller from the 1980s: a Russian property magnate, a Nigerian telecommunications baron, the richest man in the Ukraine, a billionaire from Kazakhstan, a female singer – also possibly from Kazakhstan – and the head of the treasury of the Emirate of Sharjah. Even the entrance to One Hyde Park has frosted glass and stiff security guards, and there are always a couple of Bentleys with drivers outside, obviously waiting for their owners. The apartment listings that can be found online show the materials used inside: marble, leather, expensive woods and furs – mostly in fifty shades of brown. The residents can otherwise enjoy their own spa, wine cellar, squash courts, security guards trained by elite forces, and a panic room.[4] Of course, the estate agents and professors of architecture may argue about whether or not the complex is aesthetically pleasing, but living here isn't really the point. The properties are investment instruments. And Russians naturally own several of the apartments.[5]

Right next to One Hyde Park, in a magnificent detached residence, lives a Russian who has definitely made his mark on London: Roman Abramovich, the very incarnation of everything people associate with an oligarch. Few celebrities are so enshrouded in myths as this media-shy billionaire, who was born in Saratov in 1966. What we know for certain, however, is that he seems to like London. For years he has been hoarding properties at London's most exclusive addresses – on Sloane Street and in Knightsbridge, the stronghold of British high society – and he is also the owner of Chelsea FC (or Chelski, as some nasty tongues like to call the club). In July 2018, Abramovich acquired an apartment costing £30 million in one of London's most fashionable apartment complexes: Chelsea Waterfront.[6] When they are completed in 2021, two of the towers that are part of the complex will be thirty-seven and twenty-five storeys high, respectively. The uppermost apartments will offer a 360-degree view, and each parking space will cost £85,000. The acquisition of luxury properties in world metropolises has become a popular hobby among the global elite.

But this leisure pursuit can have some unforeseen consequences, because unlike the British upper class who have traditionally owned these properties, their new owners do not become part of the neighbourhood. Abramovich and his friends do not drink beer at the local pub, nor do they organise summer fêtes with sponge cakes and Pimm's. They don't strut around with silks scarves around their necks, inspecting the streets. The buildings are more or less uninhabited, meaning that once lively neighbourhoods now appear dark and deserted. One in four properties in Knightsbridge and Belgravia stands empty, and they are exclusively bought as investment objects. In Belgravia, the shops often close in August because there is nobody there – everybody is in St Tropez or Marbella. In some cases, the properties' neighbours have also had to tolerate extensive renovation projects. In these neighbourhoods, new owners are not permitted to increase the buildings' height, but they can expand the properties downwards. Excavators have got to work, brutally digging out cellars in order to build several new floors underground, where the owners install swimming pools, gyms and cinemas. London's architects, interior designers, estate agents and lawyers have earned great sums of money from the influx of rich Russians, whose extravagant wishes know no bounds. The baths in these properties often consist of the most expensive Italian marble with detailing in real gold – even down to the flush buttons on the toilets.

The export of Russian capital is one of the main reasons why the financial differences in Russia are continuously on the rise. And the rich Russians don't just disappear off with the money – they also live in accordance with completely different rules when it comes to how long they are permitted to stay in Britain. In 2008, a special Golden Visa Scheme was developed by the British authorities for anyone with a few million pounds lying around – £2 million, to be precise. If you invested this sum in Britain, you got yourself a dedicated 'Gold Visa', and permanent residency after five years in the country. Should you randomly have £10 million lying around, you could obtain permanent residency in Britain after just two years.[7] The vast majority of those who have made use of this scheme are Russian or Chinese.

The Golden Visa Scheme is now being investigated following pressure from international corruption organisations, who believe the scheme has led to extensive money-laundering activities. When Abramovich's visa expired he was not granted a new one, and was therefore no longer permitted to stay in Britain. There was much speculation about whether the British authorities didn't want to issue Abramovich a new visa due to the country's new offensive on dirty money. But this didn't bother Abramovich. He soon acquired an Israeli passport based on his Jewish heritage, and since Israeli citizens don't need to apply for a visa to travel to Britain, he now has full access to the country.

Back at the apartment in Earl's Court, I remove my make-up and carefully hang my ballgown back on its hanger. My dream of attending an event at one of London's finest hotels has been fulfilled. As my head hits the pillow, I'm looking forward to meeting a person some refer to as a Russian prince. Others might say he's a court jester.

The freedom fighter

I'm standing in front of the entrance to Hedonism Wines in Davies Street in Mayfair. He towers over me, with a melancholic smile and the warmest handshake I've ever felt. His beard is unkempt, and a long earring dangles from one of his ears.

'What a shop!' I exclaim.

Evgeny Chichvarkin looks at me with a bashful smile. He's wearing a faded T-shirt featuring an iconic image from the painting *Liberty Leading the People* by Eugène Delacroix, and socks with multicoloured polka dots. Had I bumped into him on the street, I never would have guessed that he belongs to a line of extremely rich Russians.

'I wanted to create a business where everyone can feel at home – it doesn't matter to me whether you buy a cheap everyday wine or a more expensive type,' Chichvarkin says.

His brown hair is long in the back and bristly and short on top – a good old-fashioned mullet, although I'm not sure the hairstyle is meant to be ironic. We're surrounded by bottles of wine – over 7,000 of them, elegantly displayed on light wood shelves. I know that some of the bottles of wine here are worth hundreds of thousands of pounds each. Above the stairs that lead down to the premises, a chandelier made of wine glasses – an entire 125 Riedel glasses – has been installed. In contrast to most expensive shops, where prices are never displayed, there are small, white price tags on all the bottles I've seen. On every single one of them – even the most expensive wines. Around us runs a small team of workers and cleaners who are preparing the shop before it opens. Four men stand outside, polishing the enormous windows that frame the premises. Also outside is a beautiful black Rolls-Royce.

When Chichvarkin opened Hedonism Wines in 2012, he had examined the wine retailers in London and discovered that, despite their age and reputations, many of them lacked both service-oriented employees and a good selection. He therefore decided to start a company that would offer customers the best wines in the world, along with unparalleled customer service. Fitting out the premises cost him over £2 million. He wanted the shop to be accessible, not dark and dusty. Prize-winning Hedonism Wines is now one of Britain's most renowned wine retailers.

'When we first opened, there were several British newspapers who wrote completely crazy articles about us – saying that only Russian oligarchs shopped here and that we promoted a sort of soft-porn lifestyle – but luckily people quickly discovered that we're not like that at all, but a serious business for people interested in wine,' Chichvarkin says, before perching on a high wooden stool and setting his two iPhones on the table in front of him. His large eyes seem sorrowful.

One of the telephones rings; Chichvarkin apologises. As he takes the call in Russian I sit there, staring at him. I can't help it, even though I know it's impolite. He waves his arms around, and for somebody so tall and robust, his hands are slender and well groomed. He speaks quickly, getting up and turning around as he continues to talk. In the elegant shop, he looks like a large clown.

It wasn't love of the wine god Bacchus that led Chichvarkin to London – and he hasn't always figured on *Tatler*'s somewhat bizarre list of 'lesser-known oligarchs'. He's actually a political refugee. He was once an ordinary Russian boy from Moscow, who dreamed of the West. His journey to London began not in a private jet, but in the boot of a car. At the age of seventeen, and with initial capital of around £2,500, Chichvarkin and a friend opened a small kiosk in Moscow in 1994, where they offered passers-by cheap mobile phones. Chichvarkin had noticed that the Russians needed mobile phones. Success wasn't long in coming, and the company Euroset was born.

In just a few years, Chichvarkin opened a total of over 5,000 shops in Russia, Ukraine, Belarus, Moldova, Estonia, Latvia, Lithuania, Kazakhstan, Kyrgyzstan, Armenia and Azerbaijan, with over 27,000 employees. Euroset held over 37 per cent of the Russian mobile market, and millions of roubles streamed into the company's accounts. In a country where businessmen often have close-cropped hair and wear sleek suits, Chichvarkin quickly became known for his eccentric style of dress and haircut. But nobody earns this much money in Russia without arousing the interest of the political elite – especially if you also start to mutter about possible corruption among the country's leaders in interviews. In 2008, Chichvarkin discovered that he was under investigation. He was accused of having kidnapped a lorry driver, who had supposedly swindled him out of mobile phones worth several hundred thousand pounds. Chichvarkin denied the charges, but on Christmas Day 2008 he discovered, to his horror, that the car he was driving was being followed by what could only be the Russian intelligence service. He understood that he would be thrown in prison. Chichvarkin contacted a colleague, and in secret managed to climb into the boot of his friend's car. His friend then drove him to the airport in Moscow. For some reason, Chichvarkin happened to have both his passport and his British visa with him that day, and so was able to fly straight to London. His wife and children arrived the day after, and they have lived here ever since. Chichvarkin sold Euroset, earning a solid sum of money that shot him straight into the ranks of rich Russians living in London.

Today, Chichvarkin socialises with the British elite. He plays in the same polo games as Prince Harry, and gives talks about entrepreneurship at universities.

'I know that people in the West react to Russian spending, but this is because people have such poor memories. It actually isn't so long since we lived in bottomless poverty. I was lucky, because my dad was a pilot – he brought home clothes and other things from the West for us. I'll never forget how happy I was when he gave me jumpers and trousers that were in different colours! I'd never seen such clothes before.'

The changes the Russians have experienced have happened over a very short period of time. I tell him that I've seen the documentary *Rich, Russian and Living in London*, which includes a clip of him playing polo.[1] The programme shows rich Russians going to the best schools, buying the most flamboyant cars, the most expensive art, the most expensive houses, the most expensive food, the most expensive . . . Chichvarkin shrugs.

'There are many different types of Russians in London, such as me, and then you have a group that I don't like very much. Those are the ones who think only about money, and long to return to a time that has never really existed. They're the ones who organise balls and pretend to be aristocrats. They make me feel embarrassed to be Russian.'

He looks at me in despair as I tell him about how I went to the Russian Debutante Ball, and then buries his face in his hands for a moment.

Chichvarkin explains to me that there is no community among ordinary Russians in London. They're too marked by their time in Russia, where suspicion and scepticism got in the way of true solidarity. He believes that Russians are anxious by nature.

A young woman comes over to Chichvarkin and whispers something in his ear. I recognise her from the gossip columns that

Chichvarkin features in from time to time – it's Tatiana Fokina, his new wife, and the CEO of Hedonism. They whisper to each other a little, before Chichvarkin turns to me and apologises for the interruption. He then starts on a tirade about British bureaucracy, tardiness and poor customer service, and wonders why it's impossible to get a plumber to come out on a Saturday evening. I finally try to steer him in another direction: towards the members of the British upper class with whom I know he socialises.

'I've been welcomed with open arms. But that was only until they realised I wasn't interested in getting involved with charity work.'

I look at him, curious.

'You didn't want to contribute?'

'No. It doesn't interest me any more.'

'So you have been involved with charitable causes? In Russia?'

'Yes. I was actually extremely involved in Russia. In several organisations. But then I got tired of it.'

'How come?'

'People were so ungrateful. One day they came to me, complaining about how I had given them books when they needed washing powder. I said to them: "If you read these books, you'll soon be earning enough money to buy yourself washing powder." I don't give people washing powder.'

I'm not quite sure what to say. In the previous interviews with Chichvarkin that I've read, he's said that he doesn't understand people who have to live on unemployment benefits. He believes there's no reason people shouldn't be able to manage when they have a brain. That it's just laziness.

'Ayn Rand. I like her. Do you know her books?'

Ayn Rand. Of course. I should have seen it coming. The Russian-American author and philosopher who, putting it simply, promoted a viewpoint in which the individual is valued above the community.

'But you of all people, who comes from a society that has promoted heartless socialism, isn't it a little strange that you've jumped head-first into heartless capitalism?'

Chichvarkin snorts.

'That's exactly why! If there's going to be any hope, I have to go in the total opposite direction. And then in the end, I'll end up in a sensible place.'

A brief silence ensues. I'm curious about where Chichvarkin actually stands politically. It's a little strange to walk around wearing a T-shirt praising the French Revolution of 1830, which deposed Charles X, when you're ideologically inspired by Rand. But everything is permitted in the postmodern world, where well-known symbols take on new meanings.

Chichvarkin isn't the kind of person to keep his head down. If charity isn't his hobby, then Russian politics certainly is. He maintains close ties with opposition leader Alexei Navalny, one of the Kremlin's most vehement critics, who in 2021 was arrested and imprisoned in Russia after surviving a near-fatal nerve agent attack. Chichvarkin doesn't exactly mince his words when British journalists interview him about his opinion of Vladimir Putin ('gang leader').

'What Putin is doing is necrophilia and fascism. Russia has vast opportunities, and it's a tragedy that Putin and his accomplices manage the country the way they do. It makes me infinitely sad. It's a dream for Russians to be in Britain. The legal system here can be trusted, and you don't need to be afraid – I don't think people understand how important that is. I'm also fascinated by how solid democracy is here. That's totally unattainable for my country,' Chichvarkin says, a sad expression crossing his face again.

I have to ask Chichvarkin whether he ever fears for his life as a Russian dissident in London. He looks at me for a long time. The list of troubling incidents involving Russian citizens in the UK is starting to get a little too long.

On 23 November 2006, Alexander Litvinenko died at the age of just forty-four after having been poisoned, apparently by Russian intelligence, who are thought to have spiked the tea he drank at a meeting in London. In 2013, businessman and Putin critic Boris Berezovsky died, apparently in a suicide by hanging, but both British and American intelligence believe he was murdered.

On 4 March 2018, Sergei Skripal and his daughter Julia became gravely ill in the city of Salisbury. They were poisoned by the Novichok nerve agent developed by Russia and the Soviet Union. Skripal was a former intelligence officer in Russia, and a double agent. A total of 150 Russian diplomats were expelled from the UK as a result of the incident, as a clear indication of just how seriously the British regarded the matter. The list of suspicious deaths involving Russian citizens, or their close associates, is long. Chichvarkin is convinced that Putin is behind them. But he can't allow himself to be afraid.

'What kind of life would that be? I have to show you something!'

He picks up one of his mobile phones, and brings up a video. It shows the Russian art collective Pussy Riot waving a flag in front of the Kremlin in Moscow, wearing their famous brightly coloured balaclavas. He then shows me two other videos. In the first of them, Chichvarkin is standing on the street in front of the Russian embassy in London, along with several other men and women. With them is an open coffin, in which a woman is lying with a large piece of tape over her mouth. On the coffin is a banner featuring the words: 'Russian democracy is dead.' The next video shows numerous people shouting slogans, and a cage on a pavement. In the cage is Chichvarkin, on all fours, looking out between the bars.

'Do you still do this kind of thing?' I ask.

He wrinkles his nose.

'I used to do a lot with art and politics before, but now I don't have much time. I prefer playing polo – that's my passion,' he says.

But just before the election in Russia in March 2018, Chichvarkin stood outside the Russian embassy once again.

In March 2016, Ukrainian anti-corruption activist and businessman Roman Borisovich arranged London's first Kleptocracy Tour.[2] Kleptocracy simply means a government of thieves, or a form of government in which the leaders steal from the country. During the tour, the bus full of excited British journalists stopped in front of the Witanhurst mansion in Highgate – one of London's largest private homes, consisting of twenty-eight rooms, a 4,000 metres square cellar and its own orange grove. Only Buckingham Palace is larger. In 2008, the mansion was acquired for £50 million by Safran Holdings, a company in the Virgin Islands. Nobody knew who the owner of the property was until the *New Yorker* revealed that it was billionaire Andrey Guryev who had purchased it. Guryev had made his fortune through chemical fertilisers, and used to serve in the Russian Senate, alongside Putin.

With this, Highgate was changed – much to the frustration of local residents.

Local politician Michael Hammerson was irritated, and said that the neighbourhood didn't want 'limos with smoked windows and men in dark glasses with bulging breast pockets, and the place surrounded by CCTV. That's not Highgate.'

Highgate has traditionally been the neighbourhood of wealthy, liberal intellectuals, many of whom live in Highpoint, two modernist blocks designed by Lenin-enthusiast Berthold Lubetkin. Borisovich is clear in his speech: this is dirty money. All the properties pointed out to the journalists on the tour are dirty, he says. For the most part, money-laundering takes place through the acquisition of property. According to Transparency International, over

40,000 properties in London are owned by companies registered in tax havens. Nobody knows who the owners are or where the money to buy the properties has come from.

As I look at Chichvarkin, I think that he is brave. Being a Russian dissident is almost like playing Russian roulette. I haven't managed to get very many Russians to speak openly about politics. On the occasions I've tried, they've been reserved, and steered the conversation in another direction. I'm therefore surprised at how freely Chichvarkin speaks about politics – he's certainly not afraid to give his honest opinion, and I can understand why he's become a media favourite. Tatiana Fokina returns; Chichvarkin has to leave me now. I would have liked to have spent more time with him.

Hedonism Wines is not the only establishment Chichvarkin has founded. If you walk from Davies Street in the direction of the Ritz at Green Park, after around ten minutes you'll reach his restaurant, Hide. The place is just as exclusive and minimalistic as Chichvarkin's wine shop, and has already been awarded a Michelin star. With the motto 'There is no compromise, there is no rush', Hide will probably keep going as long as there are wealthy Russians in the city. And the area is teeming with them – on shopping trips of a more cultural nature.

In 2009, Russian Alexander Lebedev took over the *Evening Standard*.[3] The newspaper was struggling financially, and Lebedev turned it into an indispensable free paper for everyone in London. Lebedev is a former KGB agent turned oligarch. The following year, he took ownership of the *Independent*, and has made himself known as an indignant ambassador for freedom of the press. His forty-year-old son, Evgeny Lebedev, has now taken over, and has become a media darling due to his extravagant charity fundraisers at which

Raisa Gorbacheva, wife of the late Mikhail Gorbachev, is often a guest. Evgeny lives in one of London's most exclusive and historic buildings, Stud House, which lies at the centre of Hampton Court Park, where deer have roamed freely since the time of Henry VIII. Of course, such a house must be filled with both art and literature, so it is fitting if one of your Russian friends owns a bookstore. Or an entire chain of bookstores, for that matter. London's rich Russians are not only wealthy – they are also cultured. Bookstore chain Waterstones has over 300 branches in Britain, and in 2011 Russian billionaire and former advisor to Boris Yeltsin, Alexander Mamut, acquired the entire chain before selling it to the investment firm Elliott Advisors.[4] At Piccadilly Circus, just a few minutes from Savile Row and Bond Street, is the biggest Waterstones branch in London. In a beautiful art deco building from 1930, which spans six floors, over 200,000 titles are for sale. The building is a tribute to both futurism and Bauhaus architecture, and is worth a visit in itself, even if you don't intend to buy any books. A 27-metre-long light installation twists its way along the elegant steel railing from the basement and all the way up to the top of the building. Today, the top floor features the Russian Bookstore, which exclusively sells Russian books. When the Russian Bookstore opened in 2012, people joked that British intelligence service MI5 would be regular customers, because Alexander Mamut had also been one of Putin's closest advisors.

A wonderful silence always dominates the bookshop whenever I visit – the noise of Piccadilly Circus and the intensity of the gigantic, flashing advertising are magically whisked away. There is an impressive collection of books in the Russian section. Heavy wooden shelves hold 5,000 titles, including everything from classics by Leo Tolstoy and Alexander Pushkin to contemporary Russian authors. Here, you will also find the essay 'Winter Notes on Summer Impressions', which Fyodor Dostoevsky wrote after visiting London in 1862. Dostoevsky bemoaned the vulgar commercialisation of Crystal Palace, the prostitution around Haymarket and the drunks in Whitechapel. But I think he would have appreciated the Russian Bookstore. Waterstones also carries magnificent books about Russian art. The Russians in London are obsessed with art – quite understandably. Art enables them to both show off their good taste, and invest their money. Twice a year, in June and November, Russian Art Week is held, when huge sums exchange hands at auctions at Sotheby's and Christie's. In November 2014, art worth a total of £40.7 million was sold. The following year, sales totalled £17.2 million. The downturn in the market in recent years is likely due to the sanctions against Russia, which have inevitably also affected the art business.

One day, among the throng of the city's galleries, I stumble across the White Space Gallery near the National Gallery, five minutes' walk from Waterstones. The exhibition *Women at Work: Subverting the Feminine in Post-Soviet Russia* (2018) turns out to be a keen-eyed look at the expectations of Russian women. Just like in the rest of the art world, men have dominated the art scene in Russia, and the depiction of women has therefore been characterised by conservative ideals. Artist Tatiana Antoshina has challenged this through a series of photographs of historical artworks, in which the men have been replaced with women. I can't stop looking at the photograph 'Queen of the Night', an image in which an old naked woman laughs while four young men sit in a ring around her, staring in admiration.

In Russia, contemporary art is under pressure. Artists are now showing their works in their homes, rather than in public galleries, fearing the consequences. The curator at the gallery tells me that London provides a sanctuary for the artists – at least for those who can afford to live here. It can therefore pay to have ingratiated oneself with an oligarch or two. I try to get her to say something about the political pressure experienced by the artists in Russia, but she's vague, and simply shrugs.

'We're just a gallery,' she says.

London has always been a meeting place for intellectual Russians with competing world views, for political dissidents, authors and musicians, as well as more ordinary Russians – all searching for a better life. Their contribution to London isn't always heard above all the din about spies, oligarchs and attempted murders, I think one autumn evening as I walk from Holborn to Bloomsbury Square on my way to Pushkin House. In few places is London's literary heritage as entrenched as it is in Bloomsbury. This is where the Bloomsbury Group could be found in the early 1900s – an intimate circle that included the authors Leonard and Virginia Woolf and E. M. Forster, and economist John Maynard Keynes.

Back then, British authors were wildly enthusiastic about Russian literature. In 1914, thirty-four British intellectuals wrote a tribute to Russian literature in the *Sunday Times*, where they thanked Russian authors for their contributions to world literature.

Pushkin House was founded by Russian intellectuals in the 1950s in Notting Hill. At the helm was Russian Maria Zernova Kullmann, who wanted to create a neutral meeting place for Russians and British intellectuals during a time which, not unlike now, was politically polarised. Tonight is the book launch for *The Idea of Russia: The Life and Work of Dmitry Likhachev* by Russian professor of international history at the London School of Economics, Vladislav M. Zubok. Likhachev, who died in 1999, is regarded as one of Russia's foremost intellectuals, and the founder of Russian democracy. After Stalin imprisoned him for his anti-revolutionary attitudes, Likhachev decided to devote his life to restoring Russian culture. He wanted to repair the damage the revolution had done to the Russian cultural heritage, fight Russian nationalism, and unite Russia with Europe.

When the floor is opened for questions after the professor's talk, many of them are about Likhachev's legacy. I'm interested in what Likhachev would have thought of Putin. The professor laughs when I ask him this.

'I think they have extremely different views of Russian nationalism,' Zubok answers, but he doesn't expand any further.

The audience, all wearing velvet and corduroy, laugh cautiously.

After the presentation, the professor is surrounded by people eager to continue the conversation. They all speak Russian. I end up talking to Sergei, a biology researcher who has lived in London for three years.

'I'm so tired of British newspapers. They regularly publish anti-Russian propaganda. There isn't a day goes by without British journalists spreading untruths about us,' Sergei says.

I feel with him. Just weeks before the book launch, *The Times* had reported the conclusion of the neoconservative think tank the Henry Jackson Society, which claimed that half of London's 150,000 Russians should actually be regarded as spies or informants.[5] The report 'Putin Sees and Hears It All', written by Dr Andrew Foxall, who is also one of anti-corruption organisation Kleptocracy's foremost advisors, received support from British intelligence service MI6.[6]

Sergei finds the situation no laughing matter.

'American newspapers are actually more balanced than the British. My English boss comments on Russia daily in the most absurd ways. I wouldn't have been able to take living here, were it not for the fact the London is one of the world's most important places to be if you're a researcher within the natural sciences,' he says.

I leave Pushkin House, and go out to eat Russian food in a kind of act of solidarity against the accusations of espionage. London is bursting with good restaurants promoting Russian culinary culture. I take the Tube to Soho, to Frith Street, where Bar Italia is also located. Of course, the Russians have their own celebrity chef, a kind of combination of Jamie Oliver and Gordon Ramsay, in the form of burly Alexei Zimin. On Frith Street, Zimin has established the bar and restaurant Zima over three floors. I'm accompanied up to the first floor, where I'm given a menu. According to a Russian acquaintance, the thick cardboard that the menus here are printed on used to be surveillance files in the communist Soviet Union. I'm unsure whether to feel excited or shaken at the thought.

A young woman comes over to me with a bowl of hot borscht, crimson with a white blob of sour cream in the centre. It occurs to me that all the Russians I have spoken to or tried to speak to in London have been reserved and sceptical. They have all been reluctant to speak openly about what they really think of the tense political situation in their homeland, and about their lives in London. Every face stiffened. With the exception of Chichvarkin, all of them have been withdrawn, kept their distance. It has not become easier after the poisoning of Sergei and Yulia Skripal in March 2018. It got even worse in 2020 when a report from the Intelligence and Security Committee of the UK Parliament stated that the Kremlin had been involved in 'hostile foreign interference' against the UK. The relationship between London and Moscow is seen to be frozen. One of the results has been that the Russian Debutante Ball is no longer being held due the tension between the two countries.

London is often referred to as a sanctuary, but it doesn't seem so for the Russians. They appear to tread carefully, constantly looking over their shoulders. With a genuine reason, it seems.

Polish London – Hammersmith, Ealing, Streatham, Kensington

Pride and prejudice

'We've got it all here [in Albert Square]. Rubbish, rats . . .'

'And a bit of racism,' says publican Mick Carter in a serious voice as he hoses the words 'Poles go home' from the pub's entrance.

The Queen Vic is the favourite haunt of everybody in the TV series *EastEnders*. The neighbourhood residents stand around the pub, looking with sad eyes at the graffiti. The vandals have also ripped down the Polish flags the owners hung up in connection with an event the previous evening.

'It is the Britain we live in now,' says one of the Poles who live in Albert Square. Shaking his head, he folds up a Polish flag that has been cast to the ground.

Not everybody appreciated this scene in England's most popular soap opera, which aired on 21 February 2017, six months after Britain had voted to leave the EU. Twitter was seething. 'That scene about the "POLES OUT" spray painting . . . How bloody biased was that, hang your head BBC,' tweeted one viewer, while others said scriptwriter Leo Richardson ought to be sacked. Richardson quickly hit back: 'So are you saying that racism doesn't exist? And that this isn't a very real problem in Britain today?' He defended the storyline, saying that series like *EastEnders* must 'reflect the lives of people who are under-represented, so we can understand those who we didn't before.'

Richardson had good reason to problematise the hate directed at the Poles in the TV series. In the run up to the EU referendum, Labour leader at the time, Ed Miliband – who is of Polish descent himself – pointed his finger at the Poles, accusing them of being part of the reason for the decrease in British living standards, while former foreign secretary Jack Straw claimed that Poland's incorporation into the EU was an enormous mistake. The expansion of the EU changed Britain. For many Poles, the British nation was the place to be where they could finally help themselves and fulfil their dreams.

In 2003, there were 94,000 Poles in Britain. The following year, Poland became a full member of the EU, and the borders were opened. Over the course of that first year, the number of Poles in Britain increased to 162,000. Today, they are the largest group of immigrants in the country – having surpassed the Indians, who until recently comprised the biggest group. There is now close to 1 million Poles in Britain, the majority of whom live in London.[1] Polish is the language that is most spoken in Britain after English, and never before have there been so many grocery stores with Polish names on London's streets. Where there was once a newsagent's owned by Pakistanis, Polish women now stand selling pickled vegetables and pierogis in light, attractive premises.

In the wake of the tough political climate in the run up to the EU referendum, hate against immigrants began to spread. The Poles in particular suffered. A Polish man and his son were beaten bloody by English men in Upton Park, east London. Others told of hostile attitudes towards Polish staff in restaurants: 'Table next to me says to Polish waitress "How come you are so cheerful. You're going home."'

Him and his missus start laughing. Disgusting,' commented one man on Twitter.[2] In the final thirty-eight days before the Brexit vote, 1,400 hate crimes were reported; in the same period after the vote, 2,300 reports were made.[3] The promised land to which the Poles had travelled to realise their dreams was transformed into an island filled with fear. But at the same time, other stories bubbled up to the surface, about racist attacks committed by Poles – against Muslims, Jews, Caribbeans and people from the Indian subcontinent. And continually playing in the background were the news reports from Poland about a nation struggling with anti-Semitism and overt racism, especially against Africans.

One afternoon I'm at a café with my friend Sharmilla, who is Caribbean-British with Indian roots. We're both upset about the Brexit result and the hate that has spewed forth, both leading up to and in the wake of the vote. The increased antagonisms between immigrants have been especially sad to see. Sharmilla was harassed by Eastern Europeans on the train one evening, and I know several others who have experienced similar episodes.

'I don't understand it. How can Eastern Europeans – who are immigrants – harass us? We're English. British. Not foreigners – they're the ones who are foreigners,' I say, hearing how bad this sounds.

Sharmilla tells me I should talk to her friend, the Polish author A. M. Balakar, or Asia, as she's known among her friends. In her books, she explores the lives of Poles in London – no filter. 'She's married to a man of Caribbean descent,' Sharmilla says.

In Balakar's novel *Children of Our Age* (2017), we meet up-and-coming couple Karol and Milena, who will stop at nothing to become rich and powerful among the Polish community in London. They enter into a close collaboration with a staffing agency that supplies workers for hotels in west London, where Poles both young and old are tempted from their villages in Poland, only to be tricked and abused. By their own. The depictions of the characters are fairly merciless – the Poles are presented as cunning and heartless, obsessed with material wealth and sceptical of other foreigners. As I'm reading the book, I'm reminded of one of the few times I stayed at a hotel in London. One morning, I bumped into the woman who was cleaning my room because I had forgotten my jacket, and so returned to the room to get it. I tried to strike up a friendly conversation with her, but soon realised she didn't understand a word of English, only Polish. She nodded the entire time, almost as if ashamed. I've never forgotten her. What if something serious should happen to her, I wondered – how would she explain herself, or ask for help? Her situation is likely not even unique.

A couple of days later, I meet Asia on her lunchbreak. She's a chatty and funny woman in her forties, with quick quips at the ready. We find a bench in Green Park, the expansive royal park just beside Buckingham Palace, which is full of tourists and office workers eating their salads from plastic bowls. Asia's day job is at an investment bank close by. She left Poland at a young age to see the world and get an education. She tells me she was criticised by Polish readers when she published the book, because they thought she was perpetuating prejudices about Polish people. The idea for the novel came to her after a friend told her about a poor Pole who had been brought to Britain by a gang of Polish men. They took his passport and abandoned him on the street. The men then used his passport to obtain access to social benefits. Asia became curious about who these basely behaving Poles were, and began making enquiries among the Polish working class – a community she had little experience of herself. She was both shocked and impressed at how supposedly uneducated Poles managed to use the British system to their advantage. Asia emphasises that she didn't want to feed prejudices, but to tell a complex story about the ability of Polish workers to survive in London.

'I don't want to judge – Poles do what they need to do to get by. I admire their entrepreneurship enormously – they manage to build themselves up from nothing. That's commendable, and shouldn't be judged,' she says, despondent at the Brits she believes are often navel-gazing and ignorant of history.

'I have to laugh sometimes at all the British screaming and moaning about Brexit. Think about Poland! Brexit is nothing compared to what our nation has been through. Remember that Poland is a young democracy. We had no money for years, and had to fight for food. Suddenly, we could go out into the world. We got a shock. When Polish people came to England, they suddenly had the opportunity to earn huge sums of money – in their eyes, at least. They needed and still need the money, and that's why they're here. Not for cultural exchange – they're not here to become British,' Asia says.

When she talks about the failure of the British to understand how challenging it must have been to live behind the Iron Curtain, I feel offended.

'The Polish are a proud people, and they've become even more self-aware since acquiring a bad reputation. Many Europeans believe that nationalism is something to fret about, but for Poles the nation is what defines them. That's why they've created their own community here in London,' Asia says.

In *Children of Our Age*, Asia also touches on the culture shock experienced by Polish immigrants when they arrive in London. Many come from rural areas, and have never associated with people whose skin colour is anything other than white. This friction was examined in 2008, in the play *Let There Be Love* by British playwright and artistic director of the Young Vic, Kwame Kwei-Armah, who is of Caribbean descent. Prejudices run rampant in the piece, in which an older Caribbean man must relate to a young, Polish domestic worker his daughter has employed to help him at home. Through overt dialogue, Kwei-Armah turns the spotlight on the attitudes the two generations hold towards each other. The Caribbean pensioner accuses the young woman of being authoritarian, because this is seen by some as an Eastern European trait, while she believes he is lazy. Both are immigrants, but the Caribbean man regards himself as more British than the young Polish woman – after all, he came to the country first. Immigrants are specialists in establishing hierarchies, completely in line with the domination techniques of British colonialism: divide and rule.

Asia's husband's parents are from Jamaica, and when Asia and her husband visited Poland, her mother said: 'You do realise you can never live in Poland again?' Asia says she and her husband have experienced racism when they've been on holiday together.

The Poles who are accused of being racists in London make up only a marginal group within the community. But one of Poland's bestselling authors, Olga Tokarczuk, who won the International Booker Prize and the Nobel Prize in Literature in 2018, had to obtain police protection after she commented on Polish intolerance and anti-Semitism. The Poles are currently in the midst of an intense debate about their attitudes towards the Jews, both during and after the Second World War. The roots of this anti-Semitism stem from the Catholic Church.

The situation in Poland is serious. On 1 March 2018, legislation was introduced which means that anyone who publicly refers to the Nazi death camps as Polish can be fined or sentenced to up to three years in prison. Several Polish Jewish intellectuals have asked the Catholic Church in Poland to confront and challenge the growing anti-Semitism in the country.

We leave each other at Green Park Underground station. Queues of sightseeing buses wait to drive eager tourists around London's streets. I hear Italian, German and Polish being spoken among the families dressed in thick down jackets and hats, even though the weather is relatively mild. I always wonder how much they actually see, and *if* they see. Because while London's streets are enticing, they can be oh so treacherous. Behind every door in this city is a story, and not all of them are equally glamorous.

I jump on the Tube west, to Kensington. The Poles are not just a part of London's more recent history. Joseph Conrad was among the first Poles to settle in London, and the first Polish church, Saint Casimir's, opened in Shadwell in the east of the city as early as 1894. And in one of London's finer neighbourhoods, there is a very special club that was once filled with serious bridge-playing officers and glamorous women – all of them from Poland.

'People have so little knowledge about the history of Polish people in London. They think the Poles only arrived after the expansion of the EU,' says Stefan Scibor.

I feel slightly embarrassed, as I don't know that much myself. We're sitting in deep leather armchairs in the private Polish club Ognisko Polskie. Chandeliers and mahogany tables. Ornate, cast-iron railings. Oil paintings of generals on the walls. The club's premises are a magnificent white building in Knightsbridge, just next to the Brompton Oratory and one of London's finest art deco blocks.

Stefan grew up close by, in Kensington, and was educated at the University of Oxford. He's now the club's temporary director, and a good representative of the British upper class: friendly, but also reserved. I always feel slightly nervous meeting people from this kind of background because I suspect that everything they say has a subtext.

The first Polish embassy in London opened in 1919, when the Polish Republic was established, and in 1932 the Anglo-Polish Club was founded in an attempt to foster closer ties between Britain and Poland.[4] At this time, the Polish community in Britain consisted of around 5,000 people. Those who were in London worked in the confectionery industry, while others worked as coalminers in Lanarkshire or extracted salt from Cheshire's salt mines. But the lives of the Poles would be dramatically altered, in a way that still affects Poland deeply today.

In 1939, Adolf Hitler invaded Poland from the west. Joseph Stalin stomped in from the east, and sent over 1.5 million Poles to labour camps in Siberia and Kazakhstan. Over a million of them died, mainly of starvation.[5] The Polish government, led by the popular General Sikorski, fled, and established itself in London after a brief stay in Paris. Thousands of bureaucrats and supporters fled to London, settling in the south of the city in Kensington and Earl's Court, which soon became known as 'Little Poland'. Polish soldiers also fought alongside British troops in Normandy and Scotland. In 1939, 1,400 Poles were also incorporated into the Royal Air Force, and fought with the British.[6] Stefan's grandfather was among the Polish pilots in the RAF, and remained in England after the war. Throughout the war years, the Poles were regarded as heroes by the British. It was these soldiers, and individuals from the exiled government, who came together at Ognisko Polskie, which means the 'Polish hearth'.

'It was traumatic for the generals to come to London. This building was a place where they could meet other Poles in safe surroundings. They could smoke a cigar here, and relax,' Stefan says.

The club was financed by both the British and Polish governments, and the Duke of Kent opened the premises in July 1940. In the evenings, people flocked to the club to participate in literary salons, discuss politics, listen to music or watch theatrical performances. Several Polish newspapers were also soon established in London – a Polish proverb states that as soon as two Poles find themselves in a room together, they'll start a newspaper. The theatre company at the club spent a lot of time saving Polish actors from the internment camps in Siberia. I look at photographs from the club's first year, in a book that was created in connection with its fiftieth anniversary. The premises are packed with elegant men and women in suits and evening gowns.

'The men were confused and homeless – their identities were ripped away. They went from being soldiers and generals to being people of no import. The only education they had was within warfare, and the transition to civilian life was challenging,' Stefan says.

The soldiers had to make do with unskilled industrial work and shifts at factories, where no prior experience was necessary, but this was how they made lives for themselves. Among their own, the Poles were high-ranking military officials; among the English, they were refugees from the war.

Uncertainty hung over the Poles throughout the war years, even while they tried to daydream their cares away beneath the chandeliers at Ognisko Polskie. In 1943, 2,000 women who had previously been interned in Stalin's labour camps followed in the footsteps of the Polish soldiers when they found themselves on a surreal march. They began their journey from the camps in Siberia, making their way to Kitab in Uzbekistan in horse-drawn sleighs, on trains, in wheelbarrows, and sometimes on foot. The women were then sent over the Caspian Sea to a transit camp in Tehran. Here, they were divided into groups and sent by train and ship to camps in Tanzania, Uganda, Rhodesia and India.[7] Around 1,500 of them were offered refuge in Mexico. The target destination for most of the women was Britain, however, because this was where their men were. In India, when the British refused to permit a ship carrying 640 women and children to drop anchor in Mumbai, the Polish refugees were taken in by the Maharaja Digvijaysinhji Ranjitsinhji Jadeja of Nawanagar. The maharaja instructed the ship to go to the port town of Rosi, where it was able to put ashore. He gave the refugees food, and established a large camp right beside his summer palace. When the British authorities expressed their outrage at this, the maharaja declared that the refugees were his children, and issued special adoption papers for them. A square in Warsaw was named after the maharaja, as an expression of thanks.[8]

By the end of the war, 5 million Poles were spread across the world.[9]

The British had mixed feelings regarding the Poles. When soldiers from British-Polish Jewish backgrounds were sent to Polish units in 1944, it was expected they would form close bonds of comradeship with their fellow soldiers in the fight against Hitler. But the soldiers were not welcomed – instead, the lives of the British-Polish Jews were threatened by their fellow soldiers. In desperation, 200 British-Polish Jews deserted and demanded to be transferred to British divisions, even though they risked being shot. The British authorities thought the soldiers were trying to shirk their duties, and were sceptical of the request. But when the Polish foreign secretary in exile expressed his joy at being rid of them, the incident began to turn into a diplomatic crisis. The Poles' blatant anti-Semitism was a delicate problem.[10]

The status of the Polish army was left hanging throughout the war, because the loyalty of the Polish soldiers was constantly questioned. Where did their loyalties really lie? With Churchill or with their own exiled government? But at the Yalta Conference of 1945, the fate of the Poles was sealed. Poland would not be free, but ruled by a communist government supported by the Soviets – a dependency, many believed. Stalin was permitted to keep Poland as a hinterland on the condition that a free election would be held in the near future.

In the years 1946 and 1947, over 160,000 Polish refugees arrived in Britain in the form of soldiers, civilians, men, women and orphaned children. Churchill fought for the refugees, and convinced the government that they were a special case. But what should be done with the homeless Poles? Churchill had an idea, and one of the last things he managed to push through before losing the election in 1945 was the establishment of the Polish Resettlement Corps. The organisation would not be military in nature, but it would be run by the British Army. The men would contribute to the rebuilding of Britain, and were sent out to work in the industrial sector and on the country's farms. Not everybody was keen on this arrangement, however, and British unions grumbled loudly about 'Polish fascists'. At first, the National Union of Mineworkers prohibited all Poles from working in the mines, even though they needed the manpower. In the end, the union did permit the Poles to work – but only after they had negotiated themselves a quid pro quo in the form of a five-day working week.

In January 1947, 2,764 Poles worked in British industry – by October that same year, this figure had increased to 43,000. Of the 160,000 Poles who could apply for British citizenship, 120,000 applied for passports.[11] The British had no reason to fear the Poles because as soon they had acquired jobs, they bought houses and generally married among themselves. The pervading sense of home-lessness meant that the Poles actively sought to cultivate their culture. Those with higher educations continued their studies, and several obtained high-ranking academic positions. They gradually began to make up a solid middle-class community in Ealing, Earl's Court and Kensington.

This is the generation to which Stefan's parents belong. In the early 1960s there were so many Poles between Earl's Court and Exhibition Road in South Kensington that the bus drivers are said to have shouted 'the Polish corridor' as bus number 74 crossed

Cromwell Road. This was where Polish hairdressers, doctors, dentists, pharmacists, architects, estate agents and bakers could be found. Both maintaining and contributing to the Polish cultural heritage was important to the Poles, and to Stefan's parents.

'I actually didn't speak English until I started school,' Stefan says.

I'm surprised at this – I wasn't aware the Poles were so keen to preserve their language once they had settled in London. As we speak, I notice that Stefan becomes a little uncomfortable when I ask him about his childhood or his experiences as a Pole. He twists around in his chair, and begins to digress about the weather and London traffic more and more often. Stefan tells me that he noticed a significant change after Poland became part of the EU.

'Before, if I said I was Polish, nobody reacted. People didn't problematise it, I was just one of many people with an immigrant background. I was a student when things began to change, and then I found that if I mentioned my Polish background, all the Poles I met wanted to know exactly where in Poland I was from – they assumed I had just arrived. While some of the English . . . I was struck speechless the first time somebody asked me if I could fix their plumbing, I have to admit,' says Stefan, who probably hasn't the slightest knowledge of pipes or drains.

His father was a professor at the London School of Economics.

I'm fascinated by the question of Polish identity. Even Stefan, who was born and grew up here, insists that he's Polish, not English.

'You don't seem very concerned about your identity as a Londoner,' I say to him. 'If I were you, I would probably have said that I was from London. But you say you're Polish?'

'It's a complicated question. How I feel is one thing, but a lot has changed within society here. Before, I could have got away with saying that I'm from London, but now I'm almost forced to say that

I have Polish roots. I'm not particularly fond of this trend where we have to put labels on everything, it didn't used to be that way. Now everybody has to belong to an ethnic group,' Stefan says.

Stefan gradually begins to give shorter answers to my questions, and is now sitting on the very edge of the leather chair's seat.

'Let's talk about the club instead,' he says suddenly.

A number of small clubs have been incorporated into Ognisko. The objective of the various organisations is to highlight renowned Polish cultural celebrities: composer Frédéric Chopin, Marie Curie (born Marie Salomea Skłodowska) and Nicolaus Copernicus are favourites. I notice that the club seems to focus on events that promote classical music and science, and wonder whether the new Poles in London find their place here in Ognisko Polskie. As I bring this up, I notice that Stefan's expression stiffens slightly.

'Well. I suppose so.'

He pauses.

'I don't have anything in common with the new Poles beyond the language. That's why I'm a little tired of meeting Englishmen who tar us all with the same brush without thinking,' Stefan says.

He gets up.

'We're a private club for people with special interests,' he emphasises, before suddenly saying he has another meeting to get to.

It's a brisk farewell. I walk down to Cromwell Road, to what used to be the Polish corridor in the 1960s. Now the Arabs have taken over the area, and are evident at all the hotels along this road. The Poles have moved quite a bit further west. The bus drivers probably shout 'the Arab corridor' now.

Stefan's guardedness is not actually unexpected. I've met several Poles from backgrounds similar to Stefan's, and they have often seemed keen to hold at arm's length their countrymen who arrived in the UK after Poland joined the EU. The newspaper reports about loutish Poles that have dominated the media in recent years have likely also contributed to people like Stefan not wanting to be associated with the new arrivals.

In April 2015, an older Polish man made the news: a Polish prince. He was furious at the rhetoric that was beginning to characterise the debate around Brexit.

I would have loved to have been a fly on the wall when Nigel Farage, the former leader of UKIP, saw the video greeting from Prince Zylinski. Zylinski had endured enough of UKIP's hateful rhetoric against immigrants, as well as Farage's propensity to label all immigrants as parasites. 'The most idiotic example I've heard of has been Mr Nigel Farage blaming migrants for traffic jams on the M40,' Zylinski said, sitting at a marble desk in his home. With a sword in his hand, he challenged Nigel Farage to a duel in Hyde Park.[12] Unfortunately, Farage declined. The sword Zylinski showed in the video was a family heirloom, which he claims was used by his father to eradicate Nazis during the Second World War. The charismatic prince, who is also a self-made property baron, was born and raised in Lewisham, and has demonstrated that he's a warm supporter of immigration. But his somewhat unorthodox political strategy is not the only reason Zylinski has made headlines. He also owns an unusual house: a luxurious white palace in Ealing, where discretion, not vulgarity, is a virtue. The property is a reproduction of the Godzowa palace, owned by Prince Zylinski's grandmother, Jadwija. After meticulous research, that which originally was an ordinary, spacious detached property has now been converted into something much more luxurious. But not all the neighbours have been equally enthusiastic about the Polish prince's melodramatic property dreams. The prince rarely invites people in for guided tours, and I've therefore only viewed photographs taken inside the lavish property online. Marble, walnut and gold characterise the interior, but according to an acerbic commentator in the *Daily Telegraph*, the prince hasn't quite understood the meaning of the word sophisticated – Zylinski has a marble bathroom which also contains toilet paper from Tesco.[13] Such a combination bears witness to a certain lack of finesse. British journalists know exactly where to kick people who seem to be getting above their station.

But Prince Zylinski isn't just a sheltered political activist. Following the challenge he posed to Farage, he has continued his political work. In 2016, Zylinski stood as a candidate for mayor of London but lost to Sadiq Khan, and ended up in a disappointing eleventh place. He then founded the political party Polska Duma – Polish Pride – which stood in the local elections. Zylinski then ran for mayor again. The party's launch took place outside Westminster, where twenty or so supporters raised placards with texts like: 'Unite. Let's heal London' and 'Make Europhobia a Crime'. But despite his sympathetic causes, the charismatic Zylinski hasn't entirely managed to convince his countrymen in London that he's their spokesman.

'Little Poland'

Ealing, in west London, is a so-called 'leafy' neighbourhood, which implies a certain wealth, and where most of the inhabitants are white – and classified as English. In 1902, Ealing was referred to as the 'queen of the suburbs'.[1] I can easily understand the enthusiasm.

A certain degree of enlightenment and a love of high culture are essential traits for anyone living in Ealing, the area you move to if you want to belong to the middle class – and it was precisely this move that the Poles made in the years following the Second World War. There weren't so many of them back then – around 2,000 – but today that figure has risen to over 30,000 and given rise to Ealing becoming synonymous with 'Little Poland'.[2] You can't see with the naked eye that Ealing is Polish, because the district isn't like Brick Lane or Brixton where the streets are marked by Indian and Caribbean immigration. But if you listen carefully, you'll discover that Polish is the language most commonly spoken on the streets here, beside English.

The Poles came here for the job opportunities with aircraft engineering companies linked to the British Army, as well as the relatively cheap properties. Soon, the Poles began to start their own companies, and opened pharmacies, printers, bookshops, courier firms and restaurants. They also moved to the affluent neighbourhood of Chiswick close by. The Poles had strong links to the Catholic

Church, and the Pope was an important figure in their lives, much as he was for the Irish and the Italians. In their energetic way, the Poles began to make their mark on all areas of society, while also working hard to preserve a strong Polish identity in their encounter with all things British. And here, education has been key.

In 1950, the Tadeusz Kościuszko Polish Saturday School was founded – the first of many Polish Saturday schools. While other children usually slump down on the sofa with an iPhone or watch YouTube videos on an iPad on Saturday mornings, over 100 Polish girls and boys between the ages of four and sixteen attend the school in Ealing, just like hundreds of other Polish children all across Britain who go to similar Polish Saturday schools. The schools are partly financed through support from the Polish authorities, and these subsidies mean that Polish families in London can choose whether or not they wish to pay for their children to attend. The intention of the Saturday schools is to equip the children with a clear idea of who they really are: although they live in Britain, they are Polish.

The Poles have always maintained close ties to their homeland due to the political developments that followed the war. Under communism, very few Poles were able to travel out of the country. Life was tough for the Poles under the communist regime; strikes began to spread because the authorities implemented measures like increased food prices, often without warning, and a strong discontent took root. In the 1980s, people began to take to the streets to protest the communist regime and the ever-increasing economic crisis that had led to a lack of even the most necessary provisions. When the Polish government increased food prices on 1 July 1980, it was the final straw. Strikes were set in motion. And on 14 August that year, a young shipyard worker with a distinctive moustache drove into the Lenin Shipyard in Gdańsk. This uncompromising young man's name was Lech Wałęsa, and his arrival was the start of what would become Poland's first union: *Solidarność* – Solidarity.

On 13 December 1981 a state of emergency was declared in Poland. The leader of Solidarity was imprisoned and thousands were arrested; the following year, the union was banned. Ealing's streets began to seethe with activity in solidarity with the opposition back home. Poles in exile, along with second-generation Poles, began to collect money to help people back in Poland. The Polish Solidarity Campaign in Great Britain (PSC) fought for free unions and democracy in Poland, and were based here in Ealing. Throughout 1981, huge demonstrations were arranged in support of Solidarity, and many spoke out about boycotting Polish and Russian goods. Over 800 families in Warsaw received direct help from their countrymen in 'Little Poland'.

At a dinner at Ealing Town Hall, which had been arranged to promote collaboration between the British and Russians, furious Poles gathered to protest. Two hundred people demonstrated outside the building. The activists believed that the Russians were the reason that Solidarity had been banned.

The efforts of the Ealing Poles were rewarded after the fall of the Berlin Wall. On 2 December 1989, Lech Wałęsa visited Ealing in connection with a trip to London. He was welcomed as a hero.

But there was more that changed after the fall of the Berlin Wall. It became possible for Poles to travel beyond Poland's borders, and Poles abroad could now visit their loved ones. But the joy of meeting again was often tinged with bitterness. Upon arriving in what had once been their homeland, many British Poles were shook – they realised that the standard of living was much lower than they had imagined. They also met Poles who were not opposed to communism, and who were offended by their countrymen who lived abroad.

Poland underwent dramatic changes, and the Poles in Ealing became part of these political transformations. In 1990, a Polish councillor in Ealing, Wiktor Moszczyński, travelled to Poland to advise politicians there. A year later, nineteen members of the Polish government came to Ealing to refine their administrative skills, and the following year three members of Polish Parliament came to witness democracy in practice. In 1992, British Prime Minister John Major removed the visa requirement for Poles wishing to travel to the UK.

The Poles have always been keen on being politically active, and the expansion of the EU gave the Polish population in London endless opportunities within business and education. When Prime Minister David Cameron suddenly decided that the British should be given an opportunity to leave the EU, this came as a shock to the Poles.

'Leaving the EU is totally in the spirit of punk!'

Andrew Czezowski is direct. I try to hide my shock, although I'm unsure whether I succeed. All I manage to spit out is a meek: 'Could you explain what you mean by that?' I've never thought of Brexit like this – of it being a punk act. And if we're resorting to clichés, there's little that seems punk about the older Polish man sitting in front of me, next to his wife, Susan Carrington. Unconventional is perhaps a more accurate description.

'I can hardly wait until we're out. We'll be able to decide for ourselves now. It'll be wonderful. I'm tired of all the corrupt bureaucrats in Brussels,' he continues.

I'm not actually here to talk about the EU, but rather about Andrew Czezowski's Polish roots, the legendary punk club the Roxy – which managed to become a historic institution in just 100 days – and renowned nightclub the Fridge in Brixton. The Roxy was the birthplace for a philosophy of life that I've long held in high esteem, but was too young to experience.

I've come to meet the couple in Streatham, a slightly shabby area of London divided by one of the city's busiest roads, the A23. The area's current claim to fame is that the popular rapper Dave, who plays bad guy Modi in the series *Top Boy*, was raised here. Otherwise, Streatham is one of London's slightly more vapid suburbs, where you wouldn't imagine anything exciting ever takes place. But I imagine nobody will do so much as raise an eyebrow on the day a major newspaper describes Streatham as 'trendy'. It's only a matter of time.

Way back in 1978, a racy story made the headlines when a brothel run by Cynthia Payne was exposed in Streatham. When the police raided her house on Ambleside Avenue, fifty-three men were discovered, all in the midst of 'enjoying themselves'. Several of them had high-ranking jobs, and some of them were even priests – the incident became a national scandal chuckled at by all and sundry. Payne eventually became a colourful celebrity everyone had heard of.[3] But all the way at the other end of the scale, Streatham High Street was voted 'Britain's worst street' back in 2002 through a vote on BBC Radio 4's *Today* programme, due to the traffic and broken streetlights. This is actually a little unfair, because if you turn off the main road you find yourself on some of London's finest streets, with row upon row of burgundy brick houses. The properties were built taking inspiration from the Arts and Crafts aesthetic that gained popularity in the late 1800s and early 1900s. The houses almost look like Gothic churches, and several of them seem taken straight out of a fairy tale, surrounded by large trees. Andrew and Susan don't live in this kind of house, but the unassuming building is still extraordinary when you walk inside: purple carpets meet orange walls, and there's red on black and green on gold, along with Chinese vases, film posters, books, vinyl and art as far as the eye can see. The couple will soon be selling this house to move to Torquay in Devon, where a large property with a view of the sea awaits them. Andrew has recently sold his mother's home in Brixton, which has brought the couple a decent amount of money.

Andrew's parents have something in common with those of Stefan at Ognisko Polskie: it was the Second World War that brought them to London. But while Stefan's upbringing was privileged, Andrew grew up in poverty, and his parents remained at the bottom of the social ladder.

'My mother grew up in a tiny place outside Kraków. She was the daughter of a farmer and used to working hard. Because she came from a farm, she was assigned to a slave labour camp on the Dutch border. It was run by some decent Germans, who treated her well. They let her go to church every Sunday, where she met my father, who was a soldier. As a thanks for fighting for the allies, you could choose where you wanted to settle if you didn't want to go back to Poland,' Andrew says.

The choices on offer were England, Australia, South Africa and Canada. Andrew's parents decided on England. They found a home on a council estate in Brixton; by this time, the couple had five children. The kids grew up in difficult circumstances, like most of the people around them. The family settled in Brixton at the same time as the Caribbean immigrants arrived, and a community began to take shape, Andrew explains.

'We were all foreigners. My father was treated badly – he couldn't speak English properly. My mother had no friends, but together they managed to figure things out and took the challenges they faced in their stride. If something awful happened, it was just a case of getting on with it, as they had always done,' Andrew says.

He met Susan at a dance at the Ram Jam Club in Brixton when they were both sixteen. At the time, the club was one of London's most popular establishments for soul, ska and jazz. Susan came from a poor family in Walworth, in the south of the city, and because of her background received a grant to study at City of Westminster College, where she met the wealthy John Krivine. Krivine and the couple became good friends, and started hanging out on the King's Road, which has always been a place where bohemians have strutted around in their brocade dresses, paisley shirts and velvet. This was where the Antiquarius arcade was located, with over 100 small shops selling what Susan describes as English heritage: silver, tobacco and incense. In the basement, Krivine opened his own shop, named Acme Attractions, which was stuffed with rock 'n' roll retro items, art, magazines and carefully selected clothes.

Susan and Andrew began working there together. Andrew kept Krivine's accounts, without much idea of what he was actually doing. Acme Attractions soon made a name for itself, and became a competitor of Vivienne Westwood and Malcolm McLaren's more exclusive store, Let It Rock, which opened in 1974 on the same street.

It was around this time that Andrew met a young man named Donovan, who would later become known as Don Letts.

London's streets were starting to become agitated, influenced by the riots and rebellion in the US. One of the people who wanted to jump-start those under thirty was Malcolm McLaren. He'd been to the US, and seen the kinds of artistic and musical revolts that were possible. He returned home with big plans – one of which was a band called the Sex Pistols. On 6 November 1975, Andrew and Susan saw the Sex Pistols perform live for the first time at Central Saint Martins. Susan had cut off her long blonde locks, and turned up sporting a short, spiky hairstyle. The art students didn't like Johnny Rotten and the racket the band performed, and likely had no idea of what a historic event they were witnessing. But the lives of Susan and Andrew were never the same again.

The encounter with the Sex Pistols didn't just change Susan and Andrew's lives. Punk had now officially arrived in Britain, and over the subsequent years the lives of Susan and Andrew became both the incarnation and documentation of punk's first year in England. The couple decided they wanted to start their own punk club, and opened the Roxy in Covent Garden. This is where music historians and nerds will probably start to argue over the details, but one version of the story is that the Roxy became the very definition of British punk

– and that punk died the day the Roxy closed its doors. Another version is that this was the moment from which punk really took off.

At this time, Andrew was also the manager of two of England's most popular punk rock bands – Generation X, with Billy Idol on vocals, and the Damned. After trying their hand at another club in Covent Garden, Susan and Andrew decided to move south. In 1981, the Fridge opened its doors in Brixton, attracting huge crowds. The location was perfect because Brixton had always been a popular area among those interested in music. The premises soon became too small, and an alternative had to be found – a dilapidated cinema from 1913 would turn out to be the solution.

'Sade, Nick Cave and the Bad Seeds and the Eurythmics – they all played there before they became superstars. And I can promise you that you'd never have expected any of them to become big if you'd seen them live back then,' Andrew laughs.

Running the Fridge became a lot of work for the couple, and after twenty years of hard graft they sold the club. Andrew emphasises his working-class background when he looks back on how much resistance they had to endure.

'We saw how our parents struggled without complaining,' he says, drawing parallels with today's Poles in London.

Andrew becomes animated, gesticulating wildly. 'I meet Poles here in Streatham, stylish young women. They do everything they can to learn the language and find a job. They fit right in, and become British. But right next to us, there's an East African enclave. They don't mix with the English, don't learn the language, they seem to show no interest in society.' Andrew shakes his head.

I wonder why he voted for Brexit. Susan jumps in, and starts an enthusiastic monologue about the fantastic Polish hairdressers in the neighbourhood, and the wonderful Polish supermarkets in Streatham. But they don't want to visit Poland. Andrew hasn't been very interested in preserving Polish traditions.

Punk and his work with the clubs have been Andrew's foremost identity. Susan takes out a pile of photographs – she has something she wants to show me, and seems proud. In one photo, the couple are posing in front of a plaque in Neal Street, Covent Garden. Andrew is wearing an orange suit jacket and a purple shirt with ruffles down the chest. The plaque says: 'Legendary Punk Club 1976–1978' – no mean feat for a poor Polish boy from Brixton. I leave them thoughtful at how punk still inspires people, and how enthusiastic individuals like Andrew and Susan were uncompromising pioneers.

London was once marked by the craziness that went on at the Roxy. You might end up on the train from Streatham to Victoria station next to young men and women wearing ripped tights, dog collars around their necks, tartan bondage trousers covered in spikes and chains, leather coats or cut-off denim jackets. They were often loudmouthed and racist, and the worst of them spat and swigged beer. There are no punks on the train as I leave Streatham. All the passengers I see are dressed within the realms of what is regarded as 'normal' these days. And I suppose nobody would guess that I too was once a punk– there's nothing about me that even remotely signals rebellion. Tattoos have become commonplace, as have studs and brightly coloured hair. Rebellion doesn't seem the same any more. Maybe Andrew feels that, these days, Brexit is the only way he can really give the world the finger? Just like the grandfather of punk, Johnny Rotten himself.

A home for you, a home for me

Exactly how and at what moment Polish engineer Roman Wajda came up with the idea for a dedicated cultural centre in London is unknown. Perhaps he was sitting at the kitchen table drinking coffee, or taking a stroll to get some fresh air outside Battersea College where he taught. Wajda had lived in London since 1946 and was an active Polish immigrant. There turned out to be significant enthusiasm for the idea he had in 1964, and with a group of like-minded individuals he set out around Britain collecting money for the centre from other Poles who shared his vision. After years of persistent fundraising, in 1972 the foundation purchased a row of older buildings in King Street in Ravenscourt Park. Two years later, in December 1974, the Polish Social and Cultural Association (POSK) opened its doors. Sadly, Wajda would never experience the joy of seeing his dream realised – he passed away just a few weeks before the centre opened.

Just as Ognisko Polskie provided a safe base for Poles throughout the Second World War, POSK also arranged theatrical performances and grand events. The building acquired a special significance for Poles in London, and became a second home for them. The library here, which is named after Joseph Conrad, holds first editions of Conrad's books, and the walls are full of drawings signed by the author. And POSK hasn't become any less important since the

1970s. At weekends, the bar on the top floor is filled with young Poles enjoying Polish pop music they never hear anywhere else in London. In a street dominated by typical British terraced houses the building stands out; with its sharp lines, the four-storey building has a somewhat communist aesthetic. This is actually a little strange, because in the 1970s the Poles in London were none too keen on communism. Nor did they regard themselves as Eastern Europeans. They were Western Europeans, because they were Christians. You risk causing offence should you try to contradict them.

'But he's Polish?' Tomasz Furmanek looks at me, astonished.

'Yes, I was surprised, too,' I say.

I'm communicating my newfound insight into the ownership of the Roxy to another Pole, who like me probably falls into the category of retired punk. Tomasz is a passionate soul who I wouldn't hesitate to call the premier ambassador for Polish jazz in London. He's a composer and jazz vocalist himself, and came to the British capital in the early 2000s.

'Poland has become too conservative, in the most absurd way – it's completely unacceptable, as I see it. I think it's probably quite hard for young people who want to live slightly different lives than the normal lives of conformity there now. I was a punk, and later a "new waver" in the 1980s, and lived what many would probably have said was a pretty alternative lifestyle, but people didn't care back then. The space for that kind of acting out has become much narrower in Poland,' Tomasz says.

He's wearing a dark corduroy jacket and has a long fringe that he continually flicks out of his eyes. We're standing in the foyer at POSK, surrounded by families with young children. The kids run around, while some of the parents are trying to fill out forms. It looks a little chaotic, and I don't envy them the bureaucracy they have to go through to obtain their residence permits. The Polish consulate has office hours here to help Poles who want to settle in

Britain. And there are many of them. A large crucifix hangs on the wall.

Tomasz is a kind of curator for Jazz Café POSK, which has been established in the basement. Here, serious music enthusiasts can listen to Polish jazz – a genre only those with expert knowledge within the field of jazz know anything about. The Poles' relationship to jazz has been characterised by secrecy, and it was only from the mid-1950s that they were able to come out of the closet as the jazz-loving people they are.[1] While British beatniks could safely listen to Thelonious Monk and Miles Davis at Ronnie Scott's in Soho, Poles risked being arrested if the authorities found out that they were listening to jazz. During the Second World War, the Nazis banned jazz in Poland.

'The jazz in itself wasn't political, but the communist authorities regarded jazz as imperialistic, Western music, and it was forbidden from the end of the 1940s until a few years after Stalin's death. Some musicians played the music in secret, but you risked being arrested for playing or listening to jazz, or you could be thrown out of university. It was also illegal to listen to foreign radio stations, but of course there were a number of people who listened to Voice of America or Radio Berlin,' says Tomasz. Today, jazz is practically regarded as folk music in Poland. We go down to the Jazz Café. It's an intimate space, where the audience can lounge on chairs or a landing scattered with cushions.

Despite Stalin's attempts to smother it, jazz in Poland didn't die. Instead, an underground movement and unique jazz scene developed. Unlike in Paris, Oslo and Copenhagen, no American jazz artists turned up to jam with the musicians. The Polish artists had to explore jazz on their own. British jazz lovers became aware of Polish jazz after Stalin's death in 1953. Three years after Stalin passed away, some enthusiasts arranged a large international jazz festival in the city of Sopot. Thirty thousand spectators turned up to listen to Komeda Sextet, with pianist Krzysztof Komeda and Zbigniew Namysłowski's quartet. A British man in the audience was captivated by the unique music – he worked for London-based record company Decca. The album *Lola* by Zbigniew Namysłowski's quartet was released in 1964, becoming the first jazz record recorded in the West to be released by a Polish band.

During the 1960s, more Polish jazz artists came to play at Ronnie Scott's. The queues were long – hipsters had found a new music. In an old film clip from 1960s Poland, young Poles sit smoking; young women dressed in black read Norman Mailer. Tomasz is visibly proud when we talk about Polish jazz – *Polski jazz*. Today's Polish artists are at least just as innovative, he claims, and hundreds of Polish jazz albums are released each year. But I've been pondering something that doesn't quite sit right with me, and that's why I wanted to meet Tomasz.

Jazz was invented by African-American musicians. Their philosophy of life, free of prejudices and with a magnanimous and inclusive outlook, breaks radically with the news from today's Poland. News reports show a society that is increasingly turning away from the world, and back to nationalism. As we walk up to the bar on the third floor, I tell Tomasz about a report I saw recently on the BBC. Poland is in the midst of an identity crisis, according to the British reporter. 'Is this the end of liberal democracy?' the solemn reporter asked as he walked around a Polish suburb. Sombre music accompanied the images of destitution. 'We don't need to learn from the West, we have our own traditions,' said an elderly woman in the segment. Does this affect the Poles in London? And what about POSK? In the bar, Tomasz stirs his tea for a while before he answers.

'I hear what you're saying. POSK is a neutral institution where everyone can feel welcome, and as you point out, jazz is inclusive and international by nature. That's why the attitudes in Poland make me uneasy. I recently heard about a schoolboy in Poland who was wearing a pink sweater. His teacher ordered him to take it off because he looked gay. She said he might even become gay from wearing it.

I really hope these kinds of absurd prejudices don't exist among the Poles here,' Tomasz says.

But I can see from his eyes that he'd like to say more.

Immigration has become a sensitive subject in both Britain and Poland. On 26 June 2016, three days after the British voted to leave the EU, the employees at POSK were met by graffiti on the centre's front door: the words 'Fuck off OPM' had been sprayed across the glass. Nobody understood what OPM stood for. Was this vandalism by Poles directed at other Poles, or was it an act of hate triggered by Brexit? The police immediately investigated the matter as a hate crime, and the centre was filled with flowers and greetings from all across the country. After the incident, Director of POSK Joanna Młudzińska stated that Poles generally neglect to report hate crimes, because they often occur at workplaces and people don't want to complain for fear of losing their jobs.[2]

Tomasz hasn't been subjected to any racist remarks, but tells me that some of his illusions were shattered when he arrived in Britain. The country wasn't as it appeared in the captivating Merchant Ivory films he had watched throughout his childhood. In films like *A Room with a View* (1986), the English were sober, cultured beings, but Tomasz quickly experienced that Brits could be both ignorant and hostile.

'I'm a guest in this country, so I can't criticise the host. That would be extremely inelegant. But I would say that the British have been extremely adept at creating myths about themselves,' he says.

I chuckle at his diplomatic phrasing. Tomasz and I continue to reflect on the difficult situation as a young couple come into the bar with their children. The kids run around beneath the Polish flags that have been hung up. What does the future hold for them? Brexit has caused trouble for both Polish and British citizens.

*　　*　　*

'I can honestly say that I'd take a million Poles into this country before I took one Muslim.' This quote is from Jayda Fransen, leader of Britain First.[3] The organisation actively recruits supporters from among the Poles living in Britain. A few months after the EU referendum, two Poles were arrested for having thrown bacon at mosque-goers and harassing visitors there.[4] They were perhaps inspired by Polish social media personality Marcin Rola, who runs the YouTube channel Wrealu24 with over 200,000 subscribers. Some of the statements he has made include: 'In Islam paedophilia is their daily bread' and 'Muslims sell their own wives as goats'.

Slough in London, November 2017: several hundred Poles are gathered to meet a dozen or so social media personalities from Poland. Common to all of them is that they belong to the Polish right. The event has been marketed as a book fair, and among those who are gathered here is Marcin Rola, dressed in a suit. On the wall behind him hangs a banner for Polska Niepodległa, a conservative organisation. The same group has previously attempted to invite the former Catholic priest Jacek Międlar, well known for his anti-Semitic and anti-Muslim attitudes – the British authorities prevented him from coming, however, because they believe he spreads hate speech. During the discussion, which is moderated by Rola, the participants talk about how 'war is the only solution' and that 'the ethnic composition of our continent is a biological time bomb'. Such events are not uncommon. Polish skinheads have also been observed getting worryingly well acquainted with British skinheads, and Polish far-right groups arrange family days at which attendees are served anti-Islamic propaganda and can try their hand at firing weapons. This is a change in values that's on a collision course with what I perceive to be London's tolerant soul. Not long ago, one of POSK's meeting rooms was hired by a Polish organisation on the far right. It's a matter of freedom of speech, Tomasz says, with a small sigh.

The political landscape Tomasz and I bear witness to is deeply troubling. Polish researcher Michał Garapich believes that Polish far-right extremist groups' repeated visits to London may in the worst-case scenario result in the radicalisation of young Poles. Far-right extremists from the Polish Independence Movement held an anti-Semitic demonstration during a memorial day for the Holocaust – at Auschwitz, no less – in January 2019.

Tomasz and I walk slowly down to the exit, past the paintings hanging on the polished granite walls, all the way to the ground floor. POSK has a unique collection of Polish art, which has been donated by wealthy Poles. POSK is now struggling financially, and has constructed two rental apartments to supplement the centre's income. The older generation of Poles who took Polish cultural life seriously are gradually disappearing, which means that their donations are dwindling, too. The auditorium is now rented to schools in the area when they need extra space for end-of-year celebrations or performances. It's hard to say no to money.

As I leave Tomasz, I wonder what paths the next generation of Poles will follow. Many young Poles have already returned home because of Brexit – they feel uneasy about their future in London. I hope they have taken a little of London's cosmopolitan soul home with them. This seems of vital importance, at a time when conservative, national forces are gaining ground.

Luckily, London stands firm as an invincible giant.

Afterword

4 March 2021

On Sunday 23 February, 2020, Abel, Elliot and I got on one of the many local trains passing through East Croydon station heading for Gatwick airport. We had spent a week in London with my parents and enjoyed the stay. We had eaten spaghetti bolognese and apple crumble at E. Pellicci's; joked with Anna and Nevio, and Elida had promised to treat me to her exceptional meatballs the next time I visited. We had made our regular visit to Brixton looking for the coolest trainers; my sons trying to spot the notorious drill star M24. And we headed north, to Camden, just for fun. We were eager to come back, so much more to explore and of course revisit.

We had no idea we were not going to be coming back any time soon.

A month later, my parents arrived at Oslo Gardermoen airport, looking pensive. There was hardly a soul to be seen.

London did not feel safe for them any more. COVID-19 had taken hold of the capital.

The London I once knew has been paused. The restaurants and the shops are closed, the daily banter, the random conversations, the small talk between strangers on the streets of London are muted.

The Tubes and trains are empty. Nobody knows when – or even if – London will once again be the bustling metropolis we all love.

As we moved into 2021, the Brexit deal was officially sealed. Immigration to the UK has never been lower. What the consequences will be for London's fabric is impossible to foresee. There is, however, no doubt that the London I have tried to capture in this book has been created over time by those who have been arriving from all over the world for many, many years.

I have no doubt that immigrants will still want to come here and in doing so continue to make and remake the city.

A new London will surely emerge, and through it all our love for London will endure.

Acknowledgements

The dream of writing a book like this would never have been realised without a three-year writing stipend from the Norwegian Non-Fiction Writers and Translators Association (NFFO) and funding from the Fritt Ord Foundation, and I am deeply grateful for their faith in my project.

I have long been obsessed with cities, urban development and identity. In 1999, I moved to London to study at the London School of Economics (LSE), and my interest in cities led to me choosing urban studies as part of my masters in international relations. While studying at LSE, I met Professor Saskia Sassen and her husband Professor Richard Sennett, who taught there at the time. I'll never forget one lecture in which Sassen banged her fist against the lectern and cried: 'All money is dirty!' My masters thesis examined urban identity versus national identity – a hybrid of academic disciplines. Sassen and Sennett aroused an intense curiosity in me, and this book would never have been written without the inspiration they provided. Another influential person has been Oslo's own city doctor, Erling Fossen, a true urbanist.

In connection with the work this book has required, I've been surrounded by an indispensable group of helpers and advisors to whom I'm indescribably grateful. Some have read the text, others have opened doors or provided advice, discussed and reflected, while yet others have cheered me on when my energy was at its lowest. So an enormous thank you to: Abdullah Anas, Abosede Afolashade, Adeyemi Michael, Alan Dein, Alex Glinsky, Alexander Ashkurov, Amal Ghosh, Andrew Czezowski, Ann Rossiter, Anna Korjakina, Anne Hilde Neset, Andrew and Carmel Coll, Anthony Polledri, Aoife Hamill, Arun Ghosh, Asia Bakalar, Barby Asante, Bård Larsen, Ben Chikjojie, Birgitte Aasen, Birgitte Sigmundstad, Charlotte Ellis, Christine Walsh, Ciaran Thapar, Claudia Wilson, Clarie Nolan Sturley and family, Debbie Smith, Dina Brawer, Don Letts, Erling Kagge, Eva Meinich, Eva Prinz, Evgeny Chichvarkin, Friedrikke Huber, Grete Borge, Hans Petter Sjøli, Hari Kunzru, Henna Henza-Butt, Herman Betancourt, Herschel Gluck, Ingrid Schibsted Jacobsen, Ivo de Figueiredo, Jagdish Patel, Jan Olufsen, Jorun Sofie Aartun, Kealan Duigan, Kent Erlend Horne, Kwamz and Flava, Harbinder Sodhi, Hilde Ghosh Maisey, Lorraine Simpson, Louisa Olufsen Layne, Leonardo Clausi, Magda Raczynska, Maged Latif, Marius Bakke, Mary Ann Lucas, Matthew Phillip, Michelle Deignan, Mitsy Smith, Mohamed Abdi, Mohamed Kozbar, Momadou Bocoum, Monika Bobinska, Mykaell Riley, Niall McLaughlin, Neil Cole, Nicholas Okwulu, Nick Robbins, Nomy Khan, Øivind Bratberg, Paul Gilroy, the Pellicci family, Pietro Molle, Rosemari Mallett, Reza Zia-Ebrahimi, Richard Allen Greene, Richard Young, Rob Young, Roger Herz, Roman Borisovich, Samantha-Jane Ofoegbu, Shamil Thakrar, Sharmilla Beezmohun, Sheba Remy Kharbanda, Shola Amoo, Sindre Bangstad, Susan Carrington, Thomas Hegghammer, Terje Thorsen, Tomasz Furmanek, Tony Bay, Tony Murray, Tony F. Wilson, Vladimir Ashkurov, Vikram Kolmannskog and Vinay Patel.

An enthusiastic and unreserved thank you goes to Kagge, the publisher of the original 2019 Norwegian edition, and the editor Joakim Botten, who has been exceptionally patient. He's challenged me as an editor must, even when the author is riddled with doubts, and given me solid advice throughout the writing process.

I am forever grateful to my brilliant agent Thomas Mala at Northern Stories for never giving up, and Duncan Proudfoot at Robinson for fulfilling my dream. I might not have spent my life in London, but at least I was able to write a book about the love of my life.

Also, thank you to Alison McCullough for the wonderful translation of the book. It has been amazing to follow the process and see how the book was transformed.

I would also like to thank my former employers, the esteemed publishing house Aschehoug for giving me time to write this book, and a special thanks to my boss, sworn London-enthusiast and Thin Lizzy expert Jan Swensson.

A special thanks goes to my friend Kath Gifford, who was always there to give me much needed mental rest during the interviews and research, which she indeed helped me with.

My love of London comes solely from my parents, and the trust they placed in me from an early age. They were the ones who let me roam the streets of London. I hope they can forgive me for not always telling the truth about where I really was. I would like to thank them for putting up with my frequent visits, and not least for listening to all my ramblings as we've travelled around London. I don't know how many times I've said to them: 'Do you know what? The . . .'

I owe my sister Noor and her husband Amar (and Alma, Selma and Nora!) the world's biggest thank you for letting me stay at their apartment in London, which has periodically also functioned as a writing studio. There is little that beats the view of the green garden from the kitchen window there – enjoyed with a cup of tea and pistachio and almond biscuits from Marks & Spencer.

Most of all, I want to thank Olav, my dearest husband, who always encourages me, and my adorable sons Abel and Elliot, who always keep me updated on all things cool! I am truly the luckiest mum. I've tried to bribe them with English newspapers and magazines, as well as ridiculously large volumes of Rowntree's Fruit Pastilles, Cadbury's chocolate and Maltesers, each time I've returned home from London as some sort of consolation. This seems to have worked pretty well. But I think they're happy that I'm finished now – for this time, at least.

Sources

In obtaining an overview of the big picture I've greatly enjoyed the exceptional book *Bloody Foreigners: The Story of Immigration to Britain* by Robert Winder, as well as *Lovers and Strangers* by Clair Wills, which provides a collated overview of the vast and complex immigration to London, and gave me the valuable basis I needed to explore London's immigration trajectory. Also not to be missed is Peter Ackroyd's work *London*, and his *Thames: The Biography*.

I have also greatly enjoyed Iain Sinclair's books. He offers a unique perspective on all the historical layers of the city, within the fascinating field of psychogeography. I would not have walked around London's streets with such enthusiasm had I not had his books in the back of my mind: *London Overground: A Day's Walk around the Ginger Line*, *London Orbital* and *Hackney, That Rose-Red Empire: A Confidential Report* have been especially valuable, but all his books have energised me, and I am deeply indebted to him.

In many ways, the Irish are the very foundations of London, and the stories about them are numerous. I have greatly enjoyed the anthology *The Northern Ireland Troubles in Britain* edited by Graham Dawson, Jo Dover and Stephen Hopkins, and *An Unconsidered People: The Irish in London* by Catherine Dunne.

The presence of the Italians in London has mainly been documented by enthusiasts, and Olive Besagni's *A Better Life* is a treasure trove, as is the pamphlet *Little Italy: The Story of London's Italian Quarter* by Tudor Allen, along with *The Arandora Star Tragedy* edited by Peter Capella.

When it comes to the history of the people from the Indian subcontinent, Rozina Visram's *Asians in Britain: 400 Years of History* is a deeply insightful work to which I owe a deep debt of gratitude. The same applies to the photographic work *Asian Britain*, which provides unique visual documentation of Indian immigration to London and its results. Dilip Hiro's *Black British, White British* made an indelible impact on me when I first read it twenty years ago, as did *Britain's Gulag* by Caroline Elkins and *Inglorious Empire* by Shashi Tharoor – all these books offer a shocking insight into Britain's colonial past.

The lives of the Caribbeans in London are well documented. *Windrush* by Mike and Trevor Phillips has been especially important, as has Sam Selvon's novel *The Lonely Londoners* and the biography *Darcus Howe: A Political Biography* by Robin Bunce and Paul Field. I've also greatly enjoyed *Rebel Dread*, a documentary about Don Letts. The details on music history are taken from Lloyd Bradley's *Sounds Like London*.

Nobody can write about West African London without consulting David Olusoga's book *Black and British: A Forgotten History* and Bernardine Evaristo's novel *Blonde Roots*. In understanding the myths around West African witchcraft, *The Boy in the River* by Richard Hoskins has been invaluable. In the spring of 2011, I interviewed investigators Will O'Reilly and Andy Baker about the Adam case. I am deeply grateful to them, and to Emeritus Professor Jean La Fontaine, who I also met around the same time.

The traces left by the Jews in London are many, and regarding the role of football Anthony Clavane's book *Does Your Rabbi Know You're Here?* was a wonderful discovery. I have also greatly enjoyed Rachel Kolsky and Roslyn Rawson's *Jewish London: A Comprehensive Guidebook for Visitors and Londoners*. David Rosenberg's *Rebel*

Footprints: A Guide to Uncovering London's Radical History also contains much fascinating Jewish history.

The Arabs in London are a group on which little research has been conducted, so my primary source has been *Becoming Arab in London* by Ramy M. K. Aly. I look forward to the Arab British Centre completing its current research project about Arab immigration to London. Tom Bower's unauthorised biography *Fayed*, about Mohamed Al-Fayed, has also given great insight into certain circumstances regarding the situation of the Egyptians in London, if a somewhat biased one.

In understanding more about the history of the Poles in London, Piotr Stolarski's work *Polish Ealing* has been indispensable, and I learned a lot when I interviewed him. *Hello, I'm Your Polish Neighbour* by Wikto Moszczynski has also shed light on the lives of the Poles in London.

When it comes to the Russians and their arrival in London after the dissolution of the Soviet Union, *Londongrad: From Russia with Cash – The Inside Story of the Oligarchs* by Mark Hollingsworth and Stewart Lansley has been a valuable source of information. It describes this part of the Russians' story in detail, while *Other Russias* by Victoria Lomasko and *The Man without a Face: The Unlikely Rise of Vladimir Putin* by Masha Gessen have given me a certain knowledge of Russia's turbulent political situation.

I have made use of *The Times, Sunday Times, Guardian, Evening Standard, Telegraph, Daily Mail, Metro, Irish Times, Haaretz, Jewish Chronicle, Brixton Buzz, Voice, Eastern Eye, Peckham Peculiar, Independent, Sun, Al Jazeera, Financial Times* and *Morning Star.*

I have also consulted the *New Statesman, Prospect, Spectator, London Review of Books, Private Eye, Wire, Economist, Tatler, Face, New Musical Express, Elle* and *Vogue.*

Londonist.com has been a great help, as have SecretLondon. co.uk, Blackhistorywalks.co.uk and Spitalfieldslife.com.

Literature

Ackroyd, Peter, *London* (Vintage, 2000).

—, *London Under* (Vintage, 2012).

—, *Thames: The Biography* (First Anchor Books, 2007).

Adjonyoh, Zoe, *Zoe's Ghana Kitchen* (Mitchell Beazley, 2017).

Akala, *Natives: Race and Class in the Ruins of the Empire* (Two Roads, 2018).

Ali, Monica, *Brick Lane* (Doubleday, 2003).

Ali, Tariq, *Street-fighting Years: An Autobiography of the Sixties* (Verso, 2005).

Alibhai-Brown, Yasmin, *Exotic England: The Making of a Curious Nation* (Portobello Books, 2015).

—, *No Place Like Home* (Virago, 1995).

Allen, Tudor, *Little Italy: The Story of London's Italian Quarter* (Camden Local Archives, 2008).

Aly, M. K. Ramy, *Becoming Arab in London: Performativity and the Undoing of Identity* (Pluto Press, 2015).

Anas, Abdullah and Tam Hussein, *To the Mountains: My Life in Jihad, from Algeria to Afghanistan* (Hurst, 2019).

Anderson, David, *History of the Hanged: The Dirty War in Kenya and the End of the Empire – Testimonies from the Mau Mau Rebellion in Kenya* (Weidenfeld & Nicolson, 2011).

Bakalar, A. M., *Children of Our Age* (Jantar Publishing, 2017).

—, *Madame Mephisto* (Stork Press, 2012).

Barclay, Peter, *The Life and Times of Herbert Chapman, The Story of One of Football's Most Influential Figures* (W&N, 2014).

Basu, Shrabani, *Spy Princess: The Life of Noor Inayat Khan* (The History Press, 2006).

Besagni, Olive, *A Better Life* (Camden History Society, 2011).

Black, Pauline, *Black by Design: A 2-Tone Memoir* (Serpent's Tail, 2012).

Blagrove Jr, Ishmail and Margaret Busby, *Carnival: A Photographic and Testimonial History of the Notting Hill Carnival* (Rice N Peas, 2014).

Bolton, Tom, *Camden Town: Dreams of Another London* (British Library, 2017).

—, *Vanished London: London's Lost Neighbourhoods* (Strange Attractor Press, 2017).

Bower, Tom, *Fayed: The Unauthorized Biography* (Pan Books, 2001).

Bradley, Lloyd, *Sounds like London* (Serpent's Tail, 2013).

Bratberg, Øivind, *Skyggebilder av Storbritannia. Tradisjoner i en krisetid* (Cappelen Damm, 2013).

Brawer, Naftali, *A Brief Guide to Judaism* (Robinson, 2008).

Bunce, Robin and Paul Field, *Darcus Howe: A Political Biography* (Bloomsbury, 2013).

Burstein, Diana, *London: Then and Now* (Pavilion Books, 2003).

Capella, Peter (ed.), *The Arandora Star Tragedy 75 Years On: London's Italian Community Remembers* (Arandora Star London Memorial Trust, 2015).

Clavane, Anthony, *Does Your Rabbi Know You're Here? The Story of English Football's Foreign Tribe* (Quercus, 2013).

Collingham, Lizzie, *Curry: A Tale of Cooks and Conquerors* (Vintage, 2006).

Czezowski, Andrew and Susan Carrington, *The Roxy: The Club that Forged Punk in 100 Nights of Madness! Mayhem! Misfortune!* (CarrCzez Publishing, 2016).

Dawson, Graham, Jo Dover and Stephen Hopkins (eds), *The Northern Ireland Troubles in Britain: Impacts, Engagement, Legacies and Memories* (Manchester University Press, 2017).

Dee, David, 'The Hefty Hebrew. Boxing and British-Jewish Identity, 1890–1960', *Sport in History*, vol. 32, no. 3 (2012), pp. 361–81.

de Figueiredo, Ivo, *En fremmed ved mitt bord* (Aschehoug, 2016).

Dunne, Catherine, *An Unconsidered People: The Irish in London* (New Island, 2003).

Elkins, Caroline, *Britain's Gulag: The Brutal End of Empire in Kenya* (The Bodley Head, 2014).

Evaristo, Bernardine, *Blonde Roots* (Penguin, 2008).

Gessen, Masha, *The Man without a Face: The Unlikely Rise of Vladimir Putin* (Granta Books, 2014).

Gibson, Andrew and Joe Kerr (eds), *London: From Punk to Blair* (University of Chicago Press, 2004).

Gilroy, Paul, *Black Britain: A Photographic History*, with an introduction by Stuart Hall (Saqi, 2007).

—, *There Ain't No Black in the Union Jack* (Hutchinson, 1987).

Griffin, Christopher, *Nomads under the Westway: Irish Travellers, Gypsies and Other Traders in West London* (University of Hertfordshire Press, 2008).

Grinrod, John, *Concretopia: A Journey around the Rebuilding of Post-war Britain* (Old Street Publishing, 2013).

Hall, Stuart, 'The question of cultural identity', in Stuart Hall, David Held and Anthony McGrew, *Modernity and Its Futures* (Polity Press in association with the Open University, 1992), pp. 274–316.

Hamilton, Patrick, *Twenty Thousand Streets Under the Sky* (Vintage, 2010 [1987]).

Herrmann, Richard, *Mine gleders by* (Cappelen Damm, 1983).

Hiro, Dilip, *Black British, White British: A History of Race Relations in Britain* (Paladin, 1992).

Hollingsworth, Mark and Stewart Lansley, *Londongrad: From Russia with Cash – The Inside Story of the Oligarchs* (Fourth Estate, 2010).

Hoskins, Richard, *The Boy in the River* (Pan Books, 2013).

Johnson, Linton Kwesi, *Selected Poems* (Penguin, 2006).

Judah, Ben, *This is London* (Picador, 2016).

Karmi, Ghada, *The Egyptians of Britain: A Migrant Community in Transition*, Centre for Middle Eastern and Islamic Studies Occasional Paper 57 (University of Durham, 1997).

Kolsky, Rachel and Roslyn Rawson, *Jewish London: A Comprehensive Guidebook for Visitors and Londoners* (IMM Lifestyle Books, 2018).

Kureishi, Hanif, *The Black Album* (Faber and Faber, 1995).

—, *The Buddha of Suburbia* (Faber and Faber, 1990).

Letts, Don, *Dread Meets Punk Rockers* (SAF Publishing, 2007).

Lomasko, Victoria, *Other Russias* (Penguin Books, 2017).

Maconie, Stuart, *Hope and Glory: A People's History of Modern Britain* (Ebury Press, 2012).

Malkani, Gautam, *Londonstani* (Fourth Estate, 2006).

Mason, Mark, *Walk the Lines: The London Underground Overground* (Arrow Books, 2011).

McKittrick, David and David McVea, *Making Sense of the Troubles: A History of the Northern Ireland Conflict* (Viking Penguin, 2012).

Mishra, Pankah, *Raseriets tidsalder. En historie om nåtiden* (Solum Bokvennen, 2018).

Moore, Rowan, *Slow Burn City* (Picador, 2016).

Morton, James, *Gangland Soho* (Piatkus, 2008).

Moszczynski, Wictor, *Hello, I'm Your Polish Neighbour: All about Poles in West London* (Author House, 2010).

Naipaul, Shiva, *Fireflies* (André Deutsch, 1970).

Naipaul, V. S., *Among the Believers: An Islamic Journey* (André Deutsch, 1981).

—, *A Bend in the River* (Vintage, 1980).

—, *The Enigma of Arrival* (Viking, 1987).

—, *The Mimic Men* (André Deutsch, 1967).

Nasta, Susheila and Florian Stadtler, *Asian Britain: A Photographic History* (The Westbourne Press, 2013).

Olusoga, David, *Black and British: A Forgotten History* (Pan, 2016).

Orwell, George, *Down and Out in Paris and London* (Penguin, 1989 [1933]).

Phillips, Melanie, *Londonistan* (Encounter Books, 2006).

Phillips, Mike, *London Crossings: A Biography of Black Britain* (Continuum, 2001).

Phillips, Mike and Trevor Phillips, *Windrush: The Irresistible Rise of Multi-Racial Britain* (HarperCollins, 1999).

Phipps, Simon, *Brutal London* (September Publishing, 2016).

Ramamurthy, Anandi, *Black Star: Britain's Asian Youth Movements* (Pluto Press, 2013).

Razia, Ambreen, *The Diary of a Hounslow Girl* (Aurora Metro Books, 2016).

Rosenberg, David, *Rebel Footprints: A Guide to Uncovering London's Radical History* (Pluto Press, 2015).

Rossiter, Ann, *Ireland's Hidden Diaspora* (IASC Publishing, 2009).

Rushdie, Salman, *The Satanic Verses* (Viking, 1988).

—, *Shame* (Vintage, 1983).

Salih, Tayeb, *Season of Migration to the North* (Penguin, 1969).

Sardar, Ziauddin, *Balti Britain: A Journey through the British Asian Experience* (Granta, 2008).

—, *Desperately Seeking Paradise: Journeys of a Sceptical Muslim* (Granta, 2005).

Sardar, Ziauddin and Merryl Wyn Davies, *Distorted Imagination: Lessons from the Rushdie Affair* (Grey Seal/Berita Publishing, 1990).

Selvon, Sam, *The Lonely Londoners* (Penguin, 2006 [1956]).

Sherwood, Marika, *Claudia Jones: A Life in Exile* (Lawrence & Wishart, 1999).

Shukla, Nikesh, *The Good Immigrant: Fifteen Writers Explore What it Means to Be Black, Asian and Minority Ethnic in Britain Today* (Unbound Books, 2018).

Sinclair, Iain, *Hackney, That Rose-Red Empire: A Confidential Report* (Penguin, 2009).

—, *London Orbital: A Walk around the M25* (Granta, 2003).

—, *London Overground: A Day's Walk around the Ginger Line* (Hamish Hamilton, 2016).

Smith, Zadie, *NW* (Hamish Hamilton, 2012).

—, *White Teeth* (Hamish Hamilton, 2000).

Spark, Muriel, *The Ballard of Peckham Rye* (Penguin, 1999 [1960]).

Speiser, Peter, *Soho: The Heart of Bohemian London* (British Library, 2017).

Staple, Neville and Tony McMahon, *Original Rude Boy: From Borstal to The Specials* (Aurum, 2010).

Stolarski, Piotr, *Polish Ealing* (Tignarius, 2016).

Sturtevant, Katherine, *Our Sister's London: Nineteen Feminist Walks* (The Women's Press, 1991).

Suggs, *Suggs and the City: My Journeys through a Disappearing London* (Headline, 2009).

Tharoor, Sashi, *Inglorious Empire: What the British Did to India* (Penguin, 2016).

Tinker, Hugh, *The Banyan Tree: Overseas Emigrants from India, Pakistan and Bangladesh* (Oxford University Press, 1977).

Toye, Richard, *Churchill's Empire: The World that Made Him and the World He Made* (Henry Holt and Company, 2010).

Visram, Rozina, *Asians in Britain: 400 Years of History* (Pluto Press, 2002).

Wambu, Onyekachi (ed.), *Empire Windrush: Fifty Years of Writing about Black Britain* (Gollancz, 1998).

Watson, Gavin, *Skins* (Independent Music Press, 2013).

Wheatle, Alex, *Brixton Rock* (Black Amber Books, 1999).

Willetts, Paul, *Members Only: The Life and Times of Paul Raymond* (Serpent's Tail, 2010).

Wills, Clair, *Lovers and Strangers: An Immigrant History of Post-War Britain* (Penguin, 2017).

Winder, Robert, *Bloody Foreigners: The Story of Immigration to Britain* (Abacus, 2013).

Winn, Christopher, *I Never Knew That about London* (Ebury Press, 2007).

Notes

Introduction – London's global heart

1   https://www.britannica.com/topic/immigration.
2   More detail about the history of the Commonwealth can be found here: http://thecommonwealth.org/commonwealth-70.
3   There are currently fifty-three nations in the Commonwealth, which comprises around 2.4 billion people, snl.no/Samveldet_av_nasjoner.
4   On 21 January 2005, *Guardian* journalist Leo Benedictus launched the article series 'London: The World in One City'. The entire series can be found here: https://www.theguardian.com/uk-news/series/london. The series has been a great source of inspiration and material for me during the writing of this book.
5   To become an All London taxi driver who drives one of the famous black cabs, you must memorise 320 routes and maintain an overview of the 20,000 streets that exist within those 320 routes, along with 20,000 landmarks. It can take between two and four years to be granted such a licence; everyone wishing to obtain one must study the Blue Book: https://www.theknowledgetaxi.co.uk.
6   Croydon is a so-called satellite city in Greater London. The city originally belonged to the county of Surrey; in the 1960s, the city became a focus area and several office blocks were built there, including Lunar House, which is where the Visa and Immigration headquarters of the Home Office is located. Croydon is divided into three parts: South Croydon, which is mainly a quiet, affluent residential area; East Croydon, the heart of the area and where the main train station is located; and West Croydon, which is regarded as a rougher area.
7   Leo Benedictus, 'Every race, colour, nation and religion on earth', *Guardian* (21 January 2005), https://www.theguardian.com/uk/2005/jan/21/britishidentity1.
8   Afua Hirsch, 'Why a royal Meghan Markle matters', *Time* (22 May 2018), http://time.com/5281096/meghan-markle-multicultural-britain/.
9   https://www.bbc.com/news/uk-england-london-55489065.

Irish building blocks

1 Robert Winder, *Bloody Foreigners*, p. 194.
2 *Ibid.*, p. 205.
3 The Proceedings of the Old Bailey, London's Criminal Court, 1674–1913, https://www.oldbaileyonline.org/static/Irish.jsp.
4 *Ibid.*
5 Robert Winder, *Bloody Foreigners*, p. 162.
6 Catherine Dunne, *An Unconsidered People*, p. 16.
7 Graham Dawson, Jo Dover and Stephen Hopkins (eds), *The Northern Ireland Troubles in Britain*. All figures are taken from the introduction.
8 Graham Dawson, Jo Dover and Stephen Hopkins (eds), *The Northern Ireland Troubles in Britain*, p. 1.
9 Brian O'Connell, '10% of homeless are Irish', *RTE* (25 May 2000), https://www.rte.ie/archives/2015/0525/703556-irish-homelessness-in-london/. Figures from the National Audit Office show that homelessness in the UK has increased dramatically: https://www.nao.org.uk/report/homelessness/.

The dark streets of London

1 http://www.workhouses.org.uk/RowtonCamden/.
2 George Orwell, *Down and Out in Paris and London* (Penguin Books [1940], 1989 edition), p. 211.

A ballad of Camden

1 Robin Denselow, 'Madonna at Camden Palace', *Guardian* (15 October 1983), https://www.theguardian.com/century/1980-1989/Story/0,,108236,00.html.
2 This video clip effectively summarises what it was like at Camden Palace: https://www.youtube.com/watch?v=uZMvhyY3VVs.
3 Tom Bolton, *Camden Town*, p. 46.
4 Phil Lynott released the album *Solo in Soho* in 1980, on which he sings about his Caribbean heritage.
5 Simon Carsewell, 'It's become ok to make racial comments in the UK', *Irish Times* (23 April 2019), https://www.irishtimes.com/life-and-style/abroad/brexiles-it-has-become-okay-to-make-racial-comments-in-uk-1.3800551.

#IamIrish

1 https://www.londonmet.ac.uk/news/expert-commentary/2020/march/the-history-of-st-patricks-day-in-london/.
2 *Today*, BBC Radio 4 (17 April 2013).
3 John Charlton, 'London 13 November 1887', *Socialist Review*, no. 224 (November 1998), http://pubs.socialistreviewindex.org.uk/sr224/charlton.htm.
4 Ann Rossiter, *Ireland's Hidden Diaspora*, p. 23.

5 *Breaking Ground* (2013) by Michelle Deignan is a documentary that explores the Irish women's networks in London: https://vimeo.com/60492225.

The myth of Kosher Nostra

1 The analysis of Jewish footballers is taken from Anthony Clavane's book *Does Your Rabbi Know You're Here?* and the exhibition *Four Four Jew* at the Jewish Museum in 2013.

2 Anthony Clavane, *Does Your Rabbi Know You're Here?*, p. xxxvi.

3 *Ibid.*, p. 11/

4 Peter Barclay, *The Life and Times of Herbert Chapman.*

5 David Dee, ' "The Hefty Hebrew": Boxing and British-Jewish Identity, 1890–1960', *Sports in History*, vol. 32, no. 3 (September 2012), pp. 361–81, https://www.academia. edu/345584/The_Hefty_Hebrew_Boxing_and_British-Jewish_Identity_1890-1960.

6 *Jewish Chronicle* (30 August 1929).

7 Anthony Clavane, *Does Your Rabbi Know You're Here?*, p. xxvi.

8 'The Nazis at Tottenham: Why did the swastika fly at White Hart Lane?', *FourFourTwo* (16 May 2017), https://www.fourfourtwo.com/features/nazis-tottenham-why-did-swastika-fly-white-hart-lane.

9 'England v. Germany (1935)', YouTube, https://youtu.be/jaqyIn5aqUs.

10 Marcus Dysch, 'Spurs fans ready to fight "yid" charges', *Jewish Chronicle* (23 January 2014), https://www.thejc.com/news/uk-news/spurs-fans-ready-to-fight-yid-charges -1.52139.

11 'David Baddiel tackles anti-semitism in football', *BBC News* (14 April 2011), https: //www.bbc.com/news/av/uk-13089242/david-baddiel-tackles-anti-semitism-in -football,

12 Anthony Clavane, *Does Your Rabbi Know You're Here?*, p. 240; 'Avram Grant appointment makes Chelsea no more than rich man's plaything', *The Times* (21 September 2007).

13 Press Association, 'Chelsea to send racist fans on Auschwitz trips instead of banning them', *Guardian* (11 October 2018), https://www.theguardian.com/football/2018/ oct/11/chelsea-to-send-racist-fans-auschwitz-instead-banning-orders-antisemitism.

My rabbi in London

1 Alan Dein created the exhibition *After You've Gone: East End Shopfronts, 1988* in which he collected 250 photographs of shopfronts. He has also created a beautiful album: *Music Is the Most Beautiful Language in The World – Yiddisher Jazz in London's East End 1920s to 1950s*, which was released in 2018.

2 David Connett, 'Haredi: Half of Britain's Jews will soon be strictly orthodox, says new study', *Independent* (15 October 2015), https://www.independent.co.uk/news/uk/ home-news/haredi-half-of-britain-s-jews-will-soon-be-strictly-orthodox-says-new-study-a6696046.html.

An Orthodox charm offensive

1 'Canvey, the promised island', *BBC News* (9 January 2018), https://www.bbc.com/news/av/stories/42559714/why-jewish-families-are-moving-to-canvey-island.

2 http://www.kolech.org.il/en/about-us-en.html.

3 http://www.womenofthewall.org.il.

4 Helen Rumbelow, 'How I escaped my arranged marriage', *Sunday Times* (23 November 2016), https://www.thetimes.co.uk/article/how-i-escaped-my-arranged-marriage-cg35tc8xd.

5 Etan Smallman, 'samuel-613', *Independent* (20 January 2016), https://www.independent.co.uk/arts-entertainment/films/features/samuel-613-how-film-maker-billy-lumby-gained-access-to-stamford-hills-hasidic-community-a6824091.html. *samuel-613* was nominated for a BAFTA for best short film in 2016.

Cunning charlatans and comedians

1 https://www.museumoflondon.org.uk/museum-london.

2 Robert Winder, *Bloody Foreigners*, p. 185.

3 Olive Besagni, *A Better Life*, p. 10.

4 Tudor Allen, *Little Italy*, p. 24.

5 Roberto Suro, 'Italy's heroin addicts face new challenge: AIDS', *New York Times* (28 December 1987), https://www.nytimes.com/1987/12/28/us/italy-s-heroin-addicts-face-new-challenge-aids.html.

6 https://www.villascalabrini.co.uk.

7 Tudor Allen, *Little Italy*, p. 45.

8 Guy Adams, 'The man who founded Costa Coffee – then sold out for a fraction of its value now – insists he's not bitter. So . . . WHY does Mr Costa refuse to drink his own coffee?', *Daily Mail* (10 May 2013), https://www.dailymail.co.uk/news/article-2318601/The-man-founded-Costa-Coffee-sold-fraction-value-insists-hes-bitter-So-WHY-does-Mr-Costa-refuse-drink-coffee.html.

9 Robert Winder, *Bloody Foreigners*, p. 192.

10 *Ibid.*, p. 191.

A heathen dive

1 James Morton, *Gangland Soho*, p. 7.

2 Interview with the club's founder Nick Robins at Bar Italia, January 2018.

3 Biographical material on Paul Raymond taken from Paul Willetts, *Members Only*.

4 Colin MacInnes also wrote *City of Spades* (1957) and *Mr Love and Justice* (1960), which together with the novel *Absolute Beginners* (1959) make up his London trilogy.

5 Historical Resources about the Second World War, 'Mussolini: Speech of the 10 June 1940, Declaration of War on France and England', http://www.historicalresources.org/2008/09/19/mussolini-speech-of-the-10-june-1940-declaration-of-war-on-france-and-england/.

6 'Mussolini declares war 1940', https://www.youtube.com/watch?v=MBeFD9PFyTI.

7 Peter Speiser, *Soho*, p. 141.

8 The historical information on the *Arandora Star* is taken from Peter Capella (ed.), *The Arandora Star Tragedy*, and Robert Winder, *Bloody Foreigners*.

9 Clair Wills, *Lovers and Strangers*, p. 51.

Gangsters and Brexit

1 Luke Bradshaw, 'How London fell out of love with greyhound racing', *The Culture Trip* (25 January 2018), https://theculturetrip.com/europe/united-kingdom/england/london/articles/london-fell-love-greyhound-racing/.

2 'Obituary: Bert Rossi', *Sunday Times* (13 July 2017), https://www.thetimes.co.uk/article/bert-rossi-209qlbjl2.

Caribbean occupation

1 The material about Notting Hill Carnival is gathered from the book *Carnival* by Ishmail Blagrove Jr and Margaret Busby, which is regarded as the standard work on the carnival's history.

2 Mike Phillips and Trevor Phillips's *Windrush* provided the basis for my text about the years that followed the arrival of SS *Windrush*.

3 https://www.britannica.com/biography/Wyndham-Lewis.

4 Majbritt Morrison wrote the book *Jungle West 11* (Tandem Books, 1964) about her life and the attack on her husband, although it is difficult to get hold of a copy.

Notting Hill before Hugh and Julia

1 The material on Claudia Jones is taken from Marika Sherwood, *Claudia Jones*.

2 This story is taken from Robin Bunce and Paul Field, *Darcus Howe*.

3 A beautiful photographic report from the BBC can be found here: 'Notting Hill's Trellick Tower' (01 August 2017), https://www.bbc.com/news/in-pictures-40728732.

4 Lloyd Bradley, *Sounds Like London*, p. 65.

5 Mike Phillips and Trevor Phillips, *Windrush*, p. 109.

6 'John Lennon with Michael X interview' (1970), https://www.youtube.com/watch?v=EtDu73_4QIc.

7 Michael X is said to have owned a bank deposit box containing compromising photographs of Princess Margaret. Whether or not this is true is unknown, but the belief led to the film *The Bank Job* (2008) about a robbery committed in London on 11 September 1971.

A new life

1 The documentary *Black Nurses: The Women Who Saved the NHS* was broadcast on the BBC in 2016, https://www.bbc.co.uk/programmes/b083dgtb.

'The sound of rebellion'

1 The documentary *The Last Pirates: Britain's Rebel DJs* (2017) by Rodney P is well worth watching, https://www.bbc.co.uk/programmes/b096k6g1.

'Little Jamaica'

1 The speech, given on 20 April 1968, can be read in its entirety here: Enoch Powell's "Rivers of Blood" speech', *Daily Telegraph* (6 November 2007), https://www.telegraph. co.uk/comment/3643823/Enoch-Powells-Rivers-of-Blood-speech.html. The documentary *Rivers of Blood* was broadcast on the BBC on 8 March 2008. Despite significant resistance, the BBC broadcast the entire speech on the programme *The Archive on 4* in 2018.

2 Robin Bunce and Paul Field, *Darcus Howe*, p. 290.

3 Margaret Thatcher Foundation, https://www.margaretthatcher.org/document/ 104617.

4 Ty (Benedict Chijioke) sadly passed away on 7 May 2020 due to COVID-19.

5 Brixton prison has a restaurant that helps train inmates: https://theclinkcharity.org/ restaurants/brixton.

6 The Nation of Islam London Study Group: https://www.youtube.com/channel/UCtd _xmQQv6uLeUnCdgAAobg.

7 Sarah Marsh, 'How has Brixton really changed? The data behind the story', *Guardian* (14 February 2016), https://www.theguardian.com/cities/datablog/2016/jan/14/how -has-brixton-really-changed-the-data-behind-the-story.

8 United80 has since moved from its premises, and now operates using pop-ups. It can be contacted here: https://www.united80brixton.com.

Brixton's ugly duckling

1 In November 2015 the *Evening Standard* started publishing a series of reports on Angell Town. Statistics about the area are taken from this. The series also led the newspaper to set up a charitable organisation to help young people in the neighbourhood. David Cohen, 'A week in the life of Brixton's Angell Town', *Evening Standard* (28 September 2015), https://www.standard.co.uk/news/london/special-investigation-the-standard-launches-a-hardhitting-series-on-life-on-notorious-brixton-a2956876. html.

2 David Cohen, 'Standard gives Angell Town estate new challenge with 33,000 pound gym', *Evening Standard* (27 March 2019), https://www.standard.co.uk/news/london/ standard-gives-angell-town-estate-new-challenge-with-33000-outdoor-gym-a4102031.html.

3 A relatively balanced article from *The Times* by Ben Machell, 'Do drill's lyrics inspire knife crime? Or give voice to a generation that's been let down?' (4 May 2019), https: //www.thetimes.co.uk/article/do-drills-lyrics-inspire-knife-crime-or-give-voice-to-a-generation-thats-been-let-down-nqqvjzqdv.

4 Professor Paul Gilroy received the Holberg Prize on 5 June 2019.

5 Amelia Gentleman, '"I can't eat or sleep." The woman threatened with deportation after 50 years in Britain', *Guardian* (28 November 2017), https://www.theguardian.com/uk-news/2017/nov/28/i-cant-eat-or-sleep-the-grandmother-threatened-with-deportation-after-50-years-in-britain.

All mothers are queens

1 'Peckham', *Sunday Times* (19 March 2017), https://www.thetimes.co.uk/article/peckham-best-places-to-live-2017-cl6pzdmqd.
2 Tom Doyle, 'Nothing beats a Londoner', *Evening Standard* (9 February 2018), https://www.standard.co.uk/sport/football/nothing-beats-a-londoner-nike-london-advert-watch-stars-harry-kane-mo-farah-alex-iwobi-skepta-a3762356.html.
3 News Desk, 'The boy who saw angels in Peckham', *Southwark News* (8 December 2016), https://www.southwarknews.co.uk/history/boy-saw-angels-peckham/.
4 The Pioneer Health Foundation, http://thephf.org/peckhamexperiment.
5 *The Centre*, written and directed by J.B. Holmes, produced by Paul Rotha. The film is made up of archival clips from the BFI National Archive, UK Foreign Office, 1948, http://search.wellcomelibrary.org/iii/encore/record/C__Rb1676352__Spaul%20rotha__P0%2C2__Orightresult__U__X3?lang=eng&suite=cobalt.
6 Hugh Muir, 'A vision for housing, and the grim reality', *Guardian* (22 September 2005), https://www.theguardian.com/society/2005/sep/22/communities.uknews.
7 'In Depth: Damilola Taylor', *BBC News* (6 January 2003), http://news.bbc.co.uk/2/hi/in_depth/uk/2002/damilola_taylor/default.stm.
8 News broadcast, London Live (8 August 2010), https://www.londonlive.co.uk/programmes/damilola-death-of-a-ten-year-old, can be watched on YouTube: https://www.youtube.com/watch?v=JA8669b7gKk.

Idealism, fashionistas and afrobeats

1 https://www.africafashionweeklondonuk.com.
2 https://www.africafashionweeklondonuk.com/about.
3 Clare Dowdy, 'Peckham's creativity reaches a higher level in a multistorey car park', *Wallpaper** (16 March 2018), https://www.wallpaper.com/architecture/peckham-levels-carl-turner-architects-london.
4 http://saharareporters.com/2017/10/02/'kleptocracy-tour'-london-exposes-properties-purchased-laundered-funds-owned-saraki.
5 https://www.newsheadline247.com/watch-video-uncovered-kleptocracy-tour-london-exposes-properties-purchased-laundered-funds-owned-saraki-alison-madueke-others. Emma Glanfield, 'Wealthy Africans spending almost £4 million on London property every WEEK as they snap up some of the most exclusive investments in the capital', *Daily Mail* (27 October 2014), http://www.dailymail.co.uk/news/article-2808556/Wealthy-Africans-spending-4million-London-property-WEEK-snap-exclusive-investments-capital.html.
6 David Jenkins, 'The Nigerians have arrived', *Tatler* (November 2013), http://www.tatler.com/article/the-nigerians-have-arrived.

7 These figures were calculated by statistician and economist Dr Faiza Shaheen for the documentary *Will Britain Ever Have a Black Prime Minister?*, BBC Two (2016).

8 The video for 'Takeover' can be seen at: https://www.youtube.com/watch?v=6EInO2rcwcE.

A tree without roots will fall

1 An interesting analysis is this one by Todd Sanders, 'Imagining the Dark Continent: The Met, The Media and The Thames Torso', *The Cambridge Journal of Anthropology*, vol. 23, no. 3 (2003), pp. 53–66.

2 The story and details about Adam are taken from the book by Robert Hoskins, *The Boy in the River*.

3 http://news.bbc.co.uk/2/hi/uk_news/england/1695601.stm

Lost sailors, nannies and hipsters

1 'Altab Ali murdered in Whitechapel', *Runnymede Trust Bulletin*, no. 99 (1978), https://web.archive.org/web/20140419020307/http://www.runnymedetrust.org/histories/race-equality/71/altab-ali-murdered-in-whitechapel-london.html.

2 Lizzie Rivera, 'Hackney records biggest house price growth in London', *Evening Standard* (17 February 2017), https://www.homesandproperty.co.uk/property-news/buying/hackney-records-biggest-house-price-growth-in-london-average-property-prices-soar-by-700-per-cent-in-a108221.html.

3 The historic material is taken from Rosina Visram, *Asians in Britain*.

4 The material about the fight against the British Union of Fascists is taken from David Rosenberg, *Rebel Footprints*.

5 Phil Davison, 'Obituary: Shanta Gaury Pathak;, *Scotsman* (28 December 2010).

The cultural revolution

1 Tariq Ali, *Street-fighting Years*.

2 Interview with journalist John Barron and Tariq Ali, *Lateline*, Australian Broadcasting Corporation (31 May 2016), https://www.abc.net.au/lateline/interview:-tariq-ali,-british-writer-and/7465118.

3 One of the most interesting analyses of the Salman Rushdie affair is the book *Distorted Imagination* (1990) by Ziauddin Sardar and Merryl Wyn Davies.

Southall – a bell jar

1 Anandi Ramamurthy, *Black Star*.

In the footsteps of Sadiq Khan

1 There is also a 'curry mile' in Birmingham, where many from the Indian subcontinent also live.
2 Isabel Choat, 'Sadiq Khan's Tooting', *Guardian* (23 October 2014), https://www. theguardian.com/travel/2014/oct/23/sadiq-khan-tooting-london-asian-restaurant -tour.
3 'Asian African Heritage, The Railway Builders', K24Tv Live, https://www.youtube. com/watch?v=P—gzitVUNw.
4 Ian Cobain and Richard Norton-Taylor, 'Sins of colonialists lay concealed for decades in secret archive', *Guardian* (18 April 2002), https://www.theguardian.com/uk/2012/ apr/18/sins-colonialists-concealed-secret-archive.
5 'Immigration AKA New immigration bill', *Pathé News* (1968). The video shows the arrival of Kenyan Asians in London and the demonstrations: https://www.youtube. com/watch?v=t1PKCRNIiaE.
6 Catherine Elkins, *Britain's Gulag*.

The Arab and the princess

1 Fayed financed the documentary *Unlawful Killing* (2011) about the incident, which hasn't aired in the UK for legal reasons, but it can be found on YouTube: https:// www.theguardian.com/film/2012/jul/05/princess-diana-documentary-unlawful -killing.

The scent of roses

1 Little has been written about the Arab presence in London. This chapter is based on the book *Becoming Arab in London* by Ramy M. K. Aly, who is Assistant Professor of Anthropology at the American University in Cairo, and a telephone interview with the director of the Arab British Centre, Nadia El-Sebai, on 31 August 2018.
2 Saeed Taji Farouky is known for his distinguished documentary films. *Tell Spring Not To Come This Year* (2015) is about the war in Afghanistan and received critical acclaim at the Berlinale and in the *Hollywood Reporter*.

Holy war in London

1 Abdullah Anas, *To the Mountains*.
2 Danny Boyle, Chris Graham, and David Millward, 'Theresa May vows hatred and evil will never succeed as Labour warns of rise in islamophobia', *Daily Telegraph* (20 June 2017), https://www.telegraph.co.uk/news/2017/06/19/finsbury-park-mosque-latest-terror-attack-london-live/.
3 Robert Booth, Steven Morris and Ian Cobain, 'Finsbury Park attack suspect named as Cardiff resident Darren Osborne', *Guardian* (20 June 2017), https://www.theguard-ian.com/uk-news/2017/jun/19/finsbury-park-attack-suspect-named-as-cardiff-resi-dent-darren-osborne.

The revolution in Dior

1 Mark Hollingsworth and Stewart Lansley, *Londongrad*, p. 22.

2 https://workpermit.com/news/300000-russians-uk-londongrad-prime-location
-20061219n.

3 Viv Groskop, 'How the Ukraine crisis is affecting Russians in Moscow-on-Thames', *Guardian* (6 April 2014), https://www.theguardian.com/world/2014/apr/06/among-the-russians-in-london.

4 You can take a tour of One Hyde Park here: https://www.youtube.com/watch?v=Y35G5MLbVPk.

5 Nicholas Shaxson, 'A tale of two Londons', *Vanity Fair* (13 March 2013), https://www.vanityfair.com/style/society/2013/04/mysterious-residents-one-hyde-park
-london.

6 Sebastian Murphy-Bates, 'Chelsea owner Roman Abramovich puts UK visa worries aside as he kits out £30m London penthouse with sweeping views down the Thames', *Daily Mail* (14 July 2018), https://www.dailymail.co.uk/news/article-5948957/Chelsea-owner-Roman-Abramovich-puts-UK-visa-worries-aside-kits-30m-London-penthouse.html.

7 Patrick Greenfield. 'UK "Golden Visa" scheme to be suspended due to corruption fears', *Guardian* (6 December 2018), https://www.theguardian.com/uk-news/2018/dec/06/restrictions-for-2m-golden-visa-to-be-reformed.

The freedom fighter

1 *Rich, Russian and Living in London*, BBC Two (5 January 2015), https://www.bbc.co.uk/programmes/b04xndwl.

2 Roman Borisovich, ' "Kleptocracy tours" expose state failure to stop dirty money buying up London', *Guardian* (2 March 2016), https://www.theguardian.com/uk-news/2016/mar/02/kleptocracy-tours-russia-ukraine-london.

3 http://Jevgenijlebedev.com/biography/.

4 Adam Sherwin, 'Russian billionaire leads a London bookshop revolution', *Independent* (28 January 2012), https://www.independent.co.uk/arts-entertainment/books/news/russian-billionaire-leads-a-london-bookshop-revolution-6295927.html.

5 Dominic Kennedy, 'Half of us are informants, say Russian expats in UK', *Sunday Times* (5 November 2018), https://www.thetimes.co.uk/article/half-of-us-are-inform-ants-say-russian-expats-in-uk-vskn9olo2?fbclid=IwAR016IAvzMpSNpGAvZYuo4np Za4I2YaHjd5EnzWP3q3SvWu1-LyqM_FhgoI.

6 Henry Jackson Society, https://henryjacksonsociety.org/wp-content/uploads/2018/11/HJS-Putin-Sees-and-Hears-It-All-Report-web.pdf.

Pride and prejudice

1 Office for National Statistics.

2 Anthony Joseph and Mark Duell, 'BBC presenter is called "P***" on the streets as police probe racist attacks and calls to hate-crime hotline soar 60% in the wake of vote

to leave the EU', *Daily Mail* (28 June 2016), https://www.dailymail.co.uk/news/article-3662114/Reports-attacks-Poles-Muslims-wake-Brexit-vote.html.

3 Matthew Weaver, ' "Horrible Spike" in hate crime linked to Brexit vote", Met police say', *Guardian* (28 September 2015), https://www.theguardian.com/society/2016/sep /28/hate-crime-horrible-spike-brexit-vote-metropolitan-police.

4 Robert Winder, *Bloody Foreigners*, p. 318.

5 *Ibid.*, p. 319.

6 *Ibid.*, p. 320.

7 Clair Wills, *Lovers and Strangers*, p. 23.

8 'Little Poland in India', https://www.youtube.com/watch?v=rIPq-8RZxxM – http:// aakaarfilms.com/little-poland-in-india/.

9 *Ibid.*

10 Robert Winder, *Bloody Foreigners*, p. 321.

11 *Ibid.*

12 Tom McTague, 'Polish prince challenges Nigel Farage to a DUEL with swords over Ukip slurs on immigrants', *Daily Mail* (13 April 2015), https://www.dailymail.co.uk/ news/article-3037224/Polish-prince-challenges-Nigel-Farage-DUEL-swords-Ukip-slurs-immigrants.html.

13 Harry Wallop, 'Polish mayoral hopeful Prince Zylinski: "Immigration is the best thing to happen to Britain" ', *Daily Telegraph* (5 May 2006), https://www.telegraph.co.uk/ men/the-filter/polish-mayoral-hopeful-prince-zylinski-immigration-is-the-best-t/.

'Little Poland'

1 Robert Liebman, 'The queen of the suburbs', *Independent* (9 September 2000), https: //www.independent.co.uk/property/house-and-home/the-queen-of-the-suburbs-701430.html.

2 The material in this chapter is taken from Dr Piotr Stolarski's book *Polish Ealing*. Dr Stolarski is a local historian. I interviewed him in Ealing on 7 June 2018.

3 'Obituaries: Cynthia Payne, madam', *Daily Telegraph* (16 November 2015), https:// www.telegraph.co.uk/news/obituaries/11997909/Cynthia-Payne-madam-obituary. html.

A home for you, a home for me

1 Cezary L. Lerski, 'Polish jazz for dummies', *All About Jazz* (14 October 2005), https:// www.allaboutjazz.com/polish-jazz-for-dummies-60-years-of-jazz-from-poland-by-cezary-lerski.php,

2 Charlotte England, 'Poles living in the UK "scared to report hate crimes" since Brexit vote due to alleged lack of government support', *Independent* (7 January 2017), https: //www.independent.co.uk/news/uk/home-news/brexit-hate-crime-polish-eastern-european-too-scared-to-report-police-british-government-support-a7515196.htm.

3 *Newsnight*, BBC Two (26 June 2018), https://www.bbc.co.uk/programmes/p06c3yt7.

4 Emma Glanfield, 'Two Polish men who threw rashers of bacon at London mosque-goers, shouting "enjoy f***ers" as they fled the scene are jailed for eight months', *Daily*

Mail (2 November 2016), https://www.dailymail.co.uk/news/article-3897130/Two-Polish-men-threw-rashers-bacon-London-mosque-goers-shouting-enjoy-f-ers-fled-scene-jailed-eight-months.html.

Index